International Trademark Licensing

International Trademark Licensing

Edited by
Stojan Arnerstål

Wolters Kluwer

Published by:
Kluwer Law International B.V.
PO Box 316
2400 AH Alphen aan den Rijn
The Netherlands
E-mail: international-sales@wolterskluwer.com
Website: lrus.wolterskluwer.com

Sold and distributed by:
Wolters Kluwer Legal & Regulatory U.S.
7201 McKinney Circle
Frederick, MD 21704
United States of America
E-mail: customer.service@wolterskluwer.com

ISBN 978-94-035-1882-4

e-Book: ISBN 978-94-035-1920-3
web-PDF: ISBN 978-94-035-1925-8

Editor

Stojan Arnerstål is a specialist counsel and head of Life Science & Healthcare at Advokatfirman Vinge in Sweden.

Dr Arnerstål specializes in transactional intellectual property and focuses on legal and strategic advice in matters concerning IP law and contract law. His services primarily focus on IP issues and risk assessments in transactions (M&As), technology transfers, licensing structures and development agreements, including negotiations and drafting. He is in particular experienced in media, technology and life sciences-related agreements.

He is the Swedish country editor of the *Nordic Intellectual Property Law Review* and the acting chair for the trademark group of the Swedish Association for the Protection of Intellectual Property Law.

Dr Arnerstål has a background as an associate professor at the Institute of Intellectual Property, Marketing and Competition Law (IMC) at Uppsala University, Sweden, of which he was the Director for five years. Dr Arnerstål is the author of *The Anatomy of a License Agreement* (Licensavtalets anatomi) (2019), *Trademark Use* (Varumärkesanvändning) (2018), and *Trademarks as Objects of Contractual Arrangements* (Varumärket som kontraktsföremål) (2014).

Contributors

Arthur Artinian is a partner at K&L Gates in London and head of the IP and Technology Group. The intellectual property team at K&L Gates London is recognized for international trademark, design and copyright strategy and counselling, portfolio management, enforcement, litigation, and cross-border brand and technology transactions. Arthur is an internationally recognized intellectual property lawyer, representing numerous iconic brands, including leading fashion, luxury and retail brands, in complex cross-border IP counselling, litigation, enforcement and transactional matters. His work has been recognized in a number of publications, including *Chambers*, *The Legal 500*, *World Trademark Review*, *World IP Review Leaders*, *Who's Who* and *Client Choice*; he holds bar registrations in the UK, Ireland, Belgium and Australia and has worked in London, New York, Tokyo and Sydney.

Mary Atkinson is a patent attorney at K&L Gates LLP's Seattle office and is a member of the firm's IP procurement and portfolio management practice group. Mary has extensive experience assisting clients in the biotech space in patent procurement; research and development agreements; and patent licensing agreements. In addition to her patent practice, Mary assists clients in trademark licensing and trademark coexistence and consent to use agreements.

Zarina Beltrán has been an associate at Basham, Ringe y Correa, SC in Mexico since 2013. Basham is one of the leading full-service law firms in Latin America. Zarina's practice focuses on matters related to intellectual property and franchising. Zarina has been practising law in the field of intellectual property since 2010 and has experience in domestic and international matters, including in advising clients in IP matters in general; negotiating and drafting licence, franchise and confidentiality contracts; filing and prosecuting trademarks before the Mexican Institute of Industrial Property (IMPI); filing copyrights with the National Copyright Institute (INDAUTOR); due diligence in IP matters; classifying and registering product and service trademarks for Mexican and leading foreign companies; registering trademarks in South and Central America, Europe, Asia and the United States, working with local counsel in each of those regions;

counselling Mexican and international clients in intellectual property-related issues. Zarina graduated from the Instituto Tecnologico Autonomo de Mexico (ITAM) and has studied various courses on intellectual property law. She speaks Spanish and English.

Tatiana Campello is a partner at Demarest Advogados and head of the intellectual property and innovation and data privacy and cybersecurity areas. Demarest is one of the most respected law firms in Brazil and Latin America and consistently rank among Brazil's leading law firms in a wide variety of publications, including *Chambers*, *Thomson Reuters*, *Latin Lawyer*, *The Legal 500* and *IFLR*. Tatiana holds a specialization in Business Law from PUC-SP, Brazil and a BA in Law from Faculdades Integradas Cândido Mendes, Brazil. Recognized nationally and internationally in her field, she participates in several national and international associations and acts as a lecturer and speaker on topics related to her areas of expertise.

Ryan Edmondson is an associate at K&L Gates in Seattle and a member of its IP litigation practice group. He concentrates his practice in intellectual property matters, and has nearly a decade of experience representing clients in both state and federal court litigation.

Camila Garcindo Dayrell Garrote, Demarest, Brazil.

Natalia Gulyaeva is Managing Partner and heads Hogan Lovells' Global Regulatory & IP, Media and Technology (IPMT) Practice Group and Life Sciences & Healthcare Industry Group for Russia/Commonwealth of Independent States (CIS). Hogan Lovells is a leading global law firm with more than forty-seven offices worldwide and provides high-quality service across our market-leading practices: corporate & finance, global regulatory, intellectual property, media and technology, and litigation, arbitration and employment. Natalia is well known for a chain of victories in complex IP disputes before the Russian courts. She is equally creative and successful in handling disputes between international and domestic corporations in Russia and other CIS countries, and for coordinating multi-jurisdictional dispute resolution (including both litigation and arbitration). Natalia is admitted to represent clients before the Russian PTO, and enjoys rights of audience in the Chamber for Patent and Trademark Disputes and Russian courts, including the Russian IP Court. Natalia is dual-qualified and admitted for practice in Russia and England & Wales. Over the years, Natalia's team has received several World Leaders International Awards for their work in representing international and domestic companies in IP litigious and transactional matters in Russia and other CIS countries. Natalia is the winner of 2015, 2016 and 2018 'Client Choice Award' as well as the winner of Euromoney's 'European Women in Business Law' Awards 2015 and selected by her peers in *Chambers & Partners*, *The Best Lawyers* and *The Legal 500*. Natalia is a winner of 2017 'Client Choice Award' in the category 'Best in Patents (Russia)'. Natalia was also noted among the top 250 Women in IP by *IP Stars* in 2018 and 2019. Natalia's team received MIP Award 'Russia: Patent Law Firm of the Year' in 2019, 2020 and 2021 for excellence in patent litigation and 'Russia: Copyright & Design Law Firm of the Year' in 2021. Natalia is included in the lists of arbitrators of many domestic and international arbitration institutions and has experiences in acting as both counsel and arbitrator. Natalia is a tutor in the World Intellectual Property Organization (WIPO) Arbitration and Mediation Center, Associate Professor of Law Faculty at the Higher School of Economics (Moscow, Russia). She is also a member of the European Branch Committee of CIArb and chair of the Russian Chapter of the European Branch of CIArb. Natalia also serves as a chair of the IP committee of CCI France-Russie.

Seiro Hatano is a partner at TMI Associates, which is one of the largest law firms in Japan. Since the firm's founding, the IP practice has been one of the firm's most important pillars, and the firm has progressively consolidated its reputation as the best legal advisers in the IP field in Japan. Seiro Hatano's practice covers contentious and non-contentious IP-related work, with particular focus on trademark and unfair competition. He has considerable experience with contentious works regarding trademarks and unfair competition, including litigation representing foreign-based clients. In addition, he has expertise in IP transactions for brand management through licensing and M&A. Mr Hatano has experiences in trade secrets and copyright disputes, and his work also covers a wide range of sectors, including the TMT sector and protection of industrial data. He has worked at the Intellectual Property Policy Office of the Ministry of Economy, Trade and Industry of the Japanese government.

Pam Kohli Jacobson is a partner, patent attorney, and a firmwide IP practice group coordinator at K&L Gates. K&L Gates is a global law firm with more than forty offices on five continents. She has a broad intellectual property practice that ranges from portfolio management to litigating IP disputes throughout the United States. Prior to law school, she worked as a research scientist in artificial intelligence in the area of autoimmune disease research at the University of Chicago and ozone depletion research at Honeywell f/k/a Allied Signal Corp. Drawing on her experience as a former research scientist, Ms Jacobson has advised some of the largest and most innovative companies in the world in connection with the integrated management, enforcement, and licensing of their global intellectual property portfolios. She is also a well-recognized IP scholar and has served as an adjunct professor of IP Law at the University of Washington School of Law and at its Center for Advanced Study & Research on Intellectual Property.

Jan Janssen is a senior dispute resolution lawyer at PETILLION in Belgium. For more than a decade, Jan has been advising on national and international dispute resolution with a special focus on intellectual property, information technology and the liberalization of the Internet sector. Jan's practice primarily involves complex civil litigation and (international) arbitration in a variety of industries, including fashion, media, postal services, technology and telecommunications. He has ample experience in representing brand holders before national courts, EUIPO, the CJEU and arbitration institutes. He is also valued for strategic advice on online brand protection and trademark licensing and distribution agreements. Jan also provides contractual advice and assists clients in protecting, managing and enforcing their IP rights in both an online and offline environment. He assists and represents clients in transactional matters, such as distribution, agency, licensing, technology transfer, software development, outsourcing and service level agreements. Jan has been at the forefront of arbitrations concerning Internet governance assigned to the Internet Corporation for Assigned Names and Numbers (ICANN).

Sunny Kumar is a special counsel at K&L Gates in London and a member of the IP procurement and portfolio management practice group. Sunny advises on contentious and non-contentious trademark, copyright, patent, design, advertising, licensing, commercial and data privacy matters. He also has significant litigation experience and has represented clients before the High Court, Court of Appeal and Supreme Court.

Tougane Loumeau is a lawyer registered at the Paris Bar. She is a senior legal adviser within intellectual property, telecommunications, media & technology practice group at Gide Loyrette Nouel, where she shares her time between expert legal research and high-profile cases. Tougane regularly provides lectures and leads training seminars on case law developments and other notable legal issues in the field of intellectual property law for IP-specialized lawyers and corporate general counsels. Tougane is a member of several professional associations, including the AIPPI where she has served as National Group Reporter for France since 2014. She is notably the co-author of the French chapter in *International Licensing and Technology Transfer, Practice and the Law* (Wolters Kluwer). Tougane holds a Master's in Management from ESSEC Business School, France; a Postgraduate Degree (DESS) in Industrial Property Law (University of Paris II); a Master's in Business Law (University of Paris XI); and a Diploma in Law (University of Edinburgh).

Kenji Marusumi is a senior associate at TMI Associates, which is one of the largest law firms in Japan. He regularly advises clients on various contentious issues, including IP matters. He has admission to practise in Japan and New York and previously worked in London and his practice also covers cross-border issues.

Michael Meredith is an associate at K&L Gates LLP's Seattle office and is a member of the firm's IP procurement and portfolio management practice group. Michael advises clients on trade secret, trademark, and copyright matters.

Arnaud Michel is a partner within the intellectual property practice group at Gide Loyrette Nouel in France, which is one of the leading international law firms. Arnaud Michel headed the firm's Brussels office from 1986 to 1993, where he specialized in intellectual property and European law. As part of this function, he has acted as counsel to both the EU Commission and the EU Council. Arnaud has held leading positions in several professional associations. He notably acted as President of LESI (Licensing Executive Society International) from May 2014 to April 2015, of LES France (Licensing Executive Society France) from 2002 to 2004, and of APRAM (main French association for trademarks and models) in 2000 and 2002. For many years, Arnaud has lectured all over the world on IP-related issues, in particular on comparative assessment of national legal systems in the area of intellectual property law and technology licensing. He has also taken part in the drafting and implementation of trademark law in several countries of the European Union (e.g., Bulgaria and Hungary). Involved on a day-to-day basis in the most important cases in France and the EU, Arnaud Michel consistently ranks as a leading expert in intellectual property by international legal directories. He is notably the co-author of the French chapter in *International Licensing and Technology Transfer, Practice and the Law* (Wolters Kluwer).

Masakatsu Nagashima is a senior associate at TMI Associates, which is one of the largest law firms in Japan. He specializes in IP and has extensive experience in IP-related works, including entertainment areas such as movie, sports, video game (e-sports) and digital entertainment. He has international work experience in Japan, the USA and Sweden. Mr Nagashima is qualified to practise in Japan and California. He has widely published on the subject of IP and entertainment law.

Diégo Noesen is a senior dispute resolution lawyer at PETILLION in Belgium. For near to a decade, he has been focussing on European and domestic litigation with an emphasis on intellectual property. Diego's practice primarily involves complex civil litigation, both on national and on European levels, in a variety of industries, including automotive, fashion, media & entertainment, technology and telecommunications. Diégo also provides transactional advice and assists clients in protecting, managing and enforcing their intellectual property rights. He has a particular expertise in brand and copyright protection, and domain names.

Kim Parviainen works with intellectual property and digitalization-related legal issues, both contentious and non-contentious, at Castrén & Snellman in Finland. Castrén & Snellman is one of Finland's largest and most well-renowned law firms. In contentious matters, Kim Parviainen has represented clients in litigation before both national and European courts, before arbitral tribunals, as well as in a range of regulatory proceedings and appeals. In non-contentious matters, he has drafted and negotiated complex commercial contracts on everything from multi-jurisdictional licensing deals for both technology and content to R&D, consortia, standardization, selective distributorship and more.

Flip Petillion is the managing partner of PETILLION in Belgium. PETILLION is an independent law firm with a focus on dispute resolution and helps clients prevent, settle and resolve commercial disputes through compliance counselling, contract drafting, negotiation, court litigation, arbitration or other forms of alternative dispute resolution (ADR). Flip Petillion has been handling court litigations and arbitrations for over thirty years. His practice focuses on trademarks, copyrights, information technology, domains and domain names. Flip is involved in the contentious/enforcement side as well as in the advice part of the IP practice, including licensing, advertising clearance, IP-driven transactional work and strategic advice. He is also a panellist and arbitrator in different international forums. Many of his appointments are directly related to his expertise in the field of trademarks and domain names. Flip regularly lectures on various topics and teaches: (i) at the new EUIPO Trade Mark and Design Education Programme, a new training programme organized by EUIPO staff, leading IP professionals and academics; (ii) the Master of Intellectual Property and ICT Law Program of Leuven University; and (iii) at the Beneluxstichting Beroepsopleiding Merken en Modellengemachtigden (BBMM), a foundation that is supervised by the Benelux Association of Trademark and Design Law (BMM). He is also a frequent speaker at professional and academic conferences and has published several articles relating to intellectual property, including trademarks. Flip edits a yearly overview of Belgian and European IP case law in the journal *RABG*, and has edited two books on the enforcement of IP rights in Belgium and the EU, respectively:

- *Handhaving van intellectuele rechten in België / Respect des droit intellectuels en Belgique, 10 jaar implementatie van de Europese richtlijn 2004/48 / 10 ans après la transposition de la directive 2004/48*, Larcier, 2018;
- *Enforcement of Intellectual Property Rights in the EU Member States*, Intersentia, 2019.

Flip is a member, participant and representative of several international trademark and intellectual property organizations, including the International Trademark Association (INTA), Marques and the European Communities Trademark Association (ECTA).

Keisha Phippen is an associate at K&L Gates in London and a member of the IP procurement and portfolio management practice group. She concentrates her practice on intellectual property, technology, data protection and commercial matters and has experience in advising on trademark infringement, trademark licensing and trademark filing, including the filing of oppositions for a variety of global organizations.

Anthony Prenol is a co-founder of CPST Law LLP. CPST is a Canadian law firm that, together with its affiliated patent and trademark agency firm, CPST Intellectual Property Inc., provides a full range of intellectual property services. Anthony Prenol is a lawyer, patent agent and trademark agent. Anthony's practice covers the full range of intellectual property protection, enforcement and commercialization. Prior to co-founding CPST in 2020, Anthony was a partner with Blake, Cassels & Graydon LLP, where he was the head of their intellectual property practice group for ten years. Anthony has written and lectured on a wide variety of topics in the trademarks field, including the use of expert evidence in trademark litigation and on comparative advertising and official marks. Anthony is a vice-chair of the Intellectual Property Owners Association's Industrial Designs Committee and a member of the International Trademark Association's Brand Restrictions Committee.

Dr Christoph Rieken is a partner in Noerr's IP group in Germany and advises on intellectual property (IP) law, with a focus on trademark law, unfair competition law, design law and copyright law. As one of the leading European law firms, Noerr is internationally renowned with offices in eleven countries and a global network of top-ranked 'best friends' law firms. Christoph has comprehensive experience in IP-related disputes and regularly represents parties before the German courts. Moreover, Christoph advises on licence and coexistence agreements and other IP-related commercial agreements such as merchandising and sponsoring agreements. Christoph is frequently recommended for his legal advice in trademark, design and competition law by directories such as *JUVE*, *WTR1000* and *Managing Intellectual Property - IP Stars*.

Fabio Versolatto is a senior associate at RENTSCH PARTNER in Switzerland, specializing in the fields of intellectual property (IP), competition, contract and industrial law, and both advising clients on IP issues and representing them in litigation. His main areas of activity include legal disputes in trademark, unfair competition and design matters and legal advice to companies on drafting and negotiating various contracts related to IP law, such as development, distribution, licence or asset transfer (assignment) agreements. He is an author of the *iusNet Intellectual Property Newsletter* and speaker at the course for Swiss IP specialists and patent attorneys on topics of trademark law, trademark proceedings, naming laws and the law on business/company names. He has also contributed to the following publications: *Commentary on Art. 1-4 Trademark Protection Act - Basler Kommentar Markenschutzgesetz Wappenschutzgesetz* (2017), *Vorsorgliche Massnahmen bei Markenverletzung - Kommentierte Musterklagen zum Gesellschaftsrecht und zum Geistigen Eigentum* (2016), and *Corporate Brands - Wahl und Registrierung von Firmen - Schweizer IP-Handbuch* (2013).

Elizaveta Semenova, Hogan Lovells, Russia.

Dr Stefanie Weidner is a senior associate in Noerr's IP group in Germany and advises on all aspects of intellectual property (IP) and unfair competition law. She specializes in disputes involving trademarks, designs, copyrights, false advertising, as well as other commercial litigation matters such as contract/licensing disputes. Stefanie was recognized as 'Rising Star' for Germany in 2020/21 by *Managing Intellectual Property*.

Gregor Wild focuses on copyright, trademark and design law and related contractual and procedural questions. His expertise primarily extends over Swiss and international IP law, in particular to the representation before the Federal IPI, Swiss Courts and the WIPO. Gregor Wild has gained global experience in more than seventy jurisdictions where he constantly collaborates with local experts. He has acquired special knowledge regarding transnational registrations and IP portfolios. Publicity and registration issues form the focus of his academic activities. After his thesis in copyright law and his employment in the trademark division of the Swiss IPI, Gregor Wild joined RENTSCH PARTNER in 2002. RENTSCH PARTNER is a leading Swiss attorney at law and patent attorney firm that advises and represents clients in all aspects of intellectual property law - transactions, proceedings and complex cases in both a domestic and a global context. He is a member of the Special Commission of Intellectual Property Rights of the Swiss Society of Engineers and Architects (SIA) and lecturer for Private Law at the

University of Lucerne. By 1 January 2012, he was elected by the Swiss Federal Council as a member of the Federal Arbitration Board for Exploitation of Authors' and Neighbouring Rights (ESchK).

Summary of Contents

Table of Contents

Preface

Licensing of intellectual property has become an increasingly important tool for the commercializing of intangible assets. Trademark holders can take advantage of the possibility to gain revenue through brand extensions, such as merchandising, franchising and co-branding. In a globalized market, the free flow of goods and services by means of licensing often requires detailed knowledge of national legal provisions and principles that will be applicable for agreements of this type.

The book is composed of an international comparative overview on the law and application of trademark licensing in a number of jurisdictions worldwide. The chapters on the various jurisdictions are written by experienced and distinguished attorneys from around the world.

The core feature of the book is to provide a basis for an overview of similarities and differences in the covered jurisdictions and that it therefore can function as a guide for trademark holders, or as support for lawyers advising clients, contemplating trademark licensing.

I want to express my sincere gratitude towards all authors who generously have contributed with their time and knowledge in producing this book. Thank you all! Thank you Christine Robben and Wolters Kluwer for all the support and guidance in completing the project. Finally, I want to extend a thank you to Arvid Axelryd and my other colleagues at Vinge for all assistance in the project.

Stojan Arnerstål
Stockholm, May 2021

Trademark Licensing in an International Context

Stojan Arnerstål

Licensing is a frequently used method to exploit and commercialize trademarks. In trademark licensing, a trademark owner (the licensor) grants permission to another party (the licensee) to use that trademark on mutually agreed terms and conditions. Licensing is often based upon a close and ongoing collaboration between the parties.

Trademark licensing can take many different forms. A common example is *franchising*, which is a licence under which the franchisee is allowed by the franchisor to use a particular business model and trademark, with additional obligations concerning training, support, purchase of products, etc. Another example is *merchandising*, where trademarks, designs or fictional characters are licensed for use on various products such as clothes, toys, and towels. Two related concepts are *brand extension* licensing and *co-branding*. A brand extension is when two companies team up to apply a trademark on a new product, for example, if a trademark used for candy is licensed to an ice cream manufacturer who markets ice cream with that particular candy taste. Co-branding is another similar licensing form under which two trademark holders join together in creating one product, using the reputation of trademarks that complement each other. There are various other examples of licensing, for example, component or ingredient branding (e.g., 'Intel Inside' or soft drink ingredients licensed for manufacturing), etc., and the number of categories appears to be expanding with the business creativity of trademark holders.

In its most basic form, a trademark guarantees the identity of the goods or services bearing the mark. The trademark thus enables the consumer or end user to distinguish the goods or services from others with different commercial origins. This characteristic of a trademark has frequently been highlighted as the *essential function* of the trademark.[1] A central purpose of trademark law is to protect the link between the

1. From an EU perspective, cf. CJEU case C-206/01 (Arsenal) paragraph 48.

trademark, the proprietor and the relevant public.[2] Since the trademark acts as a guarantee of the commercial origin of the goods or services, the consumers or end users indirectly receive a guarantee that someone (the company owning the trademark) has exercised control over the products or services in such a way that they will satisfy the consumers' expectations as established from previous purchases or from marketing.

In addition, the trademark has the capacity to act as an abstract instrument of communication. A trademark can be used by its proprietor to acquire or preserve a reputation capable of attracting consumers and retaining their loyalty.[3] Consequently, it has been held that the essential object of trademark law is to protect proprietors against actions of third parties who might seek, by creating a risk of confusion among consumers, to damage or take advantage of the reputation accruing to the trademark.[4]

Trademark law affords protection by ensuring that the goods or services bearing the trademark are put on the market under the control of the trademark owner, which is responsible for the quality of the goods or services. Trademark licensing is in general based on the fundamental notion that all products and services put on the market under the same brand should provide the same user experience. Consumers perceive the trademark as an expression of a particular quality (understood in a broad sense) – concerning its ability to satisfy specific needs. The trademark is therefore not only a representation of the commercial origin but can also become a symbol of a particular quality and particular features. These characteristics of a trademark are safeguarded as long as the trademark holder maintains control over the use by licensees, for example, by the obligations set out in the licence agreement.

An important aspect of trademark licensing is to present a uniform image and identity to the public. Accordingly, it is an essential part of a trademark licensing structure that the licence agreement provides the licensor sufficient control mechanisms, to protect the identification and goodwill features of the trademark. Simultaneously, this will protect consumers from confusion since the trademark's capacity to provide information about the products or services is safeguarded which essentially reduces their search costs.

In essence, a trademark licence means that the licensee is given a right to use the trademark for purposes that exclusively belongs to the trademark holder – commercial usage in accordance with the functions of the trademark. Reputed trademarks are often associated with an inherent value that provides bargaining power and triggers buying impulses among consumers. In a sense, the trademark communicates a message that the trademark holder allows other actors to benefit from so-called image transfer. Under the licence, the licensee can utilize and benefit from the goodwill and connotations associated with the brand.

Through the trademark licence, a relatively small actor can provide goods and services under a well-known brand and thus take advantage of the trademark's appeal to generate customers. Because of this, the trademark licence acts as a means for faster

2. Stojan Arnerstål, Varumärket som kontraktsföremål (2014) p. 26 and Per Jonas Nordell, Varumärkesrättens skyddsobjekt – Om ordkännetecknets mening och referens (2004) p. 21.
3. Cf. CJEU case C-323/09 (Interflora) paragraph 60.
4. CJEU case C-9/93 (Ideal Standard) paragraph 16.

entrance into the market for the licensee while at the same time generating additional revenue streams for the licensor. However, for some companies licensing of their trademarks is less about revenue streams and more about increasing customer recognition. The more the trademark is used, the greater the recognition of the brand.

Further, a licensing set-up provides the trademark holder an easier access for expansion into other territories, without requiring him or her to take on all risks associated with entering into a new market. With the ongoing globalization, the international aspects of trademark licensing are increasing in importance.

An additional benefit of licensing is that it gives the trademark holder the option of taking advantage of another party's manufacturing, distribution, sales or marketing capacity, that is, without having to invest in developing such capacity within its own establishments. For these reasons, trademarks often tend to be licensed as part of a broader commercial relationship, including the transfer of other intellectual property (e.g., copyright) and know-how relating to the manufacturing of products.

A trademark licence can also provide the trademark holder access to new channels of distribution or segmentation on the market. In addition, such partnering may create efficiencies by the parties sharing common costs, for example, in relation to advertising and promotion cost.

Franchising is a good example that demonstrates not only the benefits but also the risks associated with trademark licensing. One important objective of a franchising concept is that the entire franchise network can provide a uniform user experience to customers. This means that customers should receive the same experience from different franchise operators, regardless of who owns the specific business and therefore is the actual contractual counterpart. It could even be argued that customers to a certain extent do not care who owns the particular business, as long as their brand expectations of the franchise concept are met. Such expectations can, for example, be based on previous experiences of the franchise concept or from marketing.

In many cases, it is the concept and the brand that will attract customers to a franchise location, rather than the local business as such. The brand's ability to communicate a coherent user experience is one of the main benefits for a franchisee entering into a franchise agreement. The established goodwill and customer base of the franchise concept and brand can be turned into a revenue stream by the franchisee. The economic profitability of a franchise business will to a large extent depend on maintaining the reputation and image of the network towards potential customers. For a prospective franchisee, benefiting from the accrued goodwill of a franchise may appear more attractive than the risks associated with the option of breaking totally new ground. Consequently, a well-managed franchise concept may be very beneficial for both the franchisor and the franchisee.

Nonetheless, the parties to the franchising agreement will not always have coinciding interests in this respect. One example is problems that occur when a franchisee freerides on the concept in order to maximize the profits, for example, by producing products or services of an inferior quality than is generally provided by the franchise collective. Freeriding of this nature is perhaps a particular problem in situations where the franchisee does not have recurring customers, for example, in the case of a franchise located at an airport where customers rarely return. The individual franchisee may have an incentive to reduce the quality of the products or services for cost-saving purposes. The harmful effects and costs of such behaviour are allocated to the entire franchise network, while all the benefits will be obtained by the individual franchisee. It is evident that a qualitative deterioration of this type may be detrimental to the franchise concept as a whole.

Conflicting interests of this nature may cause tension in the contractual relationship between the franchisor and the franchisee. The franchisor's main source of income is from royalties on gross sales or surcharges on the price of goods sold to the franchisees, meaning that they will naturally seek to maximize the level of sales or profit generated across the whole franchise network. In contrast, the franchisee's revenues emanate from the business outlet that they own, which will often encourage them to maximize the level of profits at their own outlet. The strategies that maximize system-wide sales in comparison to those that maximize profits at an individual franchise outlet are not the same. This may lead franchisors and franchisees to adopt different business strategies.

In summary, trademark licensing is an effective method for expanding a business and for distributing goods and services through a bilateral contractual relationship. It is therefore not surprising that the importance of trademark licensing continues to increase. However, because of the risks associated with trademark licensing, the management and protection of the trademark and control over the licensee's activities are of central importance to the trademark holder. Otherwise, the value of the trademark may deteriorate.

The cross-border aspect of trademark licensing is continuously growing in importance. The purpose of this book is to explore and discuss how issues related to protection of trademarks and use of such trademarks in contractual relationships can be dealt with from a practical and legal perspective. In the various country chapters of the book, it is discussed how national trademark law interacts with national contract law. The idea has been to highlight the transactional aspects of trademarks and the terms that apply to such transactions. The chapters provide a basis for an overview of similarities and differences in the covered jurisdictions. As such, the book can function both as a guide for practical needs and as a basis for continued theoretical discussions about transactional aspects of intellectual property in a broader and international context.

Belgium

Flip Petillion, Jan Janssen & Diégo Noesen

1. LEGAL FRAMEWORK[1]

1.1. International Regulations, Treaties and Conventions

There are two types of trademarks covering Belgium: European Union trademarks (EUTMs) and Benelux trademarks. Trademarks only covering Belgium do not exist.

EUTMs are protected under EU Trademark Regulation 2017/1001[2] and EU Directive 2015/2436.[3]

Belgium, the Netherlands and Luxembourg have applied uniform rules for the protection of trademarks since 1971. Benelux trademarks are governed by the Benelux Convention on Intellectual Property (BCIP).[4]

Belgium also protects trade names through the Paris Convention for the Protection of Industrial Property.[5] Trade names are considered to be assets covered by intellectual property rights, and can thus be licensed like registered trademarks.

1.2. Contract Law and the Code on Economic Law

As trademark holders are free to agree on the licensing of their trademarks, the agreements remain in great deal governed by the Belgian general contract law as well as specific legislation that governs specific types of agreements included in the Code on Economic Law (CEL). In this contribution, we will especially focus on the provisions of

1. This chapter was written subject to the law stated as of 1 May 2020.
2. Regulation (EU) 2017/1001 of the European Parliament and of the Council of 14 June 2017 on the European Union trademark, *OJ L 154*, p. 1 (EUTMR).
3. Directive (EU) 2015/2436 of the European Parliament and of the Council of 16 December 2015 to approximate the laws of the Member States relating to trademarks, *OJ L 336*, p. 1 (EUTMD).
4. See https://www.boip.int/en/ip-professionals/regulations-policy/regulations.
5. Paris Convention for the Protection of Industrial Property of 20 March 1883, approved in Belgium through the Law of 26 December 1974, *Belgian Official Journal* 29 January 1975, p. 869.

Book IV CEL on competition, Book X, Title 2 CEL that applies to all commercial cooperation agreements and Book X, Title 3 CEL covering the unilateral termination of exclusive distribution agreements.

Book X, Title 2 covers 'pre-contractual information in the context of commercial cooperation agreements' and aims to support and promote the development of various commercial cooperation formulas by establishing a set of rules to accompany the pre-contractual phase. A party that has been informed correctly and in good time can better evaluate the scope of its commitments and make decisions with better knowledge of the facts.[6]

Book X, Title 3 provides for specific rules to protect Belgian distributors and their network against suppliers wanting to terminate the distribution agreement.[7]

1.3. Case Law

Finally, court decisions have contributed to the legal framework applicable to trademark licensing agreements.

2. WHAT IS A TRADEMARK LICENCE?

2.1. Definition

With a licence, one party grants a specific right to another party.

Neither the BCIP nor the European legislation contains a definition of the trademark licence. One may, however, assume that in trademark licensing, a trademark owner (licensor) grants permission to another (licensee) to use that trademark on mutually agreed terms and conditions. It is a so-called reciprocal agreement whereby the owner of a trademark (licensor) grants another (licensee) the right to perform certain acts normally covered by the trademark monopoly, often subject to payment of a certain fee (royalty).

On the basis of a licence, the licensee obtains permission to affix the mark to goods produced either by himself or by the proprietor or a third party and the right to put the goods so marked into circulation. In the case of a service mark, the consent covers the right to use the mark in connection with the provision of services. This normally includes permission to use the trademark on stationery, invoices, advertising material and means of transport. A licence may or may not be exclusive.[8]

The Court of Justice of the European Union (CJEU) phrases it as follows: 'by granting a licence, the proprietor of a trade mark confers on the licensee, within the limits set out in the licence agreement, the right to use the trademark in question for purposes falling within the scope of the exclusive right conferred by that trademark, namely its commercial use in accordance with its own functions, in particular the

6. See more below, section 4.4.
7. See more below, section 10.2.
8. M.-C. Janssens, *Handboek Merkenrecht*, Intersentia, 257.

essential function of guaranteeing to consumers the origin of the goods or services in question'.[9]

2.2. Licensing and the Indication of Origin as an Essential Function of Trademarks

Trademark licensing was considered impossible at one time, given that one of the functions of a trademark is to indicate the source or origin of the goods or services. The fact that a good or service is produced or delivered by a licensee (a person authorized by the owner to use the trademark) in essence means that the good or service is emanating from a source other than the owner. As such, it would amount to a false or deceptive representation to the consumer as to the true origin of the products involved.

2.3. Licensing and Quality Control by the Trademark Holder

However, trademark licensing became acceptable where the licensor (the owner of the trademark) remained in control of the nature and quality of the goods or services sold in association with the trademark.

Quality control is, therefore, the essence of trademark licensing, providing the means for ensuring that the licensee's use is consistent with the licensor's interest in the trademark and at the same time ensuring that the consumer will get essentially the same quality good or service no matter where the trademarked good is purchased or the service is experienced.

3. BUSINESS BENEFITS OF A TRADEMARK LICENCE

There may be different reasons to grant a trademark licence or to benefit from it. We list some below, even though these will often be combined.

3.1. Territorial Expansion

It is not always easy to expand a business in a new territory with different rules and/or a different culture. A trademark holder may therefore choose to license its trademark to a local company with relevant experience. The licensee may be in a better position to import the trademark successfully.

Example: a U.S. based company active in infant and child-oriented fitness gyms had no presence in South Africa, although the company's concept can be applied internationally. This company licensed its trademark to a local business which is in charge of expanding the concept in South Africa under the U.S. company's trademark.

9. CJEU, Case C-376/11, 19 July 2012, *Pie Optiek*, ECLI:EU:C:2012:502, 47.

3.2. Mutual Benefits Related to Investments and Advertising

Partnering through licensing creates efficiencies. Licensing a trademark allows the licensor to earn additional revenue and to develop this trademark by using the licensee's structure for the manufacturing, sale or distribution of the goods and services covered by the trademark. This way, the licensor avoids having to invest in developing such capacity within its own structure. Multiple licensing deals may also quickly increase the trademark's visibility among consumers.

The licensee benefits from the licensor's previous advertising efforts to build a strong trademark. During the licensing agreement, advertising and promotion costs can be shared.

Different trademark owners may even license their trademarks to each other and combine these on a product (co-branding), creating even more value.

3.3. Expansion Through New Channels of Distribution and/or to New Markets

A trademark holder may also have issues in using a new channel of distribution, or entering a new market in the same geographical area. Licensing its trademark to someone who is already used to these distribution channels or markets can be beneficial.

A fashion brand specialized in adult clothing may, for example, use a licensee who has particular experience in children clothing to extend its trademark to this new market.

3.4. Avoid Losing a Trademark or Solve Legal Issues

Where there is a risk of losing a trademark, e.g., because of non-use, such a mark can be licensed to someone in order to keep it alive.

In some situations where a trademark is being infringed by a third party, it may be an option to convince the infringer to obtain a licence for the use of the mark instead of initiating proceedings. This type of deal is often overlooked but can be a very efficient solution. In software infringements, it has become a typical part of the settlement package offered to infringers. They must pay the value of the licence to rectify the past, and take a licence in order to be allowed to cover the use in the future.

4. CONTRACTUAL FREEDOM

4.1. Consensus Based

Benelux and EU trademarks may be licensed for all or part of the goods or services for which they are registered or applied for.

The EUTMR provides the following: 'An EU trademark is to be regarded as an object of property which exists separately from the undertakings whose goods or services are designated by it. Accordingly, it should be capable of being transferred, of being charged as security in favour of a third party and of being the subject matter of licences.'[10] 'An EU trademark may be licensed for some or all of the goods or services for which it is registered and for the whole or part of the Union. A licence may be exclusive or non-exclusive.'[11]

The BCIP provides for an identical approach: 'A trademark may be licensed for some or all of the goods or services for which it is registered and for the whole or part of the Benelux territory. A licence may be exclusive or non-exclusive.'[12]

It is worth referring to the historical analysis of the right to transfer a trademark, as explained by Professor Marie-Christine Janssens.[13] In trademark law, 'free transfer' means the rule whereby the validity of the transfer of the exclusive right to a trademark is not made dependent on a simultaneous takeover of the company. This means that trademarks may be transferred from one entrepreneur to another without the business itself being surrendered in whole or in part.

The BCIP confirms this rule of the so-called free transfer of trademarks,[14] which had already been introduced with the Benelux trademark law since 1 January 1971.

Previously this was not the case in Belgium. Article 7 of the Trademark Law of 1879 insisted that the trademark and the business would be transferred together. The transfer also had to be disclosed by registration at the registry of the Commercial Court together with the filing of an extract of the deed of transfer. However, because this rule was often infringed, irregular situations arose. These could still have repercussions after the introduction of the 'free transfer' rule in 1971: without proof of a valid transfer of an older trademark together with the related business, this old trademark can still be declared to be non-existent.

The 'free transfer' solution was found because practice had shown that the protection of the public was already guaranteed by the self-interest of the people involved, even without the link between the original business and the trademark. Someone who buys a trademark will most likely do everything to keep the trademark's strength by ensuring the quality of the goods or services. That is why a less rigid regime has been preferred, which had in the meantime been imposed by Article 21 of the Agreement on Trade-Related Aspects of Intellectual Property Rights (TRIPS).

The same rule of free transfer is incorporated in the EUTMR and EUTMD, respectively.[15]

EU legislation and the BCIP therefore allow the holder of a Benelux or EU trademark to:

- sell his trademark without transferring all or part of his business;
- sell or license parts of his trademark in the sense that the assignment or licence may apply to all or part of the goods for which the trademark was registered.

10. Preamble 26 EUTMR
11. Article 25.1, EUTMR; Article 25.1, EUTMD.
12. Article 2.32.1 BCIP.
13. M.-C. JANSSENS, *Handboek Merkenrecht*, Intersentia, 253-254.
14. Article 2.31 BCIP.
15. Article 20 EUTMR; Article 22 EUTMD.

4.2. Forms of Licensing

Licensing takes many forms, depending on the parties' intentions and business objectives as mentioned above:[16]

- Merchandising: popular trademarks (alongside designs or copyright protected fictional characters or personalities) are often licensed to be applied on ordinary products in order to increase the appeal of these products and thus raise their price. Common examples are T-shirts, mugs or hats bearing a famous trademark of a sports team or a superhero character.
- Co-branding: trademark owners can team up to create a new product or enhanced version of a product using the reputation of trademarks which complement each other. In Belgium, the famous luxury leather goods brand Delvaux created a collection inspired by the Belgian painter Magritte,[17] and Belgian watchmaker Ice-Watch made a premium collection of BMW watches.[18]
- Component branding: trademarks do not have to be on the same level on a product. A trademarked product can mention the trademark of a component of that product. The most famous example is the 'Intel Inside' campaign, through which Intel raised awareness of its trademark by mentioning it on computers from different makers such as Apple or HP who benefited from Intel's trademark reputation.
- Use of quality labels: labels certifying a certain quality obviously add value to a product. Products which comply with the required conditions will be able to mention the quality label. This will often be a trademarked logo, such as the following EU trademark which can only be used on products that have been certified as organic by an authorized control agency or body.[19]

16. See section 3.
17. https://www.delvaux.com/en/collections/focus/magritte-collection-2019?locale=en.
18. http://www.etvonweb.be/76888-collab-ice-watch-pour-bmw.
19. https://ec.europa.eu/info/food-farming-fisheries/farming/organic-farming/organics-glance/organic-logo_en.

EUTM No. 018055852.

The above list is far from exhaustive, as parties remain free to get creative or even combine different forms of licensing depending on their needs and the characteristics of the trademarks involved.

4.3. Licensing as Part of a Broader Agreement

A licensing agreement will often be part of a broader agreement, including additional conditions which do not specifically relate to the use of a trademark.

Franchising. The first agreement which immediately comes to mind is franchising. The EFF European Code of Ethics for Franchising[20] provides the following definition:

> Franchising is a system of marketing goods and/or services and/or technology, which is based upon a close and ongoing collaboration between legally and financially separate and independent undertakings, the Franchisor and its individual Franchisees, whereby the Franchisor grants its individual Franchisee the right, and imposes the obligation, to conduct a business in accordance with the Franchisor's concept.
>
> The right entitles and compels the individual Franchisee, in exchange for a direct or indirect financial consideration, to use the Franchisor's trade name, and/or trademark and/or service mark, know-how, business and technical methods, procedural system, and other industrial and /or intellectual property rights, supported by continuing provision of commercial and technical assistance, within the framework and for the term of a written franchise agreement, concluded between parties for this purpose.

A franchisee is thus allowed by a franchisor to use a particular business model or concept in return for a financial compensation. It is generally accepted that the two main characteristics of such an agreement are: (1) the licensing of intellectual property

20. https://ec.europa.eu/digital-single-market/en/content/eff-european-code-ethics-franchising.

rights in respect of trademarks or trade names and know-how and (2) the commercial or technical assistance that the franchisor usually provides to the franchisee during the term of the agreement (e.g., in relation to sales, training, marketing, etc.).

Franchising is not defined as such under Belgian law but, as will be explained below, specific pre-contractual rules apply to so-called commercial cooperation agreements.[21] Franchising is considered to be falling under the legal concept of a commercial cooperation agreement.

Distribution agreement. Another common agreement is the distribution agreement. Belgian law defines a distribution agreement as any agreement under which one or more distributors are granted the right by a principal to sell products in his own name and for his own account, which the principal manufactures or distributes himself.[22] In principle, such agreement does not necessarily involve a trademark licence, as the distributor does not manufacture any goods but simply distributes the goods bought from the principal. However, the parties will often provide for specific provisions related to the use of the principal's trademark by the distributor.

Agency agreement. Finally, Belgian law provides for a specific definition of the agency agreement: 'agreement whereby one party, the commercial agent, is permanently charged by the other party, the principal, without being under his authority, with facilitating and possibly concluding business deals in the name and on behalf of the principal, against the payment of a financial compensation. The commercial agent organizes his time and activities at his own discretion and independently'.[23]

As opposed to a distributor, a commercial agent will not buy any goods from the principal but will simply represent the principal and receive a commission on every sale. An agency agreement may include a trademark licensing agreement.

A court has the power to requalify an agreement based on a factual analysis. For example, the Court of Liège ruled that it must be assessed which element weighs most in a specific case: the provision of know-how and trademarks, or the right to purchase goods. When it appears that the specific know-how, organization and sales system are essential in the decision to be part of a network, and when the agreement implies a cooperation between the parties that goes well beyond a normal distribution agreement, this agreement may need to be requalified as a franchise agreement. This means that the general rules of contract law will apply instead of the specific rules related to distribution agreements.[24]

4.4. Importance of Pre-contractual Information

Under Belgian law, particular attention is paid to pre-contractual obligations in the context of commercial cooperation agreements.[25]

21. See section 4.4.
22. Article I.11, 3° CEL.
23. Article I.11, 1° CEL.
24. Liège Court of Appeal, 9 January 2009, JLMB 2011, No. 21, 1010.
25. Article I.11, 2° CEL and Article X.26 CEL.

These are contracts concluded between several persons, whereby one person grants the other the right to use a commercial formula in the sale of products or the provision of services in one or more of the following forms:

- a joint sign, in the sense of a sign displayed on a store or office buildings to identify a commercial undertaking;
- a joint trade name;
- a transfer of know-how;
- commercial or technical assistance.[26]

In many cases, the commercial formula includes several of these elements. However, as soon as one of the above forms is present in the commercial formula, the legal framework must be complied with.

These agreements can take many forms but, as mentioned before, the most common example is the franchise agreement.

However, all licensing agreements will not necessarily be covered by the above definition of a commercial cooperation agreement. We may think of simple agreements on the use of a trademark without any assistance or knowledge transfer from the licensor to the licensee.

Below are the most important principles of this piece of legislation, applied to licensing agreements falling under its scope.

First of all, the pre-contractual obligations are subject to Belgian law and fall under the jurisdiction of Belgian courts when the licensee's activities covered by the agreement are mainly conducted in Belgium.[27]

At least one month before the closing of the contract, the projected licensee must be provided with the following documents to enable him to make a reasoned decision:[28]

(i) a draft of the proposed agreement;
(ii) a separate document consisting of two parts:[29]
   - a first part containing the important contractual provisions; and
   - a second section containing a set of socio-economic data about the licensor, the market, expected investments, etc.

In order to ensure legal certainty but avoid unnecessary formalities and costs, a simplified version of the separate document is sufficient in the following circumstances:

- the renewal of a commercial cooperation agreement concluded for a fixed period of time;
- the conclusion of a new agreement between the same parties; or

26. Article I.11, 2° CEL.
27. Article X.33 CEL.
28. Article X.27 CEL.
29. Article X.28 CEL.

- the amendment of a commercial cooperation agreement which has been in progress for at least two years.

In the latter case, the licensor may even be exempted from providing any document if it is the licensee who requests, in writing, an amendment of the agreement in progress.[30]

Although not expressly mentioned in the relevant provisions, the projected licensee must also provide any relevant information to the licensor. The general principle of 'good faith' applies here.

The documents must be made available in writing or on a durable and accessible medium for the licensee. This means that the licensor who is providing the data electronically ensures that the other party is able to access such electronic data.

Before the expiry of the period of one month prior to the conclusion of the contract, no commitment may be made and no fee, amount or deposit may be requested or paid. This does not apply to:

- obligations relating to contracts in progress when a renewal, amendment, or a new contract between the same parties is negotiated; and
- commitments made under a confidentiality agreement.[31]

A specific provision clarifies the broad interpretation given by law to the compensation paid by the licensee and to the mention, in the separate document, of both direct and indirect compensation. A direct compensation will have to be clearly specified in the separate document. If the parties provide for an indirect compensation, its method of calculation must be explained.[32]

The law explicitly provides that all information exchanged is protected by the obligation of confidentiality. The parties may only use the information they obtain within the framework of the agreement to be concluded.[33] That being said, the parties are always free to conclude a confidentiality agreement with more specific provisions, e.g., financial penalties in case of breach.

The parties are obliged to draw up all documents in a clear and comprehensible language. In the event of any dispute as to the meaning of a term or an item of information, the interpretation shall be made in favour of the person acquiring the right.[34]

30. Article X.29 CEL.
31. Article X.27 CEL.
32. Article X.28§1,d CEL.
33. Article X.31 CEL.
34. Article X.32 CEL.

4.5. Licences and Competition

The parties' contractual freedom is also limited by European and Belgian competition rules. Infringements to these rules can be found not only in the content of the licensing agreement but also in the effective actions of the parties.[35]

Belgian competition rules are set out in Book IV CEL and essentially take over the European provisions. Moreover, it has been confirmed that the European competition principles, case law and practices are also applied by the Belgian courts and competition authorities to purely national situations which do not influence commerce between Member States, e.g., a licensing agreement which would only harm competition on the Belgian market.[36]

The validity of licensing agreements must be examined in three steps:

(1) First, it must be assessed whether the agreement is prohibited under Article 101.1 of the Treaty on the Functioning of the European Union ('TFEU') and/or Article IV.1, §1 CEL.
(2) If so, block exemption regulations may still apply. We will focus on the Vertical Block Exemption Regulation[37] applicable to selective distribution agreements.
(3) Without an applicable block exemption regulation, the agreement may still be valid if the conditions of Article 101.3 TFEU and/or Article IV.1, §3 CEL are fulfilled.

We will briefly examine each step below.

4.5.1. Article 101.1 TFEU and Article IV.1, §1 CEL

These provisions prohibit all agreements between undertakings, decisions by associations of undertakings and concerted practices which may affect trade and which have as their object or effect the prevention, restriction or distortion of competition within the EU or Belgian market. Such agreements shall be automatically void.[38]

In order to fall under these provisions, a licensing agreement must appreciably restrict competition on the relevant market(s). According to the EU Commission, a licensing agreement between non-competitors does not appreciably restrict competition if the market share held by each of the parties to the agreement does not exceed 15 % on any of the relevant markets affected by the agreement.[39]

---

35. CJEU, Joined cases 29/83 and 30/83, 28 March 1984, *CRAM and Rheinzink v. Commission*, ECLI:EU:C:1984:130.
36. F. Wijckmans, 'De nieuwe Belgische mededingingswet', R.W. 2006-07, 622, 626, No. 13-14.
37. Commission Regulation (EU) No 330/2010 of 20 April 2010 on the application of Article 101(3) of the Treaty on the Functioning of the European Union to categories of vertical agreements and concerted practices.
38. Article 101.2 TFEU; Article IV.1, §2 CEL.
39. Notice on agreements of minor importance which do not appreciably restrict competition under Article 101(1) of the Treaty on the Functioning of the European Union (De Minimis Notice), 2014/C 291/01, point 8.

However, agreements which restrict competition by including so-called hardcore limitations will in any event be prohibited. 'Hardcore' limitations are limitations which almost certainly have a negative impact on competition by their very nature or because of their purpose, e.g., a licensing agreement which purpose is to directly or indirectly fix (minimum) prices for the sale of goods to third parties.[40]

A licensor can control the distribution network of its trademarked goods by determining under which conditions these goods may be offered to the end consumer. In that regard, the licensing agreement could provide that the licensee can only sell the trademarked goods to distributors selected by certain criteria. According to the judgment of the CJEU in the '*Metro I*' case,[41] it is allowed to provide for a selective distribution network under the following conditions:

(1) the selective distribution network is necessary given the nature of the product;
(2) the selection criteria are applied without discrimination, are objective and based on quality; and
(3) the selection criteria do not reach further than necessary.

With regard to the first condition, the CJEU ruled that a selective distribution network may be justified in respect of luxury goods, as an impairment to the goods' aura of luxury is likely to affect the actual quality of those goods.[42] However, the two other conditions leave a lot of room for interpretation.

4.5.2. *Vertical Block Exemption Regulation*

The Vertical Block Exemption Regulation applies to vertical agreements; i.e., an agreement or concerted practice entered into between two or more undertakings each of which operates, for the purposes of the agreement or the concerted practice, at a different level of the production or distribution chain, and relating to the conditions under which the parties may purchase, sell or resell certain goods or services.[43] Franchise agreements including a trademark licence will usually fall under the scope of this regulation.

The EU Commission also provided guidelines for the application of the regulation.[44] Although these guidelines are considered as soft law, the Belgian Competition Authority ('BCA') and courts take these into account.[45]

The Vertical Block Exemption Regulation provides for a few conditions in order to avoid vertical agreements falling under Article 101.1 TFEU. Quite importantly, the

40. Article 4(a) Vertical Block Exemption Regulation.
41. CJEU, Case C-26/76, 25 October 1977, *Metro v. Commission*, ECLI:EU:C:1977:167.
42. CJEU, Case C-230/16, 6 December 2017, *Coty*, ECLI:EU:C:2017:941, point 25.
43. Article 1.1(a) Vertical Block Exemption Regulation.
44. Guidelines on Vertical Restraints, 2010/C 130/01
45. See, for example, BCA 24 January 2019, No. BCA 19-IO-AUD, *HM Products Benelux*; Antwerp Court of Appeal, 31 May 2018, Competitio 2018, nr. 4, 349.

Vertical Block Exemption Regulation will not apply if the main purpose of the agreement is the transfer or licence of an intellectual property right.[46]

This means that 'pure' trademark licensing agreements, such as a merchandising agreement enabling the licensee to mention a trademark on a T-shirt, fall outside the scope of this regulation and thus cannot benefit from the exemption. Conversely, a distribution agreement providing that the licensee can use the licensed trademark to show that it is a member of the licensor's official network can benefit from the exemption.

4.5.3. *Article 101.3 TFEU and Article IV.1, §3 CEL*

If no block exemption applies, a licensing agreement may still be valid if it complies with the following cumulative requirements under Article 101.3 TFEU:

(1) the agreement contributes to improving the production or distribution of goods or to promoting technical or economic progress;
(2) it allows consumers a fair share of the resulting benefit;
(3) it does not impose on the undertakings concerned restrictions which are not indispensable to the attainment of these objectives; and
(4) it does not afford such undertakings the possibility of eliminating competition in respect of a substantial part of the products in question.

Article IV.1, §3 CEL adds one element to the first requirement of the EU provision: the agreement can also allow for small and medium enterprises to strengthen their competitive position on the relevant or international market.

5. VALIDITY OF A TRADEMARK LICENCE

The EU and Benelux both provide for flexible rules regarding the validity of a trademark licence. As opposed to the transfer of a trademark, a licence does not have to be in writing and does not necessarily have to cover the entire territory of the relevant trademark.[47]

However, a licence granted for only part of the territory covered by the licensed trademark will still have to abide by general principles of European law, such as the free movement of goods and the linked exhaustion of trademark rights. As soon as goods are marketed in a particular territory within the EU with the licensor's approval, the licensor will not be able to prohibit the later distribution and sale of those goods in other parts of the EU.

Also, if the trademark licensing agreement falls under the definition of a commercial cooperation agreement as mentioned above,[48] written pre-contractual obligations will apply under Belgian law.

46. Article 2.3 Vertical Block Exemption Regulation.
47. Article 25.1 EUTMR, Article 25.1 EUTMD and Article 2.32 BCIP.
48. See section 4.4.

6. OPPOSABILITY OF A TRADEMARK LICENCE

6.1. Unregistered Licences

Unregistered licences are valid, but they are only opposable among the parties themselves. However, EU law provides for an exception: an unregistered licence has effect vis-à-vis third parties who have acquired rights in an EUTM after the date of that licence but who knew of the licence at the date on which the rights were acquired.[49]

A person who acquires the EUTM or a right concerning the EUTM (e.g., a licence) by way of transfer of the whole of an undertaking or by any other universal succession will also be bound by any existing unregistered licence, as that person becomes one of the parties to the licensing agreement.[50]

Benelux trademark law does not go into such detail. It simply provides that a licence becomes opposable against third parties only after the recordal of the licence.[51]

Both EU and Benelux case law clarified that these provisions do not preclude the holder of an unregistered licence from initiating infringement proceedings. The provisions are intended to protect a person who has, or may have, rights in a trademark and not to prevent actions initiated by a licensee against persons who infringe the trademark.[52] However, as explained below, the licensee must have the licensor's approval to initiate such proceedings (or, in case of an exclusive licence, the licensee should first inform the licensor and may take action only if the licensor does not himself within an appropriate period).[53]

6.2. Registered Licences

As mentioned in section 6.1 above, licences related to EUTMs and Benelux trademarks need to be registered in order to become fully opposable to third parties.

6.2.1. Registration of a Licence Related to an EUTM

At the request of one of the parties, the grant or transfer of a licence in respect of an EUTM is entered in the Register and published.[54] At European level, this Register is kept by the EU Intellectual Property Office ('EUIPO').[55]

The EUIPO provides an online application form to register a licence.[56] A single application for the registration of a licence for two or more EUTMs may be made only if the registered proprietor and the licensee are the same and the contracts have the

49. Article 27.1 EUTMR.
50. Article 27.2 EUTMR.
51. Article 2.33 BCIP.
52. CJEU, Case C-163/15, 4 February 2016, *Hassan v. Breiding*, ECLI:EU:C:2016:71; Gerechtshof Amsterdam, 17 February 2009, *Davidoff and Lancaster v. Coscentra*, ECLI:NL:GHAMS:2009:BH3125.
53. See section 9.1.
54. Article 25.5 EUTMR.
55. Article 111 EUTMR.
56. See https://euipo.europa.eu/ohimportal/en/online-requests-apply-now.

same conditions, limitations and terms in each case.[57] The registration is subject to the payment of a fee per EUTM, with a maximum amount in case all parties and conditions are the same and all registrations of licences are applied for at the same time.[58]

There are also some language requirements. The application for the registration of a licence for an EUTM application must be made in the first or second language of the EUTM application. When registering a licence for a registered EUTM, the application must be submitted in one of the five languages of the EUIPO, namely, English, French, German, Italian or Spanish.[59]

When an application for the registration of a licence is made by the EUTM proprietor alone, no proof of the licence is necessary. When such application is made jointly by the EUTM proprietor and its licensee, the signature of both parties constitutes proof of the licence. Proof of the licence must only be submitted when the licensee alone applies for the registration. Such proof may be an extract of the licensing agreement or a separate declaration, as long as it bears the signature of the EUTM proprietor or its representative.[60]

Parties can specify the conditions of the licence, which can be one or more of the following types:

- an exclusive licence;
- a sublicence in the event that the licence is granted by a licensee whose licence is recorded in the Register;
- a licence limited to only part of the goods or services for which the mark is registered;
- a licence limited to part of the Union;
- a temporary licence.

There are some requirements related to these different types of licences:

- exclusive licence: an explicit statement to this effect must be made in the application for registration;
- sublicence: it cannot be registered without first registering the main licence;
- limitation of goods or services: the goods or services for which the licence has been granted must be clearly indicated;
- territorially limited licence: the application must indicate the part of the European Union for which the licence has been granted. A part of the European Union may consist of one or several Member States or one or several administrative districts within a Member State;
- temporary licence: the expiry date of the licence must be specified. Mentioning the date of the commencement of the licence is optional.[61]

57. Articles 20(8) and 26(1) EUTMR.
58. Article 26.2 EUTMR; see https://euipo.europa.eu/ohimportal/en/fees-payable-direct-to-euipo.
59. Article 146(6) EUTMR.
60. EUIPO Trademark and Design Guidelines, Part E, section 3, Chapter 2, 4.1: https://guidelines.euipo.europa.eu/1922895/1786321/trade-mark-guidelines/4-1-requirements-concerning-proof.
61. Article 26.3 EUTMR.

The EUIPO notifies the party applying for a licence registration if there are any deficiencies or missing information.[62] To avoid rejection, any formal deficiencies must be remedied within the time limit established in EUIPO's communication, which will normally be two months following the date of the notification.

If the missing information relates to specific conditions of the licence, EUIPO may decide to register the licence anyway without mentioning the specific type of licence. For example, if someone does not specify the expiry date of a licence and fails to respond to EUIPO's communication in that regard, EUIPO will register the licence without mentioning that it is a temporary licence.

The party concerned may file an appeal with the EUIPO Boards of Appeal against EUIPO's decision to reject a licence or to register it without specifying the type of licence.[63]

EUIPO's examination remains limited; i.e., it will not check whether an application for registration of an exclusive licence is compatible with an existing licence which was registered before, or whether a licensee has the power to grant and register a sublicence. The parties remain responsible for any incompatibilities and have a duty to update the Register if needed.[64]

The EUIPO will only publish the type of licence as listed above, without disclosing the details such as the goods and services or territory covered by the licence.[65]

6.2.2. Registration of a Licence Related to a Benelux Trademark

To become fully opposable against third parties, a licence related to a Benelux trademark must be registered with the Benelux Office for Intellectual Property (trademarks and designs) ('BOIP').

The BOIP provides a form to be downloaded from its website, in which parties must indicate whether the registration relates to a licence or sublicence.[66]

Benelux law provides that an extract of the document establishing the licence or a corresponding declaration signed by the parties involved must be recorded and the related fees must be paid.[67] Submission of a copy of the deed evidencing a licence will suffice. If the BOIP has any reason to question the accuracy of the requested registration, the BOIP may request further information, including the submission of original documents or certified copies thereof.[68]

---

62. Article 26.4 EUTMR.
63. Article 165.1 jo. Article 162 EUTMR.
64. EUIPO Trademark and Design Guidelines, Part E, section 3, Chapter 2, 4.3 and 4.4: https://guidelines.euipo.europa.eu/1922895/1787224/trade-mark-guidelines/4-3-examination-of-specific-formalities--licences-.
65. Articles 111(3)(j) and 116(1)(a) EUTMR.
66. See https://www.boip.int/en/ip-professionals/registration-maintenance/protection-and-maintenance#modifications.
67. Article 2.33 BCIP.
68. Rule 3.1.4 Implementing Regulations under the BCIP, see https://www.boip.int/en/ip-professionals/regulations-policy/regulations.

All documents must be submitted in one of the three working languages of the BOIP (French, Dutch or English) or in German. If not, a translation in one of these four languages must be added.[69]

The fees depend on the number of Benelux trademarks covered by the licence. No additional fee applies from the sixth trademark covered by the same licence registration.[70]

7. MODIFICATION OF A TRADEMARK LICENCE

7.1. Modification of a Licence Related to an EUTM

Either party to a licence agreement may request to modify a licence in the Register.[71] Depending on the party requesting the modification and the nature of the modification, the requestor may need to provide evidence to have their request validated:

- joint request from the EUTM proprietor and the licensee: no further proof of the modification of the licence is required;
- request made by the EUTM proprietor: proof of the modification of the licence is required only where the modification for which entry in the EUTM Register is requested is of such a nature that it would diminish the rights of the registered licensee. For example, this would be the case if the licensee's name changes, if an exclusive licence becomes a non-exclusive licence, or if restrictions are imposed regarding the territorial scope of the licence, the period of time for which it is granted, or the goods or services to which it applies;
- request made by the registered licensee: proof of the modification of the licence is required only where the modification for which entry in the EUTM Register is requested is of such a nature that it would extend the rights of the registered licensee under the licence, e.g., in case of a temporary licence which becomes a permanent licence.

Where proof of the modification of the licence is necessary, it is sufficient to submit a declaration mentioning the changes to the licensing agreement or to submit an extract of the modified agreement. However, any submitted document must be signed by both parties.[72]

69. Rule 3.3 Implementing Regulations under the BCIP.
70. See https://www.boip.int/en/ip-professionals/registration-maintenance/fees#modifications.
71. Article 25.6 EUTMR.
72. EUIPO Trademark and Design Guidelines, Part E, section 3, Chapter 2, 3.2.1.2: https://guidelines.euipo.europa.eu/1922895/1789014/trade-mark-guidelines/3-2-1-2-modification-of-a-licence.

7.2. Modification of a Licence Related to a Benelux Trademark

There are no specific rules regarding the modification of a licence covering Benelux trademarks. The rules regarding registration of a licence apply.[73]

8. RIGHTS AND OBLIGATIONS OF THE LICENSOR – TRADEMARK HOLDER TOWARDS THE LICENSEE

8.1. Rights of the Licensor

EU and Benelux trademark law provides for identical rules as to the licensor's rights. The proprietor of an EU or Benelux trademark may invoke the rights conferred by that trademark against a licensee who violates any provision in his licensing contract with regard to:

- its duration;
- the form covered by the registration in which the trademark may be used;
- the scope of the goods or services for which the licence is granted;
- the territory in which the trademark may be affixed; or
- the quality of the goods manufactured or of the services provided by the licensee.[74]

These provisions allow the licensor to initiate proceedings against the licensee based on his/her exclusive trademark right, in addition to any contractual ground. This means that in the above-mentioned cases, a licensee can be liable contractually, but a licensee can also be liable for trademark infringement based on tort and/or criminal law.[75]

In its *Copad / Dior* case, the CJEU provided guidance on the last element of the applicable provisions, namely the quality of the goods covered by the licensor's trademark. A licensor can invoke the rights conferred by his trademark against a licensee who violates a provision in a licence agreement prohibiting, on grounds of the trademark's prestige, sales to discount stores of goods, provided it has been established that the violation, in the specific circumstances of the case, damages the allure and prestigious image which bestows on those goods an aura of luxury.[76]

The Advocate General had already previously indicated that the quality referred to is not limited to the material characteristics of the goods but also includes the perceived image of luxury.[77] A subjective quality perception can thus be taken into account.

In addition, the CJEU also made clear that such infringement excludes any exhaustion of trademark rights. The licensee cannot argue that the trademark holder has consented to the placing of the goods on the market, which is one of the essential

73. See section 6.2.2.
74. Article 25.2 EUTMR; Article 2.32.2 BCIP.
75. Article XV.103, §1 CEL.
76. CJEU, Case C-59/08, 23 April 2009, *Copad vs Dior*, ECLI:EU:C:2009:260.
77. CJEU, Case C-59/08, 23 April 2009, *Copad vs Dior*, ECLI:EU:C:2009:260, point 24.

conditions for exhaustion, when it is done in a way that damages the allure and prestigious image of the trademark.[78]

8.2. Obligations of the Licensor

A licensing agreement essentially implies a 'passive' duty on the licensor of allowing the licensee to take actions normally covered by the licensor's monopoly. The licensor thus undertakes to refrain from taking action against the use of its trademark by a licensee, provided that the latter complies with the licensing agreement.

However, apart from any additional obligation agreed by both parties, the licensor will in any event be bound by the general principle of good faith in the performance of the contract.[79]

Some authors even argue that a licensing agreement should be considered as a form of rental agreement, whereby the use of the trademark is rented out to the licensee.[80] This would imply that the licensor is bound by the legal provisions applicable to rental agreements. According to these rules, the licensor would have a duty to maintain the state of the trademark so as to ensure the use of it by the licensee.[81] Such maintenance is obviously done by renewing the mark but also by building and preserving the trademark's reputation. For example, a licensor may agree to reimburse all or part of the licensee's advertising costs. However, the licensing agreement will always be the main basis for the parties' duties. In that regard, the Namur Commercial Court ruled that a franchisor is not obliged to reimburse the franchisee's advertising costs in a case where the franchisee did not comply with certain criteria stated in the agreement.[82]

According to the same authors, the general rules on contract law and rental agreements would also imply that the licensor has a duty to intervene if a third party initiates trademark infringement proceedings against the licensee. The handling of such proceedings and their potential consequences harm the licensee's right to use the licensed trademark.[83] The licensor may intervene in such proceedings on a voluntary basis, but the licensor can also be forced to intervene at the request of the licensee.[84] In the majority of the cases, it will be in the licensor's interest to intervene in order to protect its trademark rights. Even if the alleged infringement is the sole consequence of the licensee's non-compliance with the licensing agreement, the licensor may still wish to intervene in order to clarify this before the court.

78. CJEU, Case C-59/08, 23 April 2009, *Copad vs Dior*, ECLI:EU:C:2009:260, point 50.
79. Article 1134, §3 and 1135 of the Belgian Civil Code.
80. B. Vanbrabant, S. De Smedt, C. Jacques, 'De distributie van goederen en de licentieovereenkomst', in X., *Bestendig Handboek Distributierecht*, VII.3, 24.
81. Article 1719 Belgian Civil Code.
82. Namur Commercial Court No. 1339/2011, 30 April 2013, DAOR 2014, No. 111, 87.
83. B. Vanbrabant, S. De Smedt, C. Jacques, 'De distributie van goederen en de licentieovereenkomst', in X., *Bestendig Handboek Distributierecht*, VII.3, 27.
84. Based on Article 813 Belgian Judicial Code.

As mentioned above, when the licensing agreement qualifies as a commercial cooperation agreement under Belgian law, the licensor will be bound by certain pre-contractual obligations as well.[85]

9. RIGHTS AND OBLIGATIONS OF THE LICENSEE TOWARDS THE LICENSOR

9.1. Rights of the Licensee

Without prejudice to the provisions of the licensing contract, the licensee of an EUTM or Benelux trademark may bring infringement proceedings only if its proprietor consents thereto. However, the holder of an *exclusive* licence may bring such proceedings if the proprietor of the trademark, after formal notice, does not himself bring infringement proceedings within an appropriate period.[86] What constitutes an appropriate period will need to be assessed on a case-by-case basis, and will often depend on the urgency related to potential damage.[87]

Benelux trademark law only recently adopted the same rule as applicable for EUTMs. The Benelux Court of Justice did previously rule otherwise, stating that a licensee could not initiate trademark infringement proceedings based on the licensed trademark, even jointly with the licensor.[88]

EU law specifically adds that if a counterclaim is brought in a legal action to which the proprietor of the EUTM is not yet a party, he will be informed thereof and will be able to join the proceedings in accordance with national law.[89] This may apply to the situation where a licensee initiated infringement proceedings based on the licensed EUTM and the alleged infringer files a counterclaim for revocation or for a declaration of invalidity of this EUTM.

A licensee is also entitled to intervene in infringement proceedings brought by the proprietor of an EUTM or Benelux trademark for the purpose of obtaining compensation for damage suffered by him.[90] The Benelux provisions add that a licensee may also request to be allocated a proportion of the profit made by the defendant and for the provision of accounts in this regard.[91]

With the permission of the Benelux trademark proprietor, the licensee can bring independent action for compensation, and even claim recall, removal or destruction measures provided that these are meant to protect the rights which the licensee has been permitted to exercise.[92]

Benelux case law confirms that the licensee may be entitled to compensation, even if the licence had not yet been registered at the time of the infringing acts.[93]

85. See section 4.4.
86. Article 25.3 EUTMR; Article 2.32.4 BCIP.
87. M.-C. Janssens, *Handboek Merkenrecht*, Intersentia, 262.
88. Benelux Court of Justice, 7 June 2002, *Adidas vs Marca Mode*, Ing.-Cons. 2002/4-5, 153.
89. Article 128.3 EUTMR.
90. Article 25.4 EUTMR; Article 2.32.5 BCIP.
91. Article 2.32.5 jo. 2.21.4 BCIP.
92. Articles 2.32.6, 2.32.7 jo. 2.22.1 BCIP.
93. Benelux Court of Justice, 28 February 2003, *Zoontjens vs Kijlstra*, RW 2004-2005, 732.

Another option provided by Benelux trademark law is for the licensor to initiate proceedings for compensation or transfer of profits in the name of the licensee.[94]

As infringement situations often include acts that can be qualified as unfair commercial practices (deception, parasitism, freeriding, etc.), a licensee may also have a personal interest and capacity[95] to bring an action for injunctive relief on these grounds.

Finally, with the trademark proprietor's consent, licensees have the right to file an opposition against an application for an EUTM or a Benelux trademark,[96] or initiate revocation or invalidity proceedings.[97]

The EU General Court held that an application for renewal of an EUTM registration always requires the express consent of the trademark proprietor.[98]

9.2. Obligations of the Licensee

The obligations of the licensee will obviously relate to the payment of the financial compensation to the licensor, as well as the compliance with all agreed conditions related to the use of the licensor's trademark.

The licensor may even impose the use of the trademark to the licensee, as the validity and the strength of a trademark depend on genuine use of the trademark.

10. END OF A LICENCE

10.1. Impact of Trademark Developments on a Licence

Trademark applications can be opposed and registered trademarks can be revoked or invalidated, which will have an impact on related licensing agreements.

By definition, a trademark application does not yet confer trademark rights on the applied-for sign. Licensing a trademark application can thus be considered as licensing an unregistered sign, which is perfectly allowed.[99] However, the purpose of a trademark application is obviously to obtain a registered right. In the framework of a licensing agreement covering a trademark application, it is thus recommended to make specific arrangements related to the upcoming registration of the application as a trademark. As registered rights confer more legal certainty, a licensor may increase the licence fee as soon as the trademark application becomes a registered trademark, for example. Conversely, if a trademark application is refused by the trademark office or successfully opposed in full, such application will not be registered and will be considered as non-existent. The consequences between the parties to a licensing agreement are best covered in the agreement. An unregistered sign may still be covered by the agreement if it has value. Otherwise, the disappearance of the trademark

94. Article 2.21.5 BCIP.
95. Within the meaning of Articles 17 and 18 of the Belgian Judicial Code.
96. Article 46.1.a EUTMR; Article 2.14.2 BCIP.
97. Article 63 EUTMR; Article 2.28.2 BCIP.
98. GC, Case T-410/07, 12 May 2009, *Jurado Hermanos vs OHIM*, ECLI:EU:T:2009:153.
99. Trademark licensing agreements will often include rules on the use of unregistered distinctive signs as well, such as the use of a specific colour together with the licensed trademark.

application may be a cause for termination of the licensing agreement. In the absence of any specifications in that regard, it can be argued that the refusal of successfully opposed trademark application would yield the same effects on the agreement as the invalidation of a licensed trademark.[100] In both cases, the right is considered to have never existed.

According to EU and Benelux trademark law, a registered trademark shall be deemed not to have had, *as from the date of the application for revocation*, the effects specified in this convention, to the extent that the rights of the proprietor have been revoked. An earlier date, on which one of the grounds for revocation occurred, may be fixed in the decision at the request of one of the parties.[101] The requesting party must show a legitimate legal interest in this respect, and it must be possible to determine the earlier date accurately on the basis of information available in the relevant case file.[102] For example, in a case before the EUIPO Board of Appeal, Musclepharm Corporation successfully revoked Monster Energy Company's trademark ASSAULT M MONSTER ENERGY for part of the goods on the basis of non-use. This revoked trademark was the basis of an opposition against an EUTM application filed by Musclepharm Corporation. Therefore, Musclepharm Corporation had an interest to fix the revocation date before the filing date of its opposed EUTM application, so that the earlier mark of Monster Energy Company, which was now revoked, could no longer be an obstacle for Musclepharm Corporation's EUTM application.[103]

An EUTM or Benelux trademark shall be deemed not to have had, *as from the outset*, the effects specified by trademark law, to the extent that the trademark has been declared *invalid*.[104]

EU trademark law adds an important clarification with regard to the revocation or invalidity of an EUTM:

> Subject to the national provisions relating either to claims for compensation for damage caused by negligence or lack of good faith on the part of the proprietor of the trademark, or to unjust enrichment, the retroactive effect of revocation or invalidity of the trademark shall not affect:
>
> (a) any decision on infringement which has acquired the authority of a final decision and been enforced prior to the revocation or invalidity decision;
> (b) any contract concluded prior to the revocation or invalidity decision, in so far as it has been performed before that decision; however, repayment, to an extent justified by the circumstances, of sums paid under the relevant contract may be claimed on grounds of equity.[105]

This means that a licensing agreement covering a revoked or invalid trademark will not be affected retroactively.

100. The consequences of the invalidation of a registered trademark are explained below, in the same section.
101. Article 62.1 EUTMR; Article 2.30nonies.4 BCIP.
102. EUIPO Trademark and Design Guidelines, Part D, section 2, 1.3.1: https://guidelines.euipo.europa.eu/1922895/1785436/trade-mark-guidelines/1-3-1-the-legal-effect-of-revocation.
103. EUIPO Fifth Board of Appeal, 14 August 2019, case No. R 94/2019-5.
104. Article 62.2 EUTMR; Article 2.30nonies.5 BCIP.
105. Article 62.3 EUTMR.

In Belgium, some authors make a distinction between revocation and invalidity of a licensed trademark, arguing that in the latter case, the invalidity of the trademark would take away the cause of the licensing agreement.[106] This agreement would thus be considered as invalid from the outset. In practice, however, this does not mean that paid royalties can be reclaimed. According to Belgian case law, reciprocal obligations performed under the agreement cannot be annulled if these cannot be returned.[107] A licensee has enjoyed the right to use the trademark before its invalidation, and this cannot be undone.

10.2. Contractual Termination

If the parties do not specify the causes for termination in the licensing agreement, the general rules on contract law will apply, such as the unilateral termination of the agreement in case of serious breach.[108]

However, unlike most other EU countries, Belgium has a specific legislation regulating the situation of a manufacturer or supplier willing to terminate an exclusive distribution agreement.[109] These provisions were introduced initially in the Law of 27 July 1961 on the unilateral termination of exclusive distribution agreements of indefinite duration. Since 31 May 2014, these provisions have been taken up in Title 3 of Book X CEL.

Belgian provisions on the termination of exclusive distribution agreements are mandatory and interfere significantly with the parties' contractual freedom to terminate such agreements. They are intended to protect Belgian distributors, who have often spent years developing a local market, and see a foreign supplier terminate the agreement, so he can take over the clients or the successful distribution network. As distribution agreements may incorporate licensing agreements, this legislation is not to be overlooked.

The provisions of Book X, Title 3 CEL do not apply to all categories of distribution agreements but only to distribution agreements:

- of indefinite duration;
- which provide exclusivity or impose substantial obligations on the distributor;
- which are unilaterally terminated without any gross negligence on the part of the distributor.[110]

In such cases, the agreement can only be terminated with a reasonable notice period or a fair compensation. Under Belgian case law, this compensation tends to be rather considerable. Depending on the circumstances, courts have held that notice periods ranging from three to forty-two months are reasonable.

106. See Y. Van Couter and B. Vanbrabant, *Handboek Licentieovereenkomsten*, Brussels, Larcier, 2008, 71.
107. Belgian Supreme Court, AR C.09.0645.F, 19 May 2011, Arr.Cass. 2011, No. 5, 1253.
108. Article 1184 Belgian Civil Code.
109. See section 4.3 for the legal definition of a distribution agreement.
110. Articles X.35 and X.36 CEL.

A notice is reasonable if it allows the distributor to find a source of income of equal importance. To determine a reasonable notice, the courts take into account all aspects of the distribution. The most significant elements are the duration of the terminated agreement, the importance of the brand, the number of manufacturers or importers who supply similar products, the extent of the territory, the importance of the distribution within the supplier's business, the profits generated by the distribution, whether the parties had a good working relationship, the distributor's obligation to invest, etc.

Further, the distributor is entitled to additional compensation in case of:

- termination by the supplier on any ground except gross negligence on the part of the distributor, or
- termination by the distributor based on gross negligence on the part of the supplier.[111]

The additional compensation is due regardless of whether sufficient notice was given. Such additional compensation includes, among others, a goodwill payment for the acquired clientele. The goodwill payment is due if the distributor proves that there was a notable increase in customers during the distribution relationship, that this increase was obtained through the distributor's marketing efforts, and that the customers will continue to buy the supplier's products after termination. This part of the compensation can be very important (six months to two years), especially for long-standing agreements and when the product was first introduced by the distributor.

10.3. Insolvency

10.3.1. General Rule: Principle of Continuity of Agreements

As a general rule, agreements continue to be in effect regardless of any insolvency proceeding under Belgian law. The sole fact that one of the parties to a licensing agreement is involved in insolvency proceedings does not automatically lead to the termination of the agreement.

However, in order to be opposable to the liquidator, a licensing agreement must comply with the requirements related to opposability of the agreement against third parties. Above, we have explained the registration requirements of a licensing agreement.[112]

10.3.2. Exceptions to the Principle of Continuity of Agreements

The main exceptions to the above-mentioned principle are related to the nature of the relationship between the parties and the provisions of the licensing agreement.

111. Article X.37 CEL.
112. See section 6.2.

So-called *intuitu personae* agreements, which are entered into because of the specific identity, experience and nature of a party, are automatically terminated in case of bankruptcy or liquidation of the party who was specifically targeted by the *intuitu personae* clause of the agreement.[113] This characteristic of the agreement has to be assessed on a case-by-case basis. In trademark licensing agreements, the person of the licensee will often be essential for the licensor as the latter will only grant a licence to a reputed or experienced person. It is recommended to specify the *intuitu personae* nature of the agreement. Bankruptcy or liquidation of the licensee does not automatically lead to the termination of the agreement, unless the *intuitu personae* nature of the agreement can be proven.

The *intuitu personae* nature may be even harder to prove by the licensee in the event of bankruptcy or liquidation of the licensor. A licensee will usually enter into a trademark licensing agreement because of the trademark and not because of the proprietor of that trademark.

A more common exception leading to the termination of the agreement are specific clauses included in the agreement. Parties can either provide that the licensing agreement will automatically end if insolvency proceedings are initiated against one of the parties or provide that one of the parties has the choice to terminate the contract based on the other party's default. There is some debate regarding the legality of the latter option because insolvency proceedings are not considered to be a default of performance of the contract, but the option has been accepted unless the trustee in bankruptcy (called the 'liquidator') warrants that the agreement will be complied with if it is not terminated. The latter option provides more freedom to the parties because the agreement will not be terminated automatically. It leaves them with a choice to continue the performance under the agreement regardless of the insolvency proceedings.[114]

10.3.3. The Liquidator's Right to Terminate Agreements

The liquidator has a right to terminate any agreement if the management of the estate so requires.[115]

However, the use of this right of the liquidator will depend on the insolvent party. A liquidator will rarely need to terminate a trademark licensing agreement if the licensee is insolvent. This situation is usually included under the automatic termination clauses of the agreement. Even if no such clause is provided, the licensor may be able to terminate the agreement on the ground of non-performance of the agreement because the insolvent licensee cannot pay the royalties or other compensation due to the licensor.

Such termination may have far-reaching implications on sub-licensees who may lose their right to use the (sub)licensed trademark. It is recommended to provide for

113. Liège Court of Appeal, 28 May 2002, JLMB 2003/4, 151.
114. J. Troussel, C. Berckmans and G. De Villegas, 'Licentieovereenkomsten en intellectuele eigendomsrechten in het licht van collectieve insolventieprocedures', TBH 2015, No. 9, 874-876.
115. Article XX.139 CEL.

solutions in the licensing agreement, for example, by providing that the licensor takes over the sublicence(s) in the event of insolvency of the licensee.

The situation is more difficult in case of insolvency of the licensor because the licensing agreement usually provides for additional funds in the estate through the licensee's payment of royalties. The termination of the agreement will therefore depend on the nature of the licensor's obligations. If the licensor's obligations are limited to its 'passive' duty not to take action against the licensee's permitted use of the licensed trademark, it will usually be difficult for the liquidator to argue that the management of the estate requires the termination of the agreement. However, the licensor may have burdensome obligations with regard to support to be provided to the licensee, or the reimbursement of part of the licensee's advertisement costs. Costs related to enforcing the licensor's trademark rights against infringers may also be significant. In that case, the liquidator may be able to justify the termination of the licensing agreement.[116]

10.3.4. Registration of Insolvency Proceedings in the Trademark Register

Competent national authorities, such as a court or the liquidator, or any of the parties involved in insolvency proceedings can request to register the fact that an EUTM is involved in these insolvency proceedings, including the liquidator's contact details.[117] It is sufficient to provide an extract of the insolvency judgment identifying the parties involved. Other confidential information may be left out.

Benelux trademark law has no specific provision for such registration.

10.4. Registration of the Cancellation of a Licence

According to EU trademark law, the cancellation of a licence can be registered at the request of one of the parties.[118] No proof is required if the request is submitted by both parties or the licensee alone. If the EUTM proprietor alleges fraud on the part of the licensee, it must submit a final decision of the competent authority to this effect. The EUIPO will not carry out any investigation in that respect.[119]

Benelux trademark law provides that a registered licence may be cancelled only at the joint request of the proprietor of the trademark and the licensee.[120] Such cancellation is done using the same form as the one provided for the registration of a licence in the Benelux trademark register.[121]

116. J. Troussel, C. Berckmans and G. De Villegas, 'Licentieovereenkomsten en intellectuele eigendomsrechten in het licht van collectieve insolventieprocedures', TBH 2015, No. 9, 872-873.
117. Article 24 EUTMR, EUIPO Trademark and Design Guidelines, Part E, section 3, Chapter 2, 2.4.1: https://guidelines.euipo.europa.eu/1922895/1788210/trade-mark-guidelines/2-4-1-applicants.
118. Article 25.6 EUTMR.
119. EUIPO Trademark and Design Guidelines, Part E, section 3, Chapter 2, 3.2.1.1: https://guidelines.euipo.europa.eu/1922895/1786739/trade-mark-guidelines/3-2-1-1-cancellation-of-a-licence.
120. Article 2.32.3 BCIP.
121. See section 6.2.2.

11. RESOLVING LICENCE DISPUTES

11.1. Disputes among Licensing Parties

Disputes among licensing parties will often be contractual in nature. However, the dispute may also concern the intellectual property right itself and therefore be considered non-contractual. The qualification of the dispute may raise important conflict of laws issues. Disputes that relate to the intellectual property right itself are traditionally governed by the *lex loci protectionis*, whereas the law governing the licence agreement may point to a different law. The *lex loci protectionis* may determine whether the trademark can be assigned or licensed, whereas the law of the contract will determine the validity and the scope of the assignment or licence.

To avoid complex questions about applicable law, parties to a licensing agreement will often include a choice of law provision. But even if the licence agreement contains an unequivocal choice of law provision, questions may remain. For example, if the licence forms part of an exclusive distribution agreement of indefinite term, mandatory provisions of Belgian distribution law may apply as soon as the distribution relationship is implemented (albeit in part) on Belgian territory.

If the law applicable to the licence agreement has not been chosen, the qualification of the agreement may be crucial. In accordance with Article 4.1 (e) and (f) of the Rome I Regulation, the law of the country where the franchisee *c.q.* distributor has his habitual residence will be the law governing the franchise *c.q.* distribution contract. However, if the franchise or distribution contract, for instance, includes a licence of a well-known trademark that is managed worldwide from the licensor's headquarters, the licensor might argue that the contract is manifestly more connected with the location of the licensor. On the basis of Article 4.3 of the Rome I Regulation, the licensor may invoke that the law of that country shall apply.

A careful analysis of conflict of law provisions at the execution of the licence agreement helps to avoid complex discussions afterwards. The same applies to defining the parties' roles and responsibilities. A licence agreement may define who is responsible for enforcing intellectual property rights towards third-party infringers, who is responsible for supporting the costs of a recall, etc. In a distribution relationship, the supplier is normally responsible for carrying out the recall, but the distributor has a duty to cooperate. Who bears the cost is an issue that often leads to discussion or litigation.

11.2. Disputes Against Third Parties

The existence of a licence agreement in and of itself will seldom lead to litigation. Questions about the validity or opposability of a licence agreement are usually raised as a defence in an infringement action. In this respect, it may not be sufficient that the licence agreement defines the parties' roles and responsibilities; the licence agreement must also be registered with the relevant trademark office to be opposable to third parties. The Benelux Court of Justice considers that a licensee can only intervene in infringement proceedings after registration of the licence.[122] However, the question remains whether this position can be maintained in view of the more recent case law of the CJEU, holding that a licensee may bring proceedings alleging infringement of an EU trademark which is the subject of the licence, although that licence has not been entered in the Register.[123]

11.3. Criminal Proceedings

Counterfeiting is criminally sanctioned in Belgium.[124] A licensee who violates the licensing conditions or a former licensee can therefore be criminally prosecuted for counterfeiting. A counterfeiter can only be criminally liable if there is a malicious or fraudulent intent. The infringement must take place in the channels of commerce, meaning that the infringer has acted in the context of a commercial activity with the aim of obtaining an economic benefit.

Criminal proceedings are initiated at the initiative of the public prosecutor. Although the public prosecutor may start investigations at his own initiative, criminal proceedings are often instigated at the trademark owner's request. A licensee may also submit a request to investigate suspected counterfeit activities. However, it is recommended that such requests are issued in concert with the trademark owner.

11.4. Alternative Dispute Resolution

Alternative dispute resolution in connection with licensing agreements is commonplace. Trademark owners value the private and less litigious character of out-of-court dispute resolution mechanisms. They allow them to make arrangements on confidentiality and to avoid negative publicity in connection with their licensed trademark.

With respect to exclusive distribution agreements of indefinite term, Belgian law provides that Belgian courts have jurisdiction on issues of mandatory law, notwithstanding any contractual provision to the contrary, as soon as the distribution relationship is implemented (albeit in part) on Belgian territory. This provision has been perceived as excluding arbitration agreements. However, with the introduction of a new Arbitration Act in 2013, it is accepted that arbitration agreements in a distribution relationship are valid, provided that the arbitrators are required to apply mandatory provisions of distribution law.[125]

---

122. Benelux Court of Justice, 28 February 2003, *TBH*, 2003, p. 599; *Ing.-Cons.*, 2003/1, p. 83; *RW* 2004-2005/19, p. 732.
123. CJEU, *Youssef Hassan v. Breiding Vertriebsgesellschaft mbH*, 4 februari 2016, C-163/15, ECLI:EU:C: 2016:71
124. See Articles XV.103-XV.111 CEL.
125. Enterprise Court Hainaut (div. Tournai), 21 December 2016, A/16/00637, *R.D.C.-T.B.H.*, 2017/9, pp. 1006-1008; Enterprise Court Antwerp (div. Hasselt), 13 July 2017, *R.W.*, 2018-2019/27, pp. 1067-1074.

Brazil

Tatiana Campello & Camila Garcindo Dayrell Garrote

1. INTRODUCTION: GENERAL OVERVIEW OF TRADEMARK PROSECUTION AND TRADEMARK LICENSE AGREEMENTS IN BRAZIL

Trademark license agreements are extremely important not only to individual businesses but also to the Brazilian economy. A survey conducted by the Brazilian Licensing Association (ABRAL) shows that there were approximately six hundred licensed companies generating an estimated BRL 18 billion in Brazil in 2019, a 7% growth over 2018[1]. Thus, trademark license agreements in Brazil are certainly an aspect of business that stimulates the economy.

The focus of this chapter is to provide some overall information about the Brazilian IP Law, touching on the subject of trademark license agreements[2] and tips to achieving a successful and potentially long-term partnership.

Before entering into a trademark license agreement in Brazil, it is important to understand some general aspects of the local trademark procedures, especially because Brazil adopts the system of first-to-file instead of first-to-use. Therefore, a trademark must be protected before the Brazilian Patent and Trademark Office (BPTO) to grant rights to its titleholder.

If a company is interested in filing a trademark in Brazil, it is also important to comprehend that the trademarks must be visually recognizable and distinctive, and not prohibited by the Brazilian IP Law No. 9,279/96 ("Brazilian IP Law").

1. For more information, see the following link: https://www.correiobraziliense.com.br/app/noticia/economia/2018/11/21/internas_economia,720570/marcas-licenciadas-crescem-acima-da-media-do-varejo.shtml.
2. This chapter is limited to certain aspects of a trademark license agreement in Brazil. If the trademark license is associated with a franchise agreement, additional comments will be needed since there is specific legislation covering this topic (Law No. 13,966/2019).

It is also relevant to note that in Brazil the use of the trademark is only mandatory after the 5th (fifth) year from the date it was granted by the BPTO. Before that, the use is not an obligation.

Unlike in other countries, in Brazil, it is not necessary to prove the use of the trademark periodically, or present Statements of Use. Brazilian IP Law states in Article 143, items I and II, that:

> Article 143—A registration will become forfeit, on the request of any person with a legitimate interest, if, after 5 (five) years from its granting, on the date of such request:
>
> I— use of the mark in Brazil has not been initiated; or
> II— use of the mark has been interrupted for more than 5 (five) consecutive years or if, within that time, the mark has been used in a modified form that implies alteration in its original distinctive character, as found on the certificate of registration.

Thus, if a legitimate third party requests forfeiture of the registration of a trademark after the period indicated above, and the titleholder cannot prove[3] its use in Brazil, the registration will be void. However, if there is a trademark license agreement between the titleholder of the trademark registration and a licensee, the mere existence of the trademark license agreement and the use of the trademark by the licensee will be sufficient to prove the use of the trademark and keep the registration alive.

Trademarks in Brazil can be:

(i) licensed, even partially; and
(ii) subject to licensing agreements if they are registered or if the registration has been applied for at the BPTO. However, trademark applications cannot generate remittance of royalties.

It is important to highlight in this regard that Article 139 of the Brazilian IP Law states that the titleholder of the licensed trademark will not lose its rights to control the specifications of the products or services subject to the licensed trademark.

Independent of the scope of the business operation, there are several benefits of a trademark license, such as additional earnings; territorial expansion; manufacturing, distributing, and marketing of another party; new channels of distribution; strategic partnerships.

Due to the very nature of the licensing agreements and the potential benefits involved, it is expected that issues between the parties will arise during the term of the agreement. However, the difference between a successful partnership and a failed one will depend on how the parties respect the rules and deal with these issues while managing the license agreement.

3. According to Brazilian IP Law, the use of the trademark must include products or services mentioned in the registration certificate, under penalty of partial forfeiture of the registration with respect to those products or services not similar or akin to those for which use of the trademark has been proved. Furthermore, the trademark will not become forfeit if the titleholder justifies the lack of use for legitimate reasons.

Therefore, before entering into a trademark license agreement, it is crucial to have a full understanding of the other party. It is imperative to confirm its capacity to be part of and respect the conditions of the deal and, in particular, build strong and fair terms and conditions for the license with clear obligations for both parties in order to avoid misunderstandings and disputes.

2. TOPIC I: BRIEF HISTORICAL CONSIDERATIONS

According to the BPTO's website, the rules and procedures that govern the registration of agreements involving industrial property rights in Brazil have a long tradition.

Based on the main constraints or contexts of public policies adopted by the country for economic development, the BPTO's practices in this regard can be presented in phases below:

(i) Between 1950 and 1970, the initial focal point was the control of royalty payments and profits abroad, and later it became the stimulus for industrial development in priority sectors. The tax deduction as a consequence of royalty payments and technical assistance services was limited to 5%. Differentiated coefficients for deduction, according to the degree of essentiality of the sectors involved, were also established.

(ii) In the second phase, between 1970 and 1990, the focus was on the regulation of the technology market, based on the national industrial development policy and its strategies. The creation of the BPTO was one of the most significant milestones of this stage, as well as the implementation of the new and current Industrial Property Code.

(iii) The period between 1990 and 2000, through state reform, marked the relaxation of rules and procedures related to the registration of agreements. Thereafter, the Intellectual Property System would seek to stimulate investments in Research and Development and promote greater international transfer of technology.

(iv) From 2000, the registration of agreements became part of the new scenario based on the coordination and strengthening of the national innovation system. Actions related to the defense of competition and the international integration of the Brazilian economy are also part of this context, in which support services to the technology market stand out.

(v) A significant change occurred in 2017. The BPTO issued Normative Instruction No. 70/2017 and Resolution 199/2017, establishing new rules and formalizing certain requirements in relation to the recordal or registration of technology transfer agreements (i.e., industrial property licensing and assignment, technology supply, specialized technical assistance services and franchise agreements). Normative Instruction No. 70/2017 introduced an explanatory note to be included in the certificate of recordal or registration of agreements, with the following content: "The BPTO has not analyzed the agreement under the fiscal perspective and under the legislation governing the remittance of capital abroad." The new rule indicates that the BPTO shall cease its inspection involving private contracts, such as proposing changes or questioning remuneration provisions agreed to by the contracting parties. The tax and remittance rules were not changed; however, the BPTO will no longer make such analysis. In addition to the changes mentioned above, Normative Instruction No. 70/2017 changed formal rules on documents that must accompany registration requests and established new guidelines for the analysis of requests, which was then further specified in the BPTO's Resolution No. 199/2017.

In summary, the BPTO's role is limited now to analyzing technical formalities of the agreement as well as to adopting a limited position that restricts its analysis. In practical terms, we have noted an increase in the number of office actions in formal procedures, and even in some cases with questions of contractual condition. It is important to be prepared to present the trademark license agreement before the BPTO in order to avoid or mitigate any of those office actions.

3. TOPIC II: REGISTRATION OF TRADEMARK LICENSE AGREEMENTS BEFORE THE BPTO

Agreements relating to industrial property rights, including trademark licenses, must be approved by and registered with the BPTO for the following purposes:

(i) *Remitting payments abroad*: For the remittance of royalties for trademark license from Brazil to a third party abroad, the agreement must first be registered at the BPTO, and after this registered at the Brazilian Central Bank (BACEN[4]) by a certified bank authorized to operate exchange rates.

(ii) *Deductibility*: Deducting payments as operational expenses for Brazilian income tax purposes: The trademark license must be registered with the BPTO to enable the payment of royalties by the Brazilian licensee, to be deducted, for purposes of calculation of its Brazilian corporate income tax.[5]

(iii) *Effectiveness before third parties*: The registration of the trademark license by the BPTO is also necessary for the agreement to be effective against third parties,

4. Rules applicable to international fund remittance in connection with contracts related to trademark, patent, and industrial design license, technical assistance and/or technology transfer include Resolutions by the National Monetary Council and Circular orders by BACEN, as follows:
   Resolution 3,568/2008 on FOREX transactions, required documents and parties' obligations and responsibilities;
   Resolution 3,844/2010, Ruling III, on Registration of Royalties and Technical Services contracts with BACEN and prior ratification with the BPTO;
   Circular 3,689/2013 on Royalties and other service credits due to foreign entities and obligatory measures prior to perfection of payment;
   Circular 3,690/2013 on FOREX contract controls & authorized contract models and numerical code identification system for classification of remittance purposes; and
   Circular 3,691/2013 on authorized institutions (including operating banks) and registration of FOREX contracts with BACEN.
   All the rules listed above are to be applied by financial institutions authorized by the Central Bank of Brazil to engage in foreign exchange transactions.
5. Regarding the taxes, it is important to note the following applicable rules: Law Nos. 4,131/62, 4,506/64, 8,383/91 and Decree-Law 1,730/79.

and to grant powers to the licensee, when expressed in the agreement, to represent the licensor before the Brazilian courts.

The registration of a trademark license agreement must comply with the following requirements:

(i) The agreement must specify the licensed trademarks (it can be in an annex, e.g., and the terms and conditions involved in such license, i.e.: payment conditions, possibility of sublicensing, exclusivity, territory and term).

(ii) The agreement must be signed by both parties' representatives and indicate their full name. It is important to have the date and office address of the representatives below the respective signatures. Regarding the signatures, the BPTO accepts electronic digital signature, based on a valid digital certificate issued by the Certification Authorities accredited by the Public Key Infrastructure in Brazil (ICP-Brasil). Digital signatures of foreign parties without a valid digital certificate issued by the Brazilian Certification Authority will be accepted when digitally notarized (e-notarization) and digitally apostilled (e-apostille). Documents that contain a handwriting signature and a digital signature on the same document will not be accepted by the BPTO.

(iii) All the pages of the agreement, including the annexes or exhibits, must contain the representative's initials. It is important to stress that if the agreement is signed with certified electronic digital signatures, the initials in all the pages will not be necessary.

(iv) The agreement must be signed by two witnesses in order to be considered an extrajudicial title. This rule is also mandatory for agreements signed in Brazil.

(v) Presentation of documents demonstrating that the parties' representatives have powers to sign the agreement on their behalf.

(vi) If the agreement is not drafted in Portuguese, it must be translated into Portuguese, or drafted and signed in both languages. In this case, if the document is signed abroad, it must be notarized or apostilled.

(vii) In the case that a power of attorney is necessary, and the document is signed abroad, such document must be notarized or apostilled.

(viii) The document must not contain any erasures or overwritten words.

(ix) The party that requests the BPTO's approval must fill in a specific form requesting the examination of the license agreement and its approval. If this requirement is filed by an attorney, a power of attorney is also needed.

(x) The BPTO's official fees for the registration of the agreement must be paid and proof of payment must be presented.

Regarding the legal requirements to request the registration of the trademark agreement at the BPTO, it is important to keep in mind the following:

Payments. Payments can be calculated as: a percentage of the net selling price of the products (or services) or the net revenue; fixed value per unit sold or fixed value.

Payment is only possible for registered trademarks. In the case of trademark license applications, these will not be entitled to remuneration. When the trademark application matures into registration, the parties will have to request from the BPTO a change in the registration certificate of the license, in which case the remuneration will retroact to the granting publication date of such decision in the Brazilian Official Gazette.

Royalties. If the parties are unrelated companies, they can agree to any value as royalty payment; however, there is a legal limitation for its tax deduction (a maximum of 1% over the net sales of products or services). The same tax deduction limitation is applicable when the parties are related companies.

Agreement renewal. The license term cannot exceed the validity of the registered licensed trademark. It is possible to renew the agreement if an addendum is signed by the parties, and this document must be presented to the BPTO before the expiration of the term in the registration certificate issued by the BPTO of the previous agreement in force. If the agreement has an automatic renewal clause, the renewal clause must be requested by means of an amendment in a registration certificate process. This procedure must be done within the term of the registration certificate, and if possible, with an explanatory letter describing what is being requested.

After the presentation of the relevant and required information and documents, the BPTO will review the license agreement to check if all the legal obligations have been met.

If everything follows the law and the BPTO's practices, the BPTO will record the agreement and publish its decision in the Official Gazette to make third parties aware. If not, the BPTO will issue office actions requesting clarifications that must be fulfilled, under the penalty of having the recordal request suspended.

4. TOPIC III: EFFECTS OF AN INVALIDATION OF THE LICENSED TRADEMARK ON THE AGREEMENT

It is important to note that, in Brazil, a trademark registration will be extinct when and if one of the provisions stated in Articles 142, 168 and 175 of the Brazilian IP Law occur:

> "Article 142—The registration of a trademark will become extinct:
>
> I— on expiry of the term of protection;
> II— on waiver, which may be total or partial with respect to the products or services indicated by the mark;
> III— by forfeiture; or
> IV— for failure to observe the provisions of Article 217.[6]
>
> Article 168—Nullity of a registration may be declared administratively if it was granted in conflict with the provisions of this law.
>
> Article 175—Nullity actions must be brought before the Federal Courts of Justice and the BPTO, when it is not the plaintiff, will participate in the action.

6. Article 217 of Brazilian IP Law states that "A person domiciled abroad must maintain permanently a duly qualified attorney resident in the country, with powers to represent him administratively and judicially, including for receiving summons."

(...) § 2—Once the decision in a nullity action is res judicata, the BPTO will publish a note for the information of third parties."

If one of the situations above occurs, the registration will be extinct, and, in such case, the trademark license agreement will lose its purpose. The same will happen in pending trademark application cases. A pending application can be shelved by the BPTO if:

(i) the BPTO maintains the rejection decision of the application (even after the filing of an appeal);
(ii) the applicant does not pay the required fees; or
(iii) the applicant does not comply with an office action issued by the BPTO.

Thus, even though the trademark license can be perpetual, the license will only be effective during the valid trademark term at the BPTO. Thus, every time a trademark is renewed, the titleholder must file a request to renew the license period. If the trademark is not renewed or, for any reason, canceled or annulled, the license will also be canceled automatically.

Therefore, to protect the licensee against these types of scenarios, the language of the agreement must be precise, particularly regarding the possible ways of terminating the agreement, stipulating fines to compensate for the potential damages.

Nevertheless, a relevant note about this topic concerns insolvency proceedings[7], a path that is, unfortunately, very common nowadays in Brazil[8]. Therefore, the trademark license agreement must be carefully worded to protect both parties in this case since:

(i) in the event of a judicial or extrajudicial recovery:
    (a) if the licensor files for judicial recovery, the effect of the license agreement remains. However, the licensor, in principle, can assign the agreement or the licensed trademark. In this case, the licensor will need: (i) judicial authorization; or (ii) that the recovery plan provides for the assignment of the trademark. If, however, the license agreement prevents the assignment of the trademark or the agreement, the clause will be valid, and the assignment of the trademark or the agreement must have the consent of the licensee;
    (b) if the licensee files for judicial recovery, any pending payment may arise in the judicial recovery, but the subsequent installments must be paid normally (if the payment is in installments). If there is a termination clause providing for the termination of the agreement in the case of nonpayment, this clause will still be valid, and the licensor will be able to terminate the agreement. However, if the licensed trademark is essential to the licensee undergoing the judicial recovery, it is possible to file a

7. Brazilian Business Insolvency Law (Law No. 11.101/ 2005) offers the following three types of insolvency proceedings: judicial recovery, extrajudicial recovery or liquidation (in insolvency).
8. For more information about the scenario in Brazil, we recommend reading: https://www.reuters.com/article/brazil-bankruptcy-serasa/brazilian-bankruptcy-filings-at-11-year-high-experian-idUSL1N1ETOVU.

lawsuit addressing the termination of the agreement exclusively based on the judicial recovery in course.

(ii) in the case of liquidation:

(a) if the licensor has entered into liquidation, a judicial administrator starts to manage the assets of the liquidation mass, including trademarks. In this case, the license agreement will not be terminated. The judicial administrator can continue with the agreement, provided that it generates receipts for the liquidation mass or decides to terminate it (Article 117 of the Brazilian Business Insolvency Law—Law No. 11,101/2005). If the judicial administrator decides to terminate it, as a rule, the licensee will receive compensation, as stipulated by the parties in the agreement;

(b) in the liquidation, prohibition of assigning the trademark is more dubious since the purpose of the liquidation is to sell the assets of the company to generate resources for creditors;

(c) if the licensee has entered into liquidation, the agreement will be terminated since it will be impossible to pay the license fee.

In light of the above, it is important to note that the parties should ensure that they are understanding and foreseeing all the risks of insolvency of each other when negotiating a trademark license. It is vital to understand the degree of insolvency protections included in the agreement and whether or not further protective measures should be taken.

It is also relevant to stress that in the case of liquidation, the sale, by the judicial administrator, of industrial property rights included in the wound-up assets should be registered at the BPTO by means of presentation of the judicial order confirming the sale.

5. TOPIC IV: CONSEQUENCES OF THE TERMINATION OR EXPIRATION OF THE AGREEMENT

The Brazilian Civil Code (Law No. 10,406/2002) provides that during the conclusion and performance of the agreement, the parties must observe the principles of honesty and good faith.

This general rule exists to avoid abusive conduct when Brazilian law is applicable in the agreement and, in the case of conflict between the parties, the local court may analyze the purposes and conditions of the agreement based on circumstances other than the written provisions.

In accordance with the Brazilian Civil Code:

- the termination of the agreement should be carried out as stated in the termination clause, which usually establishes that a prior notice of a certain period of time should be given; or
- the termination of the agreement can be unilateral, in which case it is always important that the terminating party gives notice of termination to the other party, as set in the agreement or by law. If either party wants to terminate the

agreement, the nonterminating party may be entitled to damages or indemnity of any kind as a consequence of such termination. It is also important to note that, despite the termination clause, a judge may condemn the terminating party to pay the other party an indemnity sufficient to compensate the losses resulting from the early termination of the agreement under such conditions.

Further to this, the termination of the agreement may also take into account whether the agreement is for a certain period of time or for an indeterminate period of time:

- If the agreement is for a certain period of time, the nonterminating party may request the payment of the remaining payments, if licensor, or indemnity and fine, if licensee. Thus, provisions establishing rules about the early termination of agreements with a certain period of time are very important.
- On the other hand, if the license agreement is for an indefinite period, either party may terminate it by giving advance written notice. In the case of disagreement between the parties, the judge will decide the reasonableness of the period and the amount due.

Generally (this is an example list only), the parties notify each other about the termination of the agreement if one of the events below occurs:

i. If a party fails to pay any undisputed amount due under the agreement on the due date for payment and remains in default after being notified in writing to make such payment.
ii. The licensee is using the licensed trademark in a nonauthorized or improper way.
iii. If a party commits any material breach of any of the provisions of the agreement and fails to remedy such breach.
iv. If a party goes into liquidation other than a voluntary liquidation for reorganization, reconstruction or amalgamation.
v. If a party ceases to carry on business.
vi. If a party undergoes a change affecting its voting control.
vii. When the obligations become excessively onerous to one of the parties, and a great advantage to the other party, due to exceptional and unforeseeable events.

In cases of expiration or termination of the agreement, independently of the reason, it is important to have clauses in the agreement about:

i. how the licensee will pay all outstanding sums after termination;
ii. that all rights and licenses granted would cease, and that the licensee will cease to use the licensed trademarks, as soon as the agreement is terminated or expired;
iii. if there is any sublicense agreement, such rights will need to be terminated as well; and
iv. how the licensee shall proceed after the termination of the agreement regarding the remaining stock of products involved.

Furthermore, the invalidity or expiry of registration of a trademark will usually be deemed cause for the termination of the license and any related sublicenses granted by the licensee. It is also important to address this point in the agreement since in general it is an obligation of the licensor to keep the licensed trademark alive and in force. On the other hand, the licensor will try to avoid its responsibility to a third party's decision (BPTO) if the trademark is still in an application process.

6. TOPIC V: DEFAULT RULES ON THE LICENSEE'S STANDING TO SUE THIRD PARTIES FOR TRADEMARK INFRINGEMENT

As per Brazilian IP Law, a licensee can be vested by a licensor (trademark owner) with all powers to defend the licensed trademark, without prejudice to its own rights[9]. Therefore, the parties must set out whether the licensee will have the power to sue third parties for the infringement of the licensed trademark in the defined territory.

In general, it is recommended that the agreement must determine whether the licensee can act in its sole discretion to preserve the rights and interests, or if it will be necessary to obtain the licensor's prior approval. It is important to have this power very clear in the agreement, as well as to state who will be responsible for paying all the costs involved in such actions and the time frames involved.

If a licensee receives any demand, complaint, writ, summons or other notice, it will need to be determined in the license agreement whether the licensor will assume control of the defense (including resolution by compromise and settlement) of any such claim or dispute and take all the necessary actions to compensate the licensee for potential losses and damages.

7. CONCLUSION

In general, licensed intellectual property rights are a significant and lucrative business. With such an important sector, it is vital not to waste time, money and resources when trying to navigate the requirements set out by Brazilian law and the BPTO.

Without the appropriate approvals or registrations at the BPTO and BACEN, the remittance of payments cannot be guaranteed to be made abroad, nor can the company be eligible for deductions of payments for tax purposes.

Additional important issues to be considered are the following:

- Registration—complying with the legal requirements to prevent office actions or refusals.
- Royalties—technically are unlimited for nonrelated parties (for related parties are limited to 1% of payment); however, the tax deductibility is limited to 1% over the net sales of products or services in all cases.
- Invalidation of the licensed trademark—a trademark license agreement is only effective during the term of the trademark. If that ceases, so does the license

9. As indicated in the sole paragraph of Article 139 of Brazilian IP Law: "The licensee may be vested by the titleholder with all powers to act in defense of the trademark, without prejudice to his own rights."

agreement. Precise details of termination, fines and damages must be recorded in the agreement.

- Termination—the ability to terminate and details of damages, compensation and indemnity should be specified in the agreement as well as the rights and licenses.
- Trademark infringement—licensee can be vested by licensor (trademark owner) with all powers to defend the licensed trademark, without prejudice to his own rights.

Before entering into any agreement, it is important to have a clear understanding of local rules and requirements. As legal professionals, we sometimes unfortunately receive negotiated deals that are not enforceable locally.

Together with the deal negotiation, the parties need to be assisted by a local lawyer in order to clarify the legislation and requirements imposed in the proposed transaction. As always, we recommend doing your homework before the execution of any agreement, as this will save time, and most importantly, the parties' relationship for a successful business.

BIBLIOGRAPHY

Amaral, Luiz Henrique do; Caffé, Cândida Ribeiro; Ehlers, Marc Hargen; Carneiro, Rodrigo Borges; Dannemann Siemsen Advogados. "IP in business transactions: Brazil overview" In: *Thomson Reuters Practical Law.*, August 1, 2019. Retrieved from: https://uk.practicallaw.thomsonreuters.com/7-381-1084?transitionType =Default&contextData=(sc.Default).

Barbosa, Denis Borges. "Tratado da propriedade intelectual: tomo IV." Rio de Janeiro: Lumen Juris, 2015.

Barbosa, Denis Borges. "Contratos de Propriedade Intelectual." Retrieved from: http://www.denisbarbosa.addr.com/ibmec1.doc.

Berger, Andrew. "Ten License Agreement Considerations." In: *IP in Brief.*, April 29, 2020. Retrieved from: http://www.ipinbrief.com/ten-considerations-when-entering-into-license/.

Bhering Advogados. "Licensing in Brazil." In: *Lexology*, January 4, 2019. Retrieved from: https://www.lexology.com/library/detail.aspx?g=ccaca1ae-421d-4d55-bc92-27df8eacd420.

Brasil. Lei n° 9.279, de 14 de maio de 1996. "Regula direitos e obrigações relativos à propriedade industrial." *Diário Oficial da União*: Seção 1, Brasília, 15 maio 2017.

Brasil. Lei n° 10.406, de 10 de janeiro de 2002. "Institui o Código Civil." *Diário Oficial da União*: Seção 1, Brasília, 11 jan. 2002.

Brasil. Lei n° 12.529, de 30 de novembro de 2011. "Estrutura o Sistema Brasileiro de Defesa da Concorrência." *Diário Oficial da União*: Seção 1, Brasília, 1 nov. 2011.

Brasil. Lei n° 12.846, de 1 de agosto de 2013. "Dispõe sobre a responsabilização administrativa e civil de pessoas jurídicas pela prática de atos contra a administração pública, nacional ou estrangeira, e dá outras providências." *Diário Oficial da União*: Seção 1, Brasília, 2 ago. 2013.

Caffé, Cândida, "The Role of Brazilian Universities in the Innovation Production of the Country." In: *les Nouvelles—Journal of the Licensing Executives Society*, vol. LIV No. 2, June 2019. Retrieved from: https://ssrn.com/abstract=3380596.

Cerqueira, João da Gama. "Tratado da propriedade industrial. v. II, t. II: das marcas de fábrica e de comércio, do nome comercial, das insígnias, das frases de propaganda e das recompensas industriais, da concorrência desleal." *Lumen Juris,* Rio de Janeiro: 2010.

Clarke Modet. "Changes in registration of trademarks in Brazil." October 2, 2019. Retrieved from: https://www.clarkemodet.com/en/news-posts/changes-in-registration-of-trademarks-in-brazil/.

Fekete, Elisabeth Kasznar. "Use of Unregistered and Registered Trademarks: The Brazilian System." *The Trademark Reporter: The Law Journal of the International Trademark Association*, v. 104, ed. 6, p. 1255-1274, November/December, 2014. Retrieved from: https://www.inta.org/TMR/Documents/Volume%20104/vol104_no6_a3.pdf.

Instituto Nacional Da Propriedade Industrial. Página Inicial. In: BRASIL. Ministério da Economia. 2020. Retrieved from: https://www.gov.br/inpi/pt-br.

Instituto Nacional da Propriedade Industrial. "Instrução Normativa nº 70, de 11 de abril de 2017." *Diário Oficial da União*: Seção 1, Brasília, 11 abr. 2017.

Kukula, Angela. "Knowledge Transfer and Intellectual Property in the UK: The New Challenges." In: *les Nouvelles—Journal of the Licensing Executives Society*, vol. LIV, No. 2, June 2019. Retrieved from: https://ssrn.com/abstract=3380548.

Moritz, Christian. "The Brazilian Business Insolvency Act In A Nutshell." In: *Mondaq*. [S. l.], March 21, 2017. Retrieved from: https://www.mondaq.com/brazil/insolvencybankruptcy/571604/the-brazilian-business-insolvency-act-in-a-nutshell.

Oliveira Lawyers. "Licensing Agreements Brazilian Lawyers," 2019. Retrieved from: https://oliveiralawyers.com/services/corporate-law/contracts/licensing-agreements/.

Pinheiro Neto Advogados; Machado, José Mauro Decoussau; LEITE, Márcio Junqueira; FERRER, Gustavo Gonçalves; DOTTI, Victor Rawet. "Trademarks." In: *Law and Practice*. 2019. Retrieved from: http://www.pinheironeto.com.br/Documents/Artigos/TradeMarks2019_ChambersGuides.pdf.

Santos, Manoel J. Pereira dos et al. "Propriedade intelectual: contratos de propriedade intelectual e novas tecnologia." 2. ed. *Saraiva,* São Paulo, 2009.

Schmidt, Lélio Denicoli. "Marcas: aquisição, exercício e extinção de direitos." *Lumen Juris,* Rio de Janeiro: 2016.

Stark, Lewis. "Key Financial Building Blocks of Licensing Agreements to Maximize Revenue and Protect Intellectual Properties." In: l*es Nouvelles—Journal of the Licensing Executives Society*, vol. LIV, No. 1, March 2019. Retrieved from: https://ssrn.com/abstract=3317004.

Thomson Reuters. "Brazilian bankruptcy filings at 11-year high—Experian." *Reuters: Bond News*, January 3, 2017. Retrieved from: https://www.reuters.com/article/brazil-bankruptcy-serasa/brazilian-bankruptcy-filings-at-11-year-high-experian-idUSL1N1ET0VU.

Worden, Tim; Smyth, Neil. "The impact of insolvency on licensors and licensees in the life sciences sector." In: TAYLOR WESSING. *Sinapse: Law for Life Sciences,* March 2013. Retrieved from: https://www.taylorwessing.com/synapse/march13.html.

World Intellectual Property Organization. "Trademark Licensing." In: *Learning Points.* 6. Ed, 2015. Retrieved from: https://www.wipo.int/export/sites/www/sme/en/documents/pdf/ip_panorama_12_learning_points.pdf.

World Trade Organisation. "Agreement on Trade-Related Aspects of Intellectual Property Rights," 1998. Retrieved from: https://www.wto.org/english/docs_e/legal_e/27-trips.pdf; https://aippi.org/wp-content/uploads/committees/241/GR241brazil.pdf.

Canada

Anthony Prenol

1. INTRODUCTION TO TRADEMARK LICENSING IN CANADA

1.1. Legislation on Trademark Licensing in Canada

The most important legislation in Canada explicitly addressing trademark licensing is section 50 of a federal statute, the *Trademarks Act* (the 'Act').[1]

In Canada, as in many other countries, a trademark's distinctiveness can be impaired if the public does not identify goods and services associated with the trademark owner as originating from a single source. Canadian law recognizes that a trademark owner can license others to use its mark and that, provided certain requirements are met, use by such licensees will not impair the mark's distinctiveness.

Section 50 of the Act establishes a basic set of rules for the licensing of trademarks.

Subsection 50(1) provides as follows:

> 50(1) For the purposes of the Act, if an entity is licensed by or with the authority of the owner of a trademark to use the trademark in a country and the owner has, under the licence, direct or indirect control of the character or quality of the goods or services, then the use, advertisement or display of the trademark in that country as or in a trademark, trade name or otherwise by that entity has, and is deemed always to have had, the same effect as such a use, advertisement or display of the trademark in that country by the owner.

There are several noteworthy aspects of the language in subsection 50(1).

First, the statute does not require that a licence be reduced to writing in order for the deeming provisions of subsection 50(1) to be operative. Although Canada previously had a system that required a trademark owner to register each licensee with the Trademarks Office and file a copy of at least a short-form licence agreement with such licensee, that system was abolished in 1993. Under the current system, even in the

1. R.S.C., 1985, c. T-13 as am.

absence of a written licence agreement, if a trademark owner and/or licensee can adduce evidence that satisfactorily establishes the existence of an oral licence agreement entitling the owner to exercise a sufficient level of control over the licensee's use of the mark, then the provisions of subsection 50(1) will apply and deem such use to constitute use by the owner. It is nevertheless highly recommended that any trademark owner who permits a third party to use the trademark (including a related entity) reduces the terms of their agreement to writing.

Second, subsection 50(1) applies not only to situations where the trademark owner has direct control over the character or quality of the licensed goods or services but also to situations where such control is indirect. Accordingly, in a situation where a mark has been sublicensed by a licensee, even though the trademark owner may only exercise its control over the sublicensee through the licensee, subsection 50(1) will nevertheless deem the sublicensee's trademark use to be use by the owner.[2]

Third, the operation of subsection 50(1) is not restricted to the use of a trademark *in Canada*. Although the provision in subsection 50(1) deeming a licensed use to be use of the mark by the owner only applies for the purposes of the Act in Canada, this provision can nevertheless, in certain circumstances, apply to use by a licensee outside of Canada. For example, the Act permits a person to oppose a trademark application on the basis of the person's prior making known in Canada of a trademark through its use of its mark outside of Canada combined with certain activities that took place in Canada (such as foreign advertising that spilled over into Canada).[3] In such circumstances, the opponent may cite use of its trademark that took place outside of Canada through the activities of a licensee and, as such, rely upon the provisions of subsection 50(1) to deem the licensee's foreign use of the opponent's mark to be the opponent's own use for the purpose of establishing making known of the mark in Canada.

Fourth, the wording of subsection 50(1) requires the existence of a licence agreement that gives the trademark owner control over the character or quality of the licensed goods/services, but it does not establish criteria for such character or quality or the manner in which the licensor must actually exercise such control. In practice, a trademark owner may wish to exercise its control through a variety of means such as by including criteria in a schedule to the licence agreement that the licensed products are required to meet, requiring the submission of samples of licensed goods for pre-approval, and periodically inspecting the licensee's premises where it manufactures the licensed goods or performs the licensed services.

In addition to the deeming provision contained in subsection 50(1) of the Act, subsection 50(2) contains an important presumption that can prove to be very useful in disputes. This section provides as follows:

> 50(2) For the purposes of this Act, to the extent that public notice is given of the fact that the use of a trademark is a licensed use and of the identity of the owner, it shall be presumed, unless the contrary is proven, that the use is licensed by the owner of the trademark and the character or quality of the goods or service is under the control of the owner.

2. See, for example, *Tucumcari Aero v. Cassels, Brock & Blackwell* 2010 FC 267 at paragraph 15.
3. *Trademarks Act*, sections 5, 16(1)(a) and 38(2)(c).

In order to rely upon the subsection 50(2) presumption in litigation, it is not necessary for the trademark owner or licensee to prove the existence of a licence agreement or, in particular, an agreement that entitles the trademark owner to control the character or quality of the licensed goods or services. In fact, the subsection 50(2) presumption is particularly helpful in circumstances where a trademark owner has permitted a third party to use the trademark but has not reduced their agreement to writing. In such circumstances, as long as the licensee has given public notice of the trademark owner's name and has identified that the use is under licence, the owner can rely on the presumption that the use in question is licensed and that the owner controls the character or quality of the licensee's goods or services.

It is important to note that this presumption is subject to being rebutted by other evidence. For example, if the evidence were to show that the trademark owner was unaware of the purported licensee's use of the mark or that the owner had not, in fact, approved such use, then the presumption under subsection 50(2) would very likely be successfully rebutted.

Nevertheless, the presumption contained in subsection 50(2) has proven to be quite helpful in trademark oppositions and non-use expungement proceedings. This is particularly the case where the trademark owner is seeking to rely upon use of its mark in Canada by an authorized third party but does not have a written licence agreement in place and/or would prefer not to have to incur the expense of leading evidence from the third party.

The importance of section 50 of the Act can be demonstrated by an examination of its application in non-use expungement proceedings. By way of background, section 45 of the Act permits any person to ask the Registrar of Trademarks to give notice to the owner of a registered trademark requiring it to furnish evidence showing that the trademark was in use in Canada at some point in the preceding three years in association with the goods and/or services in the registration. If the trademark owner is unable to furnish such evidence or establish the existence of special circumstances excusing its non-use, the Registrar can expunge the registration, in whole or in part, for non-use.

Under section 45, it is only the trademark owner that is permitted to submit evidence and such evidence is not subject to cross-examination by the requesting party. The Registrar of Trademarks has taken the position that, in a section 45 proceeding where the owner is relying upon use of its registered trademark by a licensee, it is not necessary for the trademark owner to file a copy of the relevant licence agreement. Instead, it is sufficient if the affidavit or statutory declaration filed by the owner states that the owner had, under a licence, direct or indirect control over the character or quality of the subject goods or services.[4]

Subsection 50(3) of the Act contains provisions regarding the commencement of proceedings for infringement by a licensee or the licensor. These provisions are discussed elsewhere in this chapter.

4. *Empresa Cubana Del Tabaco v. Shapiro Cohen*, 2011 FC 102, affirmed 2011 FCA 340.

Federal legislation, namely the *Bankruptcy and Insolvency Act* (BIA)[5] and the *Companies' Creditors Arrangement Act*,[6] provides certain protections to the licensee of a trademark in circumstances where the licensor is insolvent or is going through insolvency proceedings. These amendments not only still allow a debtor that is going through insolvency proceedings to disclaim contracts (including a trademark licence agreement) but also preserve the licensee's right to continue using licensed intellectual property provided that it continues to perform its obligations under the licence agreement in relation to the use of the intellectual property.[7]

1.2. Trademarks as Objects of Contractual Arrangements

There are no Canadian statutes that specifically address the formation, interpretation or enforcement of a trademark licence agreement. Accordingly, these questions are to be governed by: (a) the common-law rules concerning the formation, interpretation and enforcement of contracts in the Canadian provinces and territories other than Québec; and (b) the provisions of the Civil Code of Québec[8] in respect of contracts that are governed by the laws of the province of Québec, Canada's only civil law province.

For example, as is the case under the common law with respect to any other contract, a trademark licence agreement requires offer, acceptance and consideration before any agreement can be considered to have been entered by the parties.

Even in situations where the parties have reduced their agreement to writing, it is entirely possible that they may have a dispute as to the meaning of a particular provision or that the agreement may be silent on a matter. In these circumstances, Canadian courts will give the contractual terms their plain and ordinary meaning based on the understanding of an average person.

A court will, however, take into account the context of the contract including the factual matrix as it existed as of the time when the agreement was entered.[9] The factual matrix takes into account facts that were known to the parties at the time of contracting and that would bear upon the meaning to be ascribed to the contract.[10] The factual matrix can include factors such as the commercial purpose of the contract, the background to the contract and the market in which the parties were operating at the time of formation of the contract. The factual matrix does not, however, extend to the parties' subjective intentions for entering into the agreement nor is it intended to overwhelm the words chosen by the parties for their agreement.

As noted above, a trademark licence agreement need not be in writing in order to exist or to be enforceable by one of the parties. As with other contracts, the existence of a trademark licence agreement can be proved by evidence as to discussions between the parties that rise to the level of an oral agreement or by a course of conduct between the parties that establishes an intention to be bound by the terms of an agreement.

5. R.S.C., 1985, c. B-3.
6. R.S.C., 1985, c. C-36.
7. BIA, s. 65.11(7), CCAA, section 32(6).
8. CCQ-1991.
9. *Sattva Capital Corp. v. Creston Moly Corp.* 2014 SCC 53.
10. *Ibid.*, at paragraph 58.

Although two parties must have agreed upon all essential terms before a contract can be considered to exist, a term may be implied where it is necessary to give business efficacy to a contract or where the term is so obvious that it is not required to be expressly stated in the contract.[11]

The Civil Code of Québec (the 'Code') also addresses the formation and interpretation of contracts. The Code provides that a contract is formed by the exchange of consents between persons having capacity to contract.[12] The only exceptions to this general rule are where the law additionally requires a particular form to be respected as a necessary condition of its formation or where the parties subject the formation of the contract to a solemn form. There are no specific formalities that have to be observed with respect to the formation of a trademark licence agreement and so the general rules of contract formation under the Code would apply.

Under the Code, acceptance of an offer to contract may be express or tacit.[13] An offer to contract must contain all of the essential elements of the proposed contract.[14] When interpreting a contract, such as a trademark licence agreement, the court seeks to determine the common intention of the parties rather than adherence to the literal meaning of the words in the contract.[15] In interpreting a contract, the nature of the contract, the circumstances in which it was formed, the interpretation which has already been given to it by the parties or which it may have received, and usage are all taken into account.[16]

1.3. The Delimitation Between Proprietary Trademark Rules and Contract Law

A trademark licence operates as a permission to the licensee to use a trademark in circumstances that could otherwise constitute trademark infringement, passing off or depreciation of goodwill. If a licensee uses a trademark outside the scope of the licence agreement, then it could expose itself to an action by the licensor for trademark infringement, passing off and/or depreciation of goodwill.

In circumstances where a licensee breaches the terms of a licence agreement, the licensor's remedy will typically be an action for breach of contract. It is possible, however, that the licensee's actions may be so egregious as to entitle the licensor to terminate the contract. For example, the terms of a licence agreement may classify certain actions by the licensee as a breach entitling the licensor to terminate or, alternatively, the licensee's actions may constitute a fundamental breach entitling the licensor to treat the contract as at an end. Under such circumstances, if the licensor elects to terminate the contract, it can then sue the licensee for trademark infringement, passing off and/or depreciation of goodwill with respect to any ongoing uses by the former licensee of the licensor's trademarks.

11. *Energy Fundamentals Group v. Veresen* 2015 ONCA 514.
12. Section 1385.
13. *Ibid.*, section 1386.
14. *Ibid.*, section 1388.
15. *Ibid.*, section 1425.
16. *Ibid.*, section 1426.

2. TRADEMARK LICENSING AND COMPETITION LAW

As a general rule, a trademark owner is free to license or not license its trademark as it so chooses. In some circumstances, however, a trademark owner's licensing activities may have consequences under competition law. For example, if a trademark owner's refusal to grant a licence is coupled with an activity that goes beyond the scope of its trademark rights, then there may be a violation of competition laws.

In March 2019, Canada's Competition Bureau (the 'Bureau'), the entity responsible for enforcing Canada's federal competition legislation, the *Competition Act*[17], issued Intellectual Property Enforcement Guidelines (IPEGs). The purpose of the IPEGs is to articulate how the Bureau approaches the interface between competition policy and intellectual property rights and how it will determine whether conduct involving intellectual property raises an issue under the *Competition Act*.

The IPEGs describe the five steps in the Bureau's analysis for determining whether competitive harm will result from a particular type of business conduct involving IP:

(1) identifying the conduct;
(2) defining the relevant market(s);
(3) determining if the firm or firms under scrutiny possess market power by examining the level of concentration and entry conditions in the relevant market(s) as well as other factors;
(4) determining if the conduct would substantially lessen or prevent competition in the relevant market(s); and
(5) considering, when appropriate, any relevant efficiency rationales or valid business justifications.[18]

The IPEGs also make the following general observations about licensing of IP:

- licensing is the usual method by which an IP owner authorizes others to use the IP;
- in the vast majority of cases, licensing is pro-competitive because it facilitates the broader use of a valuable IP right by additional parties;
- in assessing whether a particular licensing arrangement raises a competition issue, the Bureau examines whether the terms of the licence serve to create, enhance or maintain the market power of either the licensor or the licensee; and
- the Bureau will not consider licensing arrangements involving IP to be anticompetitive unless they reduce competition substantially relative to that which would have likely existed in the absence of the licence's potentially anticompetitive terms.[19]

17. R.S.C., 1985, C-34.
18. IPEGs, paragraph 31.
19. IPEGs, paragraph 34.

Interestingly, in the IPEGs, the Bureau has expressed its support for a series of prior decisions of the Competition Tribunal in cases involving intellectual property.[20] One of those decisions, *Canada (Director of Investigation and Research) v. Tele-Direct (Publications) Inc. and Tele-Direct (Services) Inc.*[21] is particularly relevant for present purposes since it involves a refusal by the publisher of an advertising directory to license its YELLOW PAGES trademark to competing providers of directories. In that decision, the Tribunal commented as follows on the right of a trademark owner to choose whether to license its trademark:

> The respondents' refusal to license their trade-marks falls squarely within their prerogative. Inherent in the very nature of the right to license a trade-mark is the right for the owner of the trade-mark to determine whether or not, and to whom, to grant a licence; selectivity in licensing is fundamental to the rationale behind protecting trade-marks. The respondents' trade-marks are valuable assets and represent considerable goodwill in the marketplace. The decision to license a trade-mark – essentially, to share the goodwill vesting in the asset – is a right which rests entirely with the owner of the mark. The refusal to license a trade-mark is distinguishable from a situation where anti-competitive provisions are attached to a trade-mark licence.
>
> [...]
>
> While the evidence suggests that Tele-Direct is motivated, at least in part, by competition in its decision to refuse to license its trade-marks, the fact is that the Trade-marks Act allows trade-mark owners to decide to whom they will license their trade-marks. The respondents' motivation for their decision to refuse to license a competitor becomes irrelevant as the Trade-marks Act does not prescribe any limit to the exercise of that right.

It therefore appears that the Bureau still recognizes the right of a trademark owner to selectively license (or not license) its trademark.

At the same time, the IPEGs do give some examples of circumstances in which a licensor's conduct might contravene competition law:

- the licensor ties a non-proprietary product to a product covered by its IP right; or
- an IP owner acquires market power by systematically purchasing a controlling collection of IP rights and then refuses to license the rights to others, and it substantially lessens or prevents competition in markets associated with the IP rights.

It can be seen from the first example that the Bureau might take a critical view of a trademark owner that makes its agreement to license its trademark to a third party conditional upon the third party agreeing not to do something that it was otherwise entitled to do, such as making sales of its goods bearing the licensed mark in a jurisdiction where the licensor has no trademark rights. Similarly, a trademark licence agreement that goes beyond merely dictating what the licensee can and cannot do

20. IPEGs, paragraph 40.
21. 1997 CanLii 11 (CT): http://canlii.ca/t/1flnt.

using the licensed mark and places limitations on the licensee's ability to otherwise compete with the licensor could also run afoul of the *Competition Act*.

It is unlikely that the Bureau would take any issue with restrictions in a trademark licence agreement that prohibit the licensee, during the term of the agreement, from challenging the licensor's rights in the licensed trademark and/or the validity of any registration for such mark. In fact, the doctrine of licensee estoppel would, in any event, prevent a licensee from making such a challenge during the term of a licence agreement.

If, however, a licence agreement goes beyond this reasonable limitation and also prohibits a licensee from challenging the licensed mark after the expiration or termination of the agreement, then the situation is less clear.

The IPEGs also address, as an example, the scenario in which an IP rights owner decides to grant an exclusive patent licence to a third party but not to the third party's competitors.

In considering whether the parties' conduct constitutes an abuse of dominant position, the Bureau would likely consider such factors as:

- whether the IP rights owner and exclusive licensee are actual or potential competitors in the relevant market (in which case, the exclusive licence could lessen competition between the two firms);
- the reasons for the grant of the exclusive licence; and
- the competitiveness of the relevant market before and after the exclusive licence.

It is also possible that there may be circumstances in which a trademark owner's refusal to license its trademark to third parties could create an undue restraint of trade or unduly lessen competition such that it would violate the *Competition Act*. As noted in the IPEGs, the Bureau would first determine whether the refusal to license adversely affected competition in a relevant market that was different or significantly larger than the subject matter of the trademark owner's IP rights or the goods or services that result directly from the exercise of such IP rights. The Bureau would also consider the barriers to entry and whether the trademark owner's refusal to license would adversely alter other firms' incentives to innovate.

3. FORMATION OF TRADEMARK LICENCE AGREEMENTS IN CANADA

As a general rule, there are no special requirements that a trademark licence agreement has to meet in order to be valid and enforceable. As noted above, it is strongly recommended (although not essential) that a trademark licence agreement be reduced to writing.

There is also no requirement that a trademark licence agreement be recorded with the Canadian Intellectual Property Office (CIPO). Although a trademark owner or licensee can voluntarily record a trademark licence agreement with CIPO, doing so is not required for a licensee to commence proceedings to enforce rights in the trademark.

Several Canadian provinces (British Columbia, Alberta, Manitoba, Ontario, Prince Edward Island and New Brunswick) have legislation that imposes pre-contractual disclosure requirements on a franchisor in order for a franchise agreement to be valid and enforceable.[22] Therefore, if a trademark owner goes beyond merely licensing its trademark to a third party and instead imposes such further requirements on the conduct of the licensee's business that the arrangement is considered to constitute a franchise agreement, the trademark owner can find itself in a situation where it has to comply with provincial franchise legislation.

4. BREACH OF TRADEMARK LICENCE AGREEMENT

4.1. Protection of the Reputation and Goodwill of the Trademark in a Contractual Relationship

As noted above, in order for a trademark licence agreement to properly protect the rights of the trademark owner and prevent the trademark from becoming non-distinctive, the trademark licence agreement should give the owner the right to control the character and quality of the goods and services in association with which the licensed mark is permitted to be used. It is recommended that:

- a written trademark licence agreement provides the trademark owner with the right to control the character and quality of the licensed goods/services;
- the licence agreement gives the trademark owner the right to pre-approve any marketing materials or packaging that depicts the licensed trademark;
- the licence agreement gives the trademark owner the right to conduct an inspection/audit of the licensee's premises in order to verify the quality of the licensed goods/services; and
- the licensor actually exercises the foregoing rights (such as by inspecting the premises where the licensee manufactures the licensed goods or performs the licensed services, and actually exercising the right to pre-approve any materials depicting the licensed mark).

In certain circumstances, the fact that a written trademark licence agreement gives the owner the right to control the character and quality of the licensed goods/services will be sufficient to preserve the licensed mark's distinctiveness even in the absence of proof that the trademark owner actually exercised such right. For example, as discussed above, in non-use cancellation proceedings that are commenced before the Registrar of Trademarks, if the trademark owner adduces evidence that use of the trademark in Canada has been made by a licensee in circumstances where the owner has the right to control the character or quality of the licensed goods/services, then the Registrar will assume that any use that occurred in the relevant period was a licensed use that enures to the trademark owner's benefit.

In circumstances where a trademark owner has granted a licence to another person to use the trademark, there are no statutory provisions in Canada that impose

22. See, for example, Ontario's *Arthur Wishart Act (Franchise Disclosure), 2000*, S.O. 2000, c. 3

on the trademark owner an obligation to take positive action to maintain the reputation or goodwill of the licensed trademark. If the licensor and licensee specifically address this issue in a written licence agreement between them, then the terms of their agreement shall govern in this regard. In the absence of a specific agreement between them, it is nevertheless possible that a licensor's acts or omissions that result in a diminution of the regard for the licensed mark are so egregious that the licensee could have a cause of action for breach of contract.

Additionally, as noted above, several Canadian provinces (British Columbia, Alberta, Manitoba, Ontario, Prince Edward Island and New Brunswick) have legislation that imposes certain requirements on the sale and operation of franchises. Generally speaking, a franchise relationship goes beyond the mere grant from the franchisor to the franchisee of a licence of one or more trademarks and also includes the ability of the franchisor to control the franchisee's method of operation, marketing, supply of goods and other aspects of the day-to-day conduct of the franchised business.

Provincial franchise legislation typically imposes a duty of fair dealing on the parties in their performance of a franchise agreement. In most cases, this duty of fair dealing requires, among other things, that the franchisor consider the legitimate interests of the franchise network as a whole and that its activities meet the standard of commercial reasonableness. These requirements may, in certain circumstances, impose obligations on franchisors to take positive steps to protect the reputation of trademarks that are licensed to franchisees.

4.2. Licensing and Trademark Infringement

Subsection 50(3) of the Act contains provisions that allow a licensee to call upon the licensor to commence trademark infringement proceedings. This section provides as follows:

> 50(3) Subject to any agreement subsisting between an owner of a trademark and a licensee of the trademark, the licensee may call on the owner to take proceedings for infringement thereof, and, if the owner refuses or neglects to do so within two months after being called on, the licensee may institute proceedings for infringement in the licensee's own name as if the licensee were the owner, naming the owner a defendant.

It is noteworthy that the provisions in subsection 50(3) are subject to an agreement to the contrary between the licensor and licensee. Accordingly, any trademark owner would be well advised to ensure that, before it permits a third party to use the owner's trademark in Canada, it should negotiate a written agreement that governs the use of the licensed mark and, among other things, gives the owner control over the commencement and carriage of proceedings to enforce rights in the trademark.

It is also noteworthy that subsection 50(3) does not distinguish between an exclusive licence and a non-exclusive licence of a trademark. Therefore, the right of a licensee to call up its licensor to commence infringement proceedings is not contingent upon the underlying licence rights being exclusive.

Although subsection 50(3) of the Act only addresses infringement proceedings, the Act and the common law also permit a trademark owner to bring other enforcement proceedings such as an action for passing off[23] and an action to prohibit a third party from using a registered trademark in a manner that is likely to depreciate the goodwill associated with the trademark.[24]

Accordingly, a written trademark licence agreement should give the trademark owner the right to commence and prosecute enforcement actions of any kind (rather than being restricted to just actions for infringement). Even if a trademark owner is willing to include in a licence agreement provisions allowing its licensee to commence enforcement proceedings in some circumstances, it should at a minimum also include provisions that give the licensor sufficient time to consider whether to commence such proceedings itself so as to avoid the two-month default deadline set out in subsection 50(3) of the Act.

It is also recommended that a trademark licence agreement contains provisions regarding the defence of the trademark. For example, a trademark owner will likely want to impose obligations on a licensee not only to notify the licensor of third-party infringers but also to notify the licensor if any third party threatens to attack or otherwise challenge the licensor's trademark or any registration for such mark.

As noted above, although it is possible to record a trademark licence agreement with the Canadian Intellectual Property Office against particular Canadian trademark registrations and/or applications, it is not mandatory to do so. Additionally, such a recordal does not provide the trademark licensor or licensee with any additional rights nor does a failure to record a licence agreement prejudice the licensor or licensee in any manner.

The issue of infringement can also be analysed from the perspective of the actions of the licensee. Given that a trademark licence operates as a permission from the trademark owner to the licensee to use the trademark in a certain manner and subject to certain conditions, so long as the licensee is operating within the scope of its licence, it could not be said to be infringing the trademark owner's rights. If, however, the licensee's actions exceed the scope of the licence, then it could potentially be liable to the trademark owner for infringement or another cause of action under trademark law.

Under Canadian law, there is no implied warranty from the trademark owner in a licence agreement to the effect that the licensee, by carrying out its licensed activities, will not be infringing or otherwise violating the trademark rights of a third party. For this reason, a licensee may wish to take steps to protect itself by either seeking an express warranty of non-infringement in the licence agreement or conducting an infringement review prior to entering a licence agreement in order to locate potentially conflicting third-party rights.

23. Paragraph 7(b) of the Act contains what is often referred to as a statutory codification of the common law action of passing off.
24. Section 22 of the Act prohibits a person from using a registered trademark in a manner that is likely to have the effect of depreciating the goodwill associated with the mark.

5. TERMINATION OF TRADEMARK LICENCES

A properly crafted trademark licence agreement will contain provisions that deem any use by the licensee to enure to the benefit of the licensor. Even in the absence of such a deeming provision, if a court concludes that a proper trademark licence agreement existed (even in the case of an oral agreement), then all use of the licensed mark that was made by the licensee shall be deemed to constitute, for all purposes, use by the licensor. As such, if the licensor terminates a licence agreement, even in circumstances where the licensor may not have lived up to all of its obligations under the agreement, the use that the licensee made of the trademark will nevertheless still be deemed to be the trademark owner's use.

Therefore, once a trademark licence agreement has been terminated, the licensee will typically not have any right to continue using the licensed mark, nor will it have any claim to rights in the goodwill that has accumulated in the trademark, at least in part, through its efforts. Similarly, the licensee will not, in the absence of a provision to the contrary in the licence agreement, have any right to compensation for the investments that it made in the trademark.

Once a trademark licence agreement has been terminated, the right of the licensee to sub-license the mark to others would similarly be terminated. This scenario could expose the licensee to a claim for damages from sublicensees but, regardless of any claim that a sublicensee may have as against the licensee, it would not have a right to continue using the sub-licensed mark.

An interesting question that sometimes arises is what effect, if any, the invalidation or expiry of a licensed trademark has on the agreement. For example, does the agreement automatically terminate at such time? Even though a trademark registration may have lapsed for non-renewal or other reasons, a trademark owner may still have valuable common-law rights that it can continue to license to a third party. Accordingly, in the absence of a provision in the agreement providing otherwise, the expiry or invalidation of a registration for a licensed mark would not usually have any effect on the existence of the licence agreement or on the licensee's obligation to continue paying royalties.

As noted above, Canadian insolvency statutes provide some protections to licensees in circumstances where their licensor has gone bankrupt or entered insolvency protection. In such circumstances, the licensee can continue to use the licensed mark provided that it continues to comply with its obligations under the licence agreement with respect to the trademark.

Finland

Kim Parviainen

1. INTRODUCTION TO TRADEMARK LICENSING IN FINLAND

Trademarks are an important object of property in many agreements and broader licensing arrangements. Agreements on the manufacture of branded products, use of branded content, marketing cooperation and so on are all forms of trademark licences or contain elements thereof. In the below, some central principles of the Finnish law on trademark licensing will be examined in outline. These principles are largely drawn from general principles of Finnish contract law applied to an intellectual property context but also involve features specific to intellectual property and trademark law. The presentation will focus on those principles that are common to all or most trademark licences.

As will be seen, these rules are not in all respects well-settled law. One reason for this may in part be the Finnish business community's strong preference for arbitration as a dispute resolution method. While arbitration presents many advantages, one drawback is the resulting lack of published case law. Some conclusions suggested below should therefore be approached with a degree of caution until confirmed by the courts. The below presentation will generally refer to the Finnish courts, but readers should thus also note that in many instances, a concrete case would in fact be heard by an arbitral tribunal.

1.1. Main Sources of Law and Authorities

The main statutory rules on trademark licensing are now contained in section 42 of the Trademark Act (544/2019). This provision is based 'mainly'[1] on rules that predate the current 2019 Trademark Act but also serves to implement Articles 23, 25 and 26 of Directive (EU) 2015/2436 on trademarks. Additionally, section 43 of the reformed

1. HE 201/2018, p. 141.

Trademarks Act contains rules on the recordal of trademark licences. These rules are, however, either very general or narrow and their practical importance is limited.

Beyond these, the Finnish law of trademark licensing is largely governed by the general principles of Finnish contract law. These principles govern issues such as contract formation, interpretation, remedies for non-performance and the like. Generally, these rules are default rules that the parties to the contract may agree to depart from or vary as they think best.[2]

Unlike some other, e.g., Continental European jurisdictions, these general principles are not contained in any general codification, but rather arise from, e.g., the interplay of more narrowly tailored statutory rules, preparatory works to legislation, case law and commentary by legal experts.

In Finland, the Sale of Goods Act (355/1987),[3] governing the sale of movable goods, is often understood to reflect these general principles of contract law to a great degree.[4] Thus, it is comparatively common for litigants in contract disputes to cite the Sale of Goods Act by way of analogy and/or as expressive of underlying broader principles of contract law, even where the Act is not applicable in the narrower statutory sense. Caution is advised, however, as the Sale of Goods Act's rules do not mirror the underlying general rules in all respects.[5]

In respect of licensing, analogies to the Commercial Agents Act (417/1992) may also be relevant. One may also seek to draw analogies from other statutes in the broader field of intellectual property. These, however, largely already mirror each other in many respects relevant to the present discussion. As will be seen, the rules of competition law are also a factor that limits the parties' freedom of contract.

In Finland, like in the other Nordic countries, great authority also attaches to the Government's explanatory memoranda accompanying each new bill for an Act of Parliament.[6] Given the relative lack of statutory rules, there is, however, a similar lack of relevant explanatory memoranda and other preparatory works.

Finnish law is part of the Nordic branch of the civil law tradition. There is a great degree of uniformity in civil law between the Nordic countries.[7] Swedish law has been particularly influential in the development of Finnish law. It is thus common to cite legal authorities from the other Nordic countries as relevant authorities when interpreting Finnish law.[8]

2. Bärlund et al., *Finlands civil- och handelsrätt* (2013), section 4.2.1, p. 203.
3. Finland is an officially bilingual country. All statutes have official versions and titles in Finnish and Swedish only. Titles in English are translations by the author. The proper statute may be identified by the provided state book number. In some cases, an unofficial English translation is available.
4. See, e.g., Wilhelmsson et al., *Huvudpunkter i köplagen* (2006), section 1.5, pp. 26 et seq.
5. See also, Sund-Norrgård *Lisenssisopimuksen tulkinta*, Oikeustiede 45 (2012), pp. 284-333, p. 298 for a brief discussion regarding the usefulness of the Sale of Goods Act in interpreting licence agreements. See also, e.g., Wilhelmsson et al., *Huvudpunkter i köplagen* (2006), section 1.6, p. 28.
6. These are in the below cited to their Finnish-language versions as 'HE'.
7. For an English-language restatement of Nordic contract law, see Lando et al. *Restatement of Nordic Contract Law* (2016).
8. In recognition of the fact that, e.g., Swedish law will be discussed elsewhere in the present book, a preference for sources from Finland has been maintained throughout this outline, however.

Finnish law is of course also part of broader European legal traditions. Commentators, litigants and the courts will thus on occasion also cite restatements of common European contract law principles such as the *Principles, Definitions and Model Rules of European Private Law*, the 'DCFR', when considering Finnish general principles of contract law.[9]

1.2. Intellectual Property as the Object of a Contract

When discussing the law of trademark licensing, it is important to bear in mind the distinction between, one the one hand, the trademark as an *object of property* (and the owner's rights attached to the property) and, on the other hand, *agreements* in respect of that object of property. The rules each are subject to should not be conflated.

1.2.1. Breach of Agreement and Infringement

First, it should be noted that trademark infringement is distinct from breach of contract in respect of, e.g., a licence agreement. Thus, if a licensee oversteps the rules of the licence agreement, this will generally amount to breach of contract. It may *also*, however, amount to trademark infringement. These two kinds of wrongs are subject to distinct rules.

These issues will be discussed in greater detail below in sections 6.1 and 6.2.

1.2.2. Law Applicable to Agreement Versus Trademark as Property

Second, it should be noted that even if a Finnish trademark, as an object of property, is governed by Finnish law,[10] this does not necessarily mean that *agreements* in respect of that property also must be governed by Finnish law. Conversely, there is nothing in Finnish law that would prevent parties from using an agreement governed by Finnish law to dispose of a trademark that, as an object of property, is governed by the laws of another country. Indeed, this is common.

The fact that a non-Finnish trademark is the object of an agreement under Finnish law does not, for instance, mean that the Finnish Trademarks Act's remedies for infringement would become applicable to the non-Finnish trademark. Instead, the law of the place where the trademark exists and is enforced (the *lex loci protectionis*) would apply to questions of whether the trademark has been infringed and what the aggrieved party's remedies against such infringement are.

Nevertheless, e.g., Swedish works such as Arnerstål, *Varumärket som kontraktsföremål* (2014) or Runesson, *Licens till patent och företagshemligheter i avtals- och kontraktsrätten* (2014) would likely be relevant when considering the Finnish law of licensing as well.

9. See, e.g., the Market Court MAO:659/18, *Haahtela-kehitys v. Rapala*, and the Supreme Court in KKO 2015:26 and KKO 2018:37, *Suomen Kerta v. Meira*, for examples of judicial citations to the DCFR.

10. For brevity, the present outline omits the specific case of European Union trademarks. Pursuant to Article 19 of Regulation (EU) 2017/1001 on the European Union trademark, these will, as objects of property, generally be governed by the law of the proprietor's residence.

These issues may also have practical relevance. While Finnish law, for instance, will not require that trademark licences are executed in writing, enforcement of that licence in other countries (in respect of intellectual property registered in that country) will in many cases in practice require a written agreement.

1.2.3. *Registered Versus Non-registered Trademark Rights*

It should also be noted that the Finnish Trademarks Act provides for the existence of both registered and non-registered trademarks. Under section 4 of the Trademarks Act, a non-registered trademark is established where it 'in its target group, is commonly known as a sign for the rightholder's products or services'. Both registered and non-registered trademarks are capable of being transferred and licensed, subject to essentially the same rules.

Additionally, however, the Finnish Unfair Competition Act (1061/1978) also, to simplify, provides for causes of action in respect of, e.g., passing off or freeriding on goodwill. Such causes of action are distinct from trademark rights and generally understood to be more tied to accrued goodwill value and not be objects of property in the same sense as trademarks. Nevertheless, a trademark licence agreement may in many cases need to address these rights also.

2. SCOPE AND FORMATION OF LICENCE AGREEMENTS

In Finland, licences are generally contractual in nature. Finnish intellectual property law does not, e.g., recognise bare licences or deed licences as distinct legal categories. Rather, questions such as whether a valid licence has been established will generally be covered by the same contract law analysis.

The same rules will generally also apply for licences to both registered and non-registered trademarks (but see, e.g., section 2.3 regarding recordal).

2.1. Freedom of Licence and Contract

The Trademarks Act, in section 42.1, provides generally that trademark proprietors and applicants may licence their marks. This is taken to mean that they may grant a licence which is exclusive (i.e., to the exclusion of all other use) or parallel (meaning that others may also have rights in use of the mark). The licence may also, e.g., be territorially limited or have as its object only some of the goods or services for which the mark is registered.[11]

This list is not, however, an exhaustive *numerus clausus* of permitted licence types, but rather a set of examples. Subject to other mandatory rules, e.g., of competition law, the parties to a licence agreement will in most cases have the freedom to craft whatever licence and limitations they deem appropriate for their venture.[12]

11. HE 201/2018, p. 141.
12. While recognising that some limitations may be of a purely contractual nature, i.e., subject only to the remedies for breach of contract, others may also allow for infringement-based remedies. See sections 6.1 and 6.2 for details.

In international licensing practice, a distinction is often also drawn between exclusive and sole licences. The former is taken to exclude further exploitation by the rightholder itself, while the latter would allow the rightholder to also continue to use the right (but not grant parallel licences). These categories are not well established in Finnish law, even if often referred to in practice. Given that Finnish law also emphasises party intent in interpreting contracts (see discussion below), parties are advised to specifically define the intended effect if they wish to use these terms in contracts.

Thus - subject to the limitations discussed below - the details of trademark licences will to a great extent be subject to the freedom of contract. Parties will, in other words, largely be free to craft their own licence terms as they see fit. Parties will also usually not be compelled to 'force' their arrangements into specific predefined statutory categories to give them effect.

Finnish law also does not provide for any language requirements for business-to-business contracts. Parties are thus generally free to conclude the agreement in whatever language they feel best, provided that all parties understand what they are committing to. English-language contracts are in practice extremely common.

2.2. Formation of Agreement

The Trademarks Act does not regulate the formation of licence agreements. This issue is thus subject to general principles of Finnish contract law. These principles in turn provide for a large degree of freedom in how contracts are formed.

2.2.1. Offer–Acceptance Template Not Mandatory

The Finnish Contracts Act (228/1929) provides a basic offer–acceptance template for contract formation, as indeed the contract laws of most countries do.

Thus, one party may, e.g., proffer a draft agreement that the other party may accept or reject. A modified acceptance is deemed a rejection of the original offer and the making of a new counter-offer, that the original offeror may then in turn accept or reject. Once a party accepts the other party's offer, a valid contract is formed.

This offer–acceptance mode of contract formation is not mandatory or even typical, however.[13] In most cases, contract negotiations will take place by exchanging non-binding agreement drafts on the specific understanding that a binding agreement will be formed only upon signature by the duly authorised representatives of both parties (and/or subject to some other agreed-upon requirement).

13. For ways of concluding an agreement, see, e.g., Bärlund et al., *Finlands civil- och handelsrätt* (2013), section 5.2.2, p. 266 *et seq.*

2.2.2. *Agreement on Price May Not Be Necessary*

Interestingly, agreement on price may not be part of the essential requirements (sometimes referred to as the *essentialia negotii*) for a valid licence agreement to be formed.[14] In this, Finland may depart from many other countries.

Thus, the parties may in principle establish a trademark licence but leave the royalty rate, or other price terms, undecided or open. The price being undefined does not prevent a valid licence from having come into effect. Arguably, however, given the crucial nature of agreement on price in real-life commercial transactions, the burden of proof should be high for a court to find that a valid licence has been established without any term as to price.

Where a valid licence has been established without agreement on price, the courts will imply into the agreement an obligation to pay 'reasonable remuneration'.[15] Given that payment of reasonable compensation (often in the form of a fictitious licence rate) in many cases would be part of an infringement damage analysis,[16] the courts would likely apply a similar analysis in this context also.

2.2.3. *No Requirement as to Written Form*

Finnish law also does not provide for any general requirement as to written form, signatures or other 'proof' of the contract.[17] A licence may thus in principle also be oral, implied and/or established by the conduct of the parties. In practice, written form is virtually always to be preferred.

Nevertheless, a rightsholder forbearing from action against a potential licensee, e.g., in the context of negotiations that have dragged out until after use has started, could thus in some contexts also be deemed to have established a valid licence by 'implied acceptance'.[18]

Parties should thus be mindful of the risk of inadvertently establishing a licence during, e.g., prolonged contract negotiations. Parties may also wish to consider entering into a pre-agreement agreeing on the modalities for a final agreement to be formed or at least include specific language in all draft agreements as to execution modalities and their effect on contract formation.

Memorialising the licence agreement into a written contract is of course also strongly advised for documentation and evidentiary purposes. If parties to litigation do not raise any challenges, courts will most often take the written contract as evidence of the parties' agreement, e.g., without additional oral testimony to this effect. Even if the agreement is written, parties to litigation are not, however, prevented from introducing oral testimony concerning the parties' intent, e.g., behind a specific term, or even from claiming that the parties' actual agreement included a term not memorialised into the

14. See, e.g., Wilhelmsson et al., *Huvudpunkter i köplagen* (2006), section 5.2.1, p. 138.
15. See, e.g., the Finnish Market Court in MAO:513/19, *Teosto v. MTV*, paragraphs 95-96 (albeit in the context of a copyright licence).
16. For details, see section 6.2.3 below.
17. Compare, e.g., French-style rules on *prevue des obligations* or statute of frauds requirements of written form for all transactions exceeding a specific monetary value.
18. See, e.g., the Finnish Market Court in MAO:513/19, *Teosto v. MTV*, paragraph 93.

contract. In this sense, Finnish law does not provide for a 'parol evidence' or 'four corners' rule as found in, e.g., some other jurisdictions.[19] In practice, however, parties will in many cases want to introduce an 'entire agreement' clause to exclude oral or other side agreements concerning the subject matter of the written agreement.

On the more practical level, parties are also advised to consider that the licence agreement may end up being relevant in other jurisdictions where written form is more strongly preferred. This could be the case if, e.g., a Finnish law-governed contract also concerned non-Finnish trademarks. In this context, a need will often arise for a certified true copy of the agreement. Such certification will often need to be sought from a Finnish notary public.[20] For this, the notary will require a written agreement that clearly and unambiguously identifies all annexes and exhibits that form part of the agreement. On occasion, side letters and similar arrangements, not expressly referred to in the agreement text itself, may present challenges when certification is sought before a notary public.

2.3. Recordal and Perfection of Licence

The Trademarks Act, in section 43, provides that parties may seek to record a trademark licence in the Finnish register of trademarks. Recordal is not required for the underlying licence to be effective, however.[21] Rather, a valid licence is established as explained above.

Pursuant to section 43.2 of the Trademarks Act, however, a trademark licence that has not been recorded will not be binding on third parties or the rightholder's good faith creditors. If, for instance, a licensor grants putatively exclusive licences to A and thereafter B, B will also have obtained a valid licence, on condition that B had a good faith belief that no prior exclusive licence existed, and that A had failed to record A's licence. Similarly, a validly recorded trademark licence agreement will be binding upon, e.g., pledgees receiving the mark as a security interest for the licensor's debts. Recordal of the licence will also have benefits in the event of the rightholder's bankruptcy (see section 8 below).

A licence may be recorded against pending trademark applications and registered trademarks, but not against non-registered trademarks.[22] If a licence is recorded against an application for a trademark, the recordal will upon registration also cover the granted mark.

The applicant (for a trademark application), the rightholder (for a granted registration) and the licensee may all apply for recordal of the licence. They may do so by right without agreeing to this in the licence agreement or otherwise. Given, however, that the trademark register in some instances may require proof of the

19. See generally, e.g., Sund-Norrgård, *Lisenssisopimuksen tulkinta*, Oikeustiede 45 (2012), p. 284–333, p. 293 regarding comparisons to the four corners rule.
20. See the Public Notaries Act (420/2014). Note that Finland does not have a Continental civil notary profession. Notaries are public officials with a much more limited role than in, e.g., Continental jurisdictions.
21. HE 201/2018, p. 141.
22. HE 201/2018, p. 142.

agreement, parties would generally be advised to agree on an obligation to reasonably assist in recording the licence agreement (also to avoid a party, e.g., ending up compelled to make unnecessarily broad disclosures of agreement materials to prove, e.g., the scope of the licence).

For recordal to be granted, the licensor must be the registered rightholder for the mark at issue. In, e.g., various grant-back arrangements, the transfer of title must therefore be recorded first, before the trademark registry will accept recordal of a licence granted by the new rightholder.[23]

3. INTERPRETATION OF LICENCE AGREEMENTS

After a valid licence agreement has taken effect, the need often arises for the *interpretation* of the terms thereof. Most licence agreements will be subject to the normal maxims of interpretation of Finnish contract law. For reasons of brevity, these will not here be explained in full.[24]

3.1. Common Subjective Intent as a Starting Point

In Finnish law, the analytical starting point for contract interpretation is often understood to be the *parties' common intent*. Thus, the process of interpreting an agreement is often analytically understood as an exercise in discovering the parties' common intention underlying the agreement or a term thereof. The exercise in principle does not seek to discover, e.g., what a reasonable person objectively speaking would understand the agreement to mean. Rather the key issue is what the parties' subjective intent was. In this, Finnish law may deviate from certain other jurisdictions with more objective interpretative traditions.

If the parties' common intent can be proven, the courts will thus generally give this effect, even where this might depart from the ordinary meaning of the words used in the contract. If, to use a contrived example, the parties genuinely thought they were in the process of licensing a trademark but, for lack of experience, mistakenly referred to the object of the licence as a *patent*, the courts generally would enforce the agreement in respect of the trademark – if the parties' genuine common intent to this effect could be established.

When negotiating contracts, parties should thus bear in mind that negotiating materials, emails and the like will frequently be referred to in litigation over unclear contract terms. Oral testimony of the conduct of the negotiations and the parties' (alleged) intentions is also comparatively common, even where the agreement is in written form.

23. HE 201/2018, p. 143.
24. But see generally, e.g., Bärlund et al., *Finlands civil- och handelsrätt* (2013), section 5.3.2.1, p. 292 *et seq*. For the specific issue of interpreting licence agreements, see also, e.g., Sund-Norrgård, *Lisenssisopimuksen tulkinta*, Oikeustiede 45 (2012), p. 284–333 and Sund-Norrgård, *Lojalitet i licensavtal* (2011), section 5.3, p. 123 *et seq*., advocating a modern interpretative approach. The below is largely a summary of the traditional approach as explained in these.

3.2. Other Maxims of Interpretation

As a more practical matter, however, interpretation of an agreement will of course generally start with the words of the agreement text itself, either in plain language meaning or in the specific usages and customs of the industry at hand. The party claiming that the common intention in fact was something else than the wording would suggest would have the burden of proof for this.[25] Thus, the wording of the agreement will be decisive in most instances.

Additionally, the courts will generally try to look at the agreement as a whole and give each term an interpretation that is harmonious with that whole and which best gives effects to the overall intention of the agreement. Courts may, e.g., wish to give a narrow interpretation to terms that somehow run counter to this main purpose.

Parties often also argue that unclear terms should be interpreted against the parties that proffered them (*in dubio contra proferentem* or *contra stipulatorem*). In practice, however, the scope of this rule, especially in individually negotiated licence agreements between businesses, has not become as wide as perhaps in some other countries.[26]

Finally, there has historically existed, at least as regards copyrights, a principle according to which licence terms should be interpreted in favour of the licensor (e.g., in favour of a narrower grant of licence).[27] In recent case law, the scope of this principle has arguably narrowed even in copyright law, however, to apply mostly to situations where a significant power balance exists in favour of the licensee. As such the principle would mostly serve to protect licensors who are clearly the weaker party in negotiations for, e.g., licensing a creative work to a large company.[28]

It is thus unclear if much scope remains for a generally pro-licensor maxim of interpretation, at least in the context of business-to-business trademark agreements.

4. SUBSTANTIVE AND IMPLIED CONTRACTUAL REQUIREMENTS

The question of what – if any[29] – substantive requirements and standards of conduct are implied by law into a licence agreement is highly unclear in Finnish law. There is very little to no public case law addressing the various situations that might arise and how they should be dealt in the event the parties have not specifically addressed the issue in their agreement. While some analogies as to, e.g., the licensor's responsibility

25. Saarilehto et al., *Varallisuusoikeus* (2012), section III.5, p. 440
26. See Sund-Norrgård, *Lisenssisopimuksen tulkinta*, Oikeustiede 45 (2012), p. 284–333, p. 299. See also Bärlund et al., *Finlands civil- och handelsrätt* (2013), section 5.3.2.1, p. 294.
27. See Sund-Norrgård, *Lisenssisopimuksen tulkinta*, Oikeustiede 45 (2012), p. 284–333, p. 299 for a summary of various positions advanced on the question.
28. The Finnish Market Court in MAO:59/17, *A and B v. Lumon Oy*, paragraph 24, noting that the principle of narrow interpretation has been based on the power imbalance between licensor and licensee. But see MAO:540/19, *Fiskars Finland Oy Ab v. Kuovi Oy*, applying the doctrine.
29. See generally Sund-Norrgård, *Lojalitet i licensavtal* (2011), discussing the possibility of a caveat emptor (buyer beware) approach and rejecting this at, e.g., pp. 19, 125 and passim.

for the licensed trademark could be drawn from the Sale of Goods Act, given the very different subject matters, it is unclear how far such analogies really would carry.[30]

The possible interpretations referred to below are thus speculative at best. It is also not possible in this context to review all possible requirements that could be implied into the agreement and/or could be beneficial to agree on expressly. Parties should ensure that their licence agreement is reasonably comprehensive in terms of the parties' obligations and responsibilities and avoid leaving central issues subject to highly uncertain legally implied terms.[31]

4.1. General Duties of Good Faith and Cooperation

Finnish law imposes a general duty of good faith and loyal cooperation on parties. The longer-term or more profound the parties' cooperation is, the more extensive the courts will generally consider this obligation.[32] The scope of the obligation will in many instances be vague and will often require case-by-case consideration.[33] Nevertheless, it has been argued that the scope of these general obligations has expanded in recent years.[34]

The parties are often understood to be, e.g., under an obligation to warn each other if they become aware of factors that would materially impede the performance of the agreement or materially endanger the key goals envisioned by the parties.[35] Similarly, the parties may also be under an obligation to provide reasonable assistance to each other to ensure the performance of the contract.[36] Arguably the parties could also be under a duty to notify each other if they become aware of a third party infringing on the licensed trademark (see section 7 below). As noted, these obligations will typically be understood as more wide-ranging in the case of longer-term cooperation agreements or where the cooperation is otherwise more profound.

Parties could also be under an obligation to confirm the existence of the licence agreement to a third party, where this is necessary for using the licensed trademark and, e.g., to provide reasonable quality digital files enabling the use of a licensed figurative mark. To a very great degree, this will, however, depend on the other specifics of the licensing arrangement at hand.

30. See also Sund-Norrgård, *Lisenssisopimuksen tulkinta*, Oikeustiede 45 (2012), p. 284–333, p. 298 for a brief and sceptical discussion on the usefulness of the Sale of Goods Act in interpreting licence agreements.
31. But see also, e.g., Sund-Norrgård, *Lojalitet i licensavtal*, JFT 3/2011 sections 311–315 warning against the danger of 'overregulating' and supporting more open and relational contracting in licence agreements.
32. Sund-Norrgård *Lisenssisopimuksen tulkinta*, Oikeustiede 45 (2012), p. 284–333, p. 291.
33. There is also a degree of disagreement of the extent to which such principles will impose independent obligations, above and beyond, e.g., the express terms of the agreement. See, e.g., Klami-Wetterstein, *Från förhandlingsfrihet till förhandlingsbundenhet* (2016), p. 120 et seq. (and p. 77 for an example of criticism of case law failing to give the principle independent effect).
34. Bärlund et al., *Finlands civil- och handelsrätt* (2013), section 5.3.4, p. 302.
35. See, e.g., Bärlund et al., *Finlands civil- och handelsrätt* (2013), section 5.3.4, p. 302. Compare also, e.g., DCFR IV. C. - 2:102: Pre-contractual duties to warn (in respect of service contracts).
36. See also the Sale of Goods Act, section 15, on the duty to contribute to the performance of the contract. Compare also, e.g., DCFR III. - 1:103: Good faith and fair dealing and DCFR III. - 1:104: Co-operation as general principles of contract law.

Given the vague nature of these general obligations, however, parties should where feasible expressly agree on, e.g., such assistance and informational obligations as may be appropriate for the arrangement. On the other hand, however, some modern legal commentators instead would prefer there to be more room for general duties of loyal cooperation.[37] To such ends, the parties may of course also elect to agree on an express term requiring good faith cooperation but specifying it in greater detail to best match their purposes.

4.2. Validity and Scope of the Licensed Mark

Parties may also wish to agree on what the licensor's liability for the validity and existence of the licensed trademarks is.

Absent such specific agreement, this responsibility is uncertain. At least where a licensed registered trademark specifically is identified in the agreement, it seems likely that the courts would understand this to imply a warranty that the identified mark was valid at least at the time the licence agreement was concluded. If the agreement identified the specific goods and services for which the mark was registered, it also seems possible that a court would conclude the same in respect of these specifically identified elements of protection. It also seems likely that courts would conclude that the licensor also was under an implied obligation to pay all necessary renewal fees to keep the mark in effect.

The situation can quickly become ambiguous, however, e.g., where the licence is for an unidentified set of marks (such as a licence for all marks protective of a specific brand, without further specification). If no specific registration or scope of protection is identified at any point, it may also be hard for the licensee to argue that it entered into the agreement in reliance of the existence of a specific element of protection if that element was never conclusively identified between the parties.

The situation is also more unclear in terms of the licensed marks later being invalidated. It is not clear, e.g., what the licensor's liability is if the licensed mark later is invalidated for, e.g., in fact infringing on a third-party right. The analysis may also depend on whether the licensor knew of this risk or not when concluding the licence agreement.

The parties may thus wish to consider incorporating express terms concerning these issues into their agreement.

4.3. Infringement of Third-Party Rights

Parties should also agree on what the licensor's liability would be if use of the licensed trademark turned out to infringe third-party rights. In other words, the parties should likely agree on appropriate indemnities and indemnification procedures for the event that the licensee had to pay damages to a third party for use of the licensed trademark.

From the perspective of Finnish infringement rules, the licensee cannot escape infringement liability towards a third party merely due to having used the trademark in

37. See generally, e.g., Sund-Norrgård, *Lojalitet i licensavtal* (2011), passim.

reliance of the licence agreement. While the degree of negligence or intent under Finnish law to some extent may affect the assessment of damages, it is nevertheless clear that infringement as such is subject to strict liability.[38]

The question therefore becomes to what extent the licensee has recourse under the licensee agreement or otherwise to require the licensor to offset these damages to third parties and its other related costs. This question is very uncertain in Finnish law. It is relevant to note that that commentators have expressed a degree of uncertainty even on the principles to be applied to the traditional sale movables under the Sale of Goods Act,[39] so even this source for analogies is somewhat unclear on the issue of third-party infringements.

Arguably, Finnish courts may consider the nature of the overall arrangement. If the trademark licence was, e.g., part of a broader 'turnkey' business model licence (franchise), one may speculate that the Finnish courts could be more likely to consider the licensor liable for these costs than in 'bare' arrangements where the licensor's responsibilities are very limited overall.

Ultimately, however, the question remains highly uncertain if left to underlying legal rules only. Parties should therefore consider agreeing on procedures to be observed in the event of such claims, on the control of the defence, and on the ultimate apportionment of liabilities.

Such terms would often take the form of an 'indemnity clause'. The terminology of such clauses ('Licensor shall indemnify and hold harmless…') is in many cases patterned on common law usages that may not fully fit in the overall system of Finnish contractual liabilities. Absent qualifications, a Finnish court may consider an indemnity clause an 'express warranty' and undertaking of strict liability in respect of the subject matter of the indemnity clause.[40] In market practice, it is also not unusual for liability under such indemnities to be carved out from general liability caps or subject to their own specific caps.

4.4. Maintaining Goodwill

Given that the goodwill of the licensed trademark typically will have value to both licensor and licensee, it is generally in both parties' long-term interest to ensure the preservation of that value. The parties will therefore likely wish to agree on the specifics of both parties' obligations in maintaining this value.

The nature of the specific licensing arrangement will often determine who will be responsible for what. An arrangement wherein the licensor itself will not use the mark during the term of the agreement will be materially different from arrangements wherein the licensor will have primary responsibility for, e.g., national marketing and coordinate a group of parallel licensees (as in the case of franchising). Often, however, the licensor will want to draw up a brand manual and quality standards and generally

38. See, e.g., section 69.2 of the Trademarks Act providing for liability irrespective of fault.
39. See, e.g., Wilhelmsson et al., *Huvudpunkter i köplagen* (2006), section 4.1.6, p. 103 *et seq.*
40. Whereas otherwise Finnish law often would exclude liability for factors beyond the control of the liable party. See also section 40.3 of the Sale of Goods Act, providing for stricter liability when there is a breach of an 'express warranty'.

require the licensee to refrain from any action that would be injurious to the brand. The licensee might wish to require a reasonable level of marketing efforts by the licensor.

Finnish law is largely silent on the rules that apply absent such specific agreements. Likely the parties' general duties of good faith cooperation (see section 7) at least require them to refrain from actions that cause material harm to the brand. The parties may also be required to conduct themselves in accordance with good business practices when conducting business under the brand.

The licensor may not, however, be able to unilaterally foist detailed brand guidelines or quality requirements on a licensee, without the licensee first agreeing to this in the licence agreement or otherwise. Perhaps, however, the licensee in some cases could be deemed to have tacitly accepted, e.g., marketing and brand guidelines, if it was aware of the expectation to comply with them prior to the conclusion of the agreement.

While the licensee's general duties of good faith cooperation in some cases could be understood to include an obligation to provide the licensor with reasonable information on the licensee's activities, or even limited site access, in order to allow for basic quality assurance, the parties will in most cases want to specifically agree on audit rights or the like to avoid any disagreements, as the scope of such rights would be unclear.

The question of the *licensor's* obligation to maintain the goodwill of the brand is also uncertain. The DCFR suggests that franchisors are under an obligation to 'make reasonable efforts to promote and maintain the reputation of the franchise network' and, e.g., 'design and co-ordinate the appropriate advertising campaigns aiming at the promotion of the franchise network'.[41]

No express rule to this effect exists in Finnish law. Potentially an obligation like this could be considered part of a franchisor's general duties of good faith cooperation, but even this would be uncertain. Finnish courts may also look at the level of marketing efforts the franchisor is undertaking at the time the agreement is concluded and/or the materials provided to the franchisee and potentially prefer to imply into the agreement a requirement to maintain similar or proportional efforts going forward as well.

Many franchisors, however, require that franchisees pay a separate marketing fee.[42] In these cases, the franchise agreement may specify the scope of the franchisor's services provided in consideration of the fee. Even absent detailed marketing requirements, a Finnish court would be much more likely to imply a requirement of reasonable marketing efforts into the agreement where the franchisees specifically pay for such services.

It does not seem very likely, however, that Finnish courts would consider extensive marketing obligations to apply to trademark licences generally, however. Given the broad range of licensing arrangements and commercial terms surrounding them, parties should prefer to agree expressly on their expected contributions to maintaining the brand's goodwill.

41. DCFR IV. E. – 4:207: Reputation of network and advertising.
42. The Finnish Franchising Association maintains a public list of its members with some of their key franchise terms. See franchising.fi/jasenesittelyt.

See also section 5 on the use of selective distribution schemes as a tool for maintaining goodwill.

4.5. No Onward Transfer Absent Agreement

The Trademarks Act, in section 42.2, furthermore forbids the licensee from transferring the licence to a third party, except where the parties to the licence agreement have agreed on this. The rule also applies to sublicensing.[43] Thus, the parties need to agree on such a right to sublicense, without which this would not be possible.

While the rule is plain and intuitive, parties are still advised to pay the issue due regard. For instance, independent contractors performing such work for the licensee that would constitute infringement of the trademark absent a licence would need their own direct licence or sublicence. Under section 6.2 of the Trademarks Act acts such as importing or exporting products or stocking them for the purposes of placing them on the market are actions that also come within the scope of the exclusive right granted by the trademark.

Independent contractors performing such functions for the licensee could thus require a sublicence to do so. Some contractors may, however, instead be deemed to work on behalf of, and for the account of, the primary licensee. In this case, the actions of the contractor may be covered by the primary licence. This will likely be the case at least in, e.g., respect of staffing agency employees, even if they strictly speaking are not employed by the licensee.

Licensees should thus review their supplier and independent contractor chains to identify participants that need licence coverage. Given that the Finnish Trademarks Act takes a negative view of implied sublicensing rights, licensees should ensure all appropriate scenarios are appropriately considered and, where necessary, addressed in the agreement.

5. LIMITATIONS ON SUBSTANTIVE TERMS OF LICENCE AGREEMENT

As noted above, trademark licensing is generally subject to extensive freedom of contract in Finland. Even where requirements may be implied into the contract by law, the parties are generally free to vary them at will. There are, however, rules that limit this freedom significantly.

Many key limitations are found in competition law. Most of the central competition law principles are found in European Union law and mirrored in Finnish law. A full review of these rules is beyond the scope of the present presentation, but a few key points are noted below.

In addition to limitations in respect of the substance of the agreement itself, competition law will also limit the parties' conduct prior to the agreement being

43. The wording of the 2019 Act is potentially somewhat ambiguous as to what constitutes a transfer' of the licence, but the Government's explanatory memorandum clarifies that sublicensing also is caught by the prohibition. See HE 201/201, p. 141.

concluded, e.g., during negotiations. Competition law may, e.g., limit information sharing between companies.

5.1. Arrangements That Restrict Competition Between Undertakings

Article 101 of the Treaty on the Functioning of the European Union (TFEU) prohibits arrangements between companies that have as their 'object or effect the prevention, restriction or distortion of competition'. Even where an arrangement might be caught by Article 101(1), however, an exception is provided for in Article 101(3).[44] Under this latter provision, the arrangement might still be permitted if it, subject to certain conditions, 'contributes to improving the production or distribution of goods or to promoting technical or economic progress'. Many licence agreements will thus either not be caught by the prohibition in Article 101(1) or in any event benefit from the exemption provided for in Article 101(3).

The European Commission has issued several so-called Block Exemption Regulations. An arrangement that meets the criteria of a block exemption is considered to benefit from an Article 101(3) safe harbour automatically, even if otherwise caught by the prohibition in Article 101(1). The Commission has also issued several guidelines interpreting these rules and relevant case law in certain contexts. Local Finnish rules are largely interpreted in line with these European Union principles and guidelines.

In respect of trademark licence agreements, the EU Technology Transfer Block Exemption Regulation (TTBER) and the Vertical Block Exemption Regulation (VBER), and the guidelines that interpret these, will likely in practice be the most important. They do not cover pure trademark licences,[45] but are often also referred to when considering licence agreements more broadly.[46]

5.1.1. *Selective Distribution Schemes*

One context in which trademark licensing typically has an important role, and which *is* specifically addressed by the VBER and related guidelines, is *selective distribution schemes*. In these, a brand owner will seek to restrict the sales channels of its products to ensure they are sold only in outlets and channels deemed appropriate to the brand. Such schemes are generally used in connection to products with a perceived high brand value, e.g., luxury goods, and to retain that value.

44. These are largely mirrored by sections 5-6 of the Finnish Competition Act (948/2011).
45. The TTBER applies to transfers of 'technology rights', understood as patents, software copyrights and the like. The TTBER is thus not directly applicable to trademark licence agreements. The VBER in turn applies to 'vertical agreements' between undertakings operating 'at different level[s] of the production or distribution chain, and [which relate to] to the conditions under which the parties may purchase, sell or resell certain goods or services'. The VBER applies to licensing of intellectual property in such vertical arrangements, but only if the IP-related provisions 'do not constitute the primary object of [the] agreements and are directly related to the use, sale or resale of goods or services by the buyer or its customers'.
46. The fact that a specific arrangement does not benefit from a block exemption does not in itself mean that it is prohibited. Rather, a case-by-case analysis must be undertaken. In that analysis, block exemptions may also be referred to, as expressing broader principles, even if not applicable by their subject matter.

Such arrangements may be permitted in connection to selective distribution schemes 'designed, primarily, to preserve the luxury image of those goods [provided that] that resellers are chosen on the basis of objective criteria of a qualitative nature that are laid down uniformly for all potential resellers and applied in a non-discriminatory fashion and that the criteria laid down do not go beyond what is necessary'.[47]

In connection to such schemes, brand owners have also been considered to be permitted to use contract terms that prohibit distributors from selling the products on separately branded internet websites on 'condition that that [the term restricting third-party internet sales] has the objective of preserving the luxury image of those goods, that it is laid down uniformly and not applied in a discriminatory fashion, and that it is proportionate in the light of the objective pursued'.[48]

There are, however, several detailed concerns and issues to consider in assessing selective distributorship schemes. Parties entering into such arrangements should consider the overall competition law implications of their agreement carefully.

5.1.2. Other Potentially Problematic Terms

Both the TTBER and the VBER contain lists of so-called hardcore restrictions. The EU Commission considers that these hardcore restrictions are restrictive by their very object and are thus unlikely to fulfil the conditions for exemption of Article 101(3).[49] They should thus be avoided in most licensing arrangements. Both regulations also contain separate lists of 'excluded restrictions'. While these are viewed somewhat more favourably than hardcore restrictions, they also present risks of incompatibility with competition law.[50]

Without here conducting a full review of such terms (these will also be the same in most EU countries), one can generally note that, e.g., the following terms will often be problematic or prohibited:

- Terms restricting the licensee's ability to determine its prices when selling products to third parties.
- Terms restricting passive sales into other jurisdictions than the primarily licensed jurisdiction.
- Terms restricting the licensee's right to challenge the licensed trademark in court.[51]

47. *Coty Germany GmbH v. Parfümerie Akzente GmbH,* case C-230/16, paragraph 36.
48. *Coty Germany GmbH v. Parfümerie Akzente GmbH,* case C-230/16, paragraph 36.
49. See, e.g., Guidelines on the application of Article 101 of the Treaty on the Functioning of the European Union to technology transfer agreements, paragraph 43: 'It is only where agreements contain hardcore restrictions of competition, that it can normally be presumed that they are prohibited by Article 101.'
50. See, e.g., Guidelines on the application of Article 101 of the Treaty on the Functioning of the European Union to technology transfer agreements, paragraph 128: 'It is only the individual restriction in question that is not covered by the block exemption, implying that individual assessment is required.'
51. See, however, Sund-Norrgård, *Lojalitet i licensavtal* (2011), section 7.3.5, p. 272, adopting a somewhat positive view of no-challenge clauses, subject to limitations.

- Terms restricting the licensee's right to conclude licensing agreements with other licensors, e.g. exclusivity clauses or non-compete undertakings.[52]

As noted, Finnish law mirrors EU law to a great extent with little local deviations. In any event, however, parties are generally advised to consider the competition law aspects of their licensing arrangement with some care.

5.2. Abuse of Dominance

Article 102 TFEU and section 7 of the Finnish Competition Act also prohibit abuse of dominant market position. Such abuse can include using market power to, e.g., impose unfair contract terms, limiting production or product development, discriminatory practices, and the like.

In the field of intellectual property, the doctrine on abuse of dominance has been applied to, e.g., the conduct of copyright organisations, the licensing of standard essential patents and some instances of refusal to license. Pure trademark licences have to date not been the focus of Article 102 enforcement.

Nevertheless, a dominant standards organisation discriminatorily refusing to license, e.g., a certification mark that is a practical requirement for market entry could conceivably be the subject of scrutiny under Article 102. There are also other contexts where similar concerns could become relevant.

Whenever a dominant company is party to a trademark licence agreement, the parties should take care to ensure that all relevant competition law obligations are complied with. A full review of these requirements is beyond the scope of the present presentation, however.

6. BREACH OF LICENCE AGREEMENT

A party that acts in a manner contrary to the licence agreement is in breach of the agreement. Generally, this will be in respect of express obligations of the agreement text, but as discussed above, certain requirements might also be implied into the licensing relationship by law, even without an express contract term to that effect.

6.1. Remedies for Breach of Agreement

The remedies applicable to breach of a licence agreement will generally be those of general Finnish contract law principles. The parties are typically free to vary these in their agreement, however. These remedies include specific performance, price reduction, damages, and termination for cause.

52. See, however, Sund-Norrgård, *Lojalitet i licensavtal* (2011), section 6.3.7.1, p. 157 *et seq.*, adopting a somewhat positive view of non-competition undertakings, subject to limitations.

6.1.1. *Specific Performance and Cure of Breach*

Unlike some other jurisdictions, Finnish law provides for a general right to obtain specific performance. In other words, the aggrieved party may generally seek a court order compelling performance.[53] The aggrieved party may also, subject to certain limitations, require that the breaching party cure defects in its performance.

In licence agreements, the practical relevance of these remedies is somewhat limited. In most cases, the licence will be established directly by virtue of the agreement and thus not require any specific performance order. The parties would in any event often also be uninterested in continuing the relationship if a party actively refuses to comply with the agreement.

This being said, non-payment of royalty fees will often require obtaining a money judgment, ordering payment, before a competent court. In the event of a dispute as to the expiry of the licence, the licensor may also need to obtain a court order prohibiting further use of the mark.

6.1.2. *Price Reduction*

In some cases, the licensee may also have the right to require a reduction in the price, e.g., the royalty rate.[54] While it is not fully settled law that price reduction is available in all contract types as a general principle of contract law (i.e., absent agreement to that effect), there has been increasing recognition in Finland that price reduction likely will be generally available in connection to most contracts.[55] The parties would generally, however, have the right to agree to exclude price reduction as a relevant remedy.

In brief, the remedy of price reduction allows an aggrieved party to claim a reduction in price that is proportional to any reduction in value due to a defect in the other party's performance. Unlike damages, price reduction does not require any fault (e.g., negligence) attributable to the other party. It is sufficient that there has been a defect in the party's performance, which has caused the benefit conferred to have lesser value that it would have had if all contractual requirements were met. For trivial non-conformities price reduction may not be available, however.

The remedy is not very commonly sought in licensing disputes, but arguably could be relevant, e.g., where the object of the licence is partly invalidated. Thus, the aggrieved party could argue that loss of exclusive rights for some goods or services constitutes a reduction in the value of the licence that should be offset by a corresponding reduction in the royalty rate. In these contexts, price reduction may present certain advantages as a distinct remedy given that it applies irrespective of any fault on the part of the licensor.

53. Save for a few exceptions, such as where the performance is personal in nature.
54. For international comparisons, it may be helpful to note that the modern remedy is an evolution of the *actio quanti minoris* of Roman law. Compare, e.g., Kaser et al., *Romersk privaträtt* § 41.39 *et seq*.
55. See, e.g., Bärlund et al., *Finlands civil- och handelsrätt* (2013), section 5.4.3, p. 304, presenting price reduction as a general principle of contract law and Sisula-Tulokas, *Felpåföljden prisavdrag* (1990) for a historical discussion of the remedy in Finnish law. See also DCFR III. – 3:601: Right to reduce price.

6.1.3. *Damages*

The aggrieved party will also typically be entitled to damages. There is some disagreement among Finnish commentators on whether liability in damages requires that the party in breach conducted itself negligently (referred to as 'negligence liability') or if it is sufficient that the factor that gave rise to the loss was within the control of the party in breach (referred to as 'control liability').[56] The matter is not settled in respect of trademark licence agreements. Generally, however, the trend has been towards stricter forms of liability for damages.

The aggrieved party will generally be entitled to full damages for all its losses. The quantum of damages will in these cases typically be set to put the aggrieved party in the (fictional and counterfactual) position it would have been without the breach.[57] The specific quantum will thus of course depend on the nature and consequences of the breach.

Where evidence of the quantum cannot be obtained or obtaining evidence would be unreasonably burdensome in relation to, e.g., the value of the matter, Finnish courts may, pursuant to section 17:2.3 of the Code of Judicial Procedure, estimate the quantum.

In market practice, it is very common for parties to limit liability for indirect loss or injury. Where the scope of this limitation has not been defined in the agreement (by, e.g., contractually defining indirect loss), the Finnish courts will generally look to the Sale of Goods Act. According to section 67.2 of the Act, indirect loss includes:

- loss in consequence of reduction in production or turnover;
- loss in consequence of the object of the contract not being usable for its intended purpose (loss of 'use value');
- loss of profit in consequence of a loss or non-performance of an agreement with a third party;
- loss in consequence of injury to goods other than the product sold (generally not relevant to trademark licensing);
- other similar losses that are hard to predict.

While often advisable to include an express definition of indirect loss tailored to the case at hand, it is comparatively common in Finnish agreements to exclude liability for indirect loss with the understanding that the courts will look to section 67.2 of the Sale of Goods Act for the definition.[58] There are also several Supreme Court cases that may serve to clarify the definition in the Sale of Goods Act.[59]

56. Wilhelmsson et al., *Huvudpunkter i köplagen* (2006), section 1.5, p. 28.
57. But other methods of calculating damages also exist. See generally, Hemmo, *Vahingonkorvauksen määräytymisestä sopimussuhteissa* (1994).
58. Indeed, this was a stated purpose for introducing the statutory definition in the Sale of Goods Act. See Wilhelmsson et al., *Huvudpunkter i köplagen* (2006), section 3.2.5.2, p. 83.
59. See the Supreme Court in, e.g., KKO 2009:89, KKO 2012:101 and KKO 2014:61.

Similarly, parties may also agree to introduce specific monetary caps on liability. Note, however, that limitations of liability generally under Finnish law may not be relied on to reduce liability for wilful misconduct or gross negligence.[60]

In Finnish law, claims for, e.g., restitution by way of price reduction or return of the price (in the context of termination for cause) are often *not* understood as *damages*. This may be very significant if the parties have, e.g., limited *damages* liability by using such a cap on liability, often set as a percentage of payments made under the agreement. In these cases, a party may have a claim for damages up to the cap *and* a separate claim for return of some payments made under the agreement. Parties are generally advised to be explicit as to whether such liability caps are intended to cover only damages or also all other forms of monetary liability.

6.1.4. Termination for Cause

The aggrieved party will also have the right to terminate the licence agreement for cause[61] if the breach was fundamental or material in nature.[62] In many cases, parties will agree to vary this rule by, e.g., introducing a requirement that the party in breach be reserved a number of days to fix the breach.

Generally, Finnish law does not *require* that such an additional time for performance be fixed by the terminating party,[63] unless so has been agreed. If, however, the aggrieved party voluntarily sets an additional *reasonable* time for correct performance, further failure will often be taken as a factor supporting the existence of a right to terminate for cause.[64]

If the agreement is terminated for cause, the parties may be ordered to return or make restitution for their respective performances (i.e., get their money back). Where returning a performance is not possible, a party may be required to make restitution of the value of the benefit received.[65] Where conforming performance by one party has been met by conforming performance by the other, restitution may potentially also be waived.[66]

In this context a point of linguistic caution may also be relevant. In Finnish law, a terminological distinction is made between termination for cause (*purkaminen, hävning*) and termination for convenience (*irtisanominen, uppsägning*). The right and obligation to return performances only attaches to the former.

60. See generally, Sund-Norrgård, *Friskrivningsklausuler i köpeavtal*, JFT 2/2015 sections 115–141.
61. For international comparisons, it may be helpful to note that the modern remedy is an evolution of the *actio redhibitoria* of Roman law. Compare, e.g., Kaser et al., *Romersk privaträtt* § 41.39 *et seq*.
62. DCFR III. - 3:502 uses the term 'fundamental breach' in English. Most agreements will, however, use the English term 'material breach' in Finnish market practice. Typically, these two terms tend to be considered interchangeable, both referring to breaches that are '*olennainen*' in Finnish and '*väsentlig*' in Swedish.
63. Compare the Consumer Protection Act which, under the influence of EU law, in some instances requires that an additional period for performance be fixed prior to termination for cause.
64. Compare section 25.2 of the Sale of Goods Act.
65. Compare, e.g., DCFR III. - 3:510: Restitution of benefits received by performance.
66. Compare, e.g., DCFR III. - 3:511: When restitution not required. See also, e.g., Sund-Norrgård, *Lojalitet i licensavtal* (2011), section 7.3.5.1, p. 264.

As this distinction is not reflected in the English-language concept of 'termination', it is often advisable to clarify whether termination *for cause* or *convenience* is intended. Translation issues may also arise in connection to this terminological point. Agreements drafted in Finnish or Swedish (the official languages) might attach significant meaning to the parties' choice of terminology. Merely translating both terms as 'termination' without further qualifications risks losing key information in the translation. Where, e.g., an international agreement refers to 'terminating' an agreement, it may for Finnish purposes also be of importance to determine which form of termination is intended and use the proper term in translation.

6.2. Remedies Against Infringement

In some cases, conduct that constitutes breach of agreement can *also* constitute infringement of the licensed trademark. In such cases, the aggrieved licensor-claimant may potentially, in addition to the remedies for breach of agreement (see section 6.1 above), also use the remedies provided for trademark infringement.

These 'infringement remedies' include interim and final injunctive relief and damages. Significantly, they also include certain information disclosure obligations not available in breach of agreement actions and a system of assessing the quantum of damages that to some extent departs from the system in contractual liability.

6.2.1. Breach of Agreement Versus Infringement

Pursuant to section 42.3 of the Trademark Act, a breach of a term of the agreement may also constitute trademark infringement in respect of the following:

(1) The duration of the agreement.
(2) The registered form in which the mark may be used.
(3) The scope of the goods or services covered by the licence.
(4) The geographic scope of the licence.
(5) The quality of the goods or services provided by the licensee.

Where the breach of agreement concerns one of the above, the breach will also constitute infringement, allowing the licensor to alternatively used infringement-based remedies against the licensee. This provision is novel in Finnish law.

After the CJEU's holding in *IT Development*,[67] these remedies arguably also should be available in the same proceedings as in which the breach of agreement matter is heard. Given that Finland generally requires infringement claims to be heard

67. *IT Development SAS v. Free Mobile SAS*, case C-666/18, paragraph 49: 'the breach of a clause in a licence agreement for a computer program relating to the intellectual property rights of the owner of the copyright of that program falls within the concept of 'infringement of intellectual property rights', within the meaning of [the IP Enforcement] Directive 2004/48, and that, therefore, that owner must be able to benefit from the guarantees provided for by that directive, regardless of the liability regime applicable under national law'.

before the Market Court,[68] this may now mean that claimants may use both sets of remedies irrespective of their choice of venue.[69] There is no national case law on the issue, however.

It remains to be seen to what extent the express rule in section 42.3 of the Trademark Act, potentially in conjunction with the holding *IT Development*, will lead to litigants increasingly referring to 'mixed remedies' in licensing disputes.

6.2.2. Information Disclosure

The Finnish IP Evidence Act (344/2000) implements the EU IP Enforcement Directive (2004/48). The Act provides for certain evidentiary tools that are not available in standard breach of contract actions in Finland.

Finnish law generally does not provide for broad discovery-like rights to obtain information from counterparties in litigation. The IP evidence regime represents a partial expansion of the scope of information the claimant may require, while still being very limited in comparison to, e.g., US-style discovery.

Without here addressing the full gamut of tools under the 2000 Act, it may be noted that the Act, in section 7a, allows rightholder-claimants to ask the court to order defendants to disclose information such as names of companies participating in the production chain and the quantities and prices for such goods. In case law, the Act has been held to also allow for disclosure order in respect of related documentary evidence.[70]

The traditional view has been that such an order should be issued only after the infringement has been sufficiently established (i.e., before moving on to the damages phase of the case),[71] but in recent case law the Supreme Court has also approved pretrial disclosure orders.[72] While still far short of, e.g., US-style discovery proceedings, case law has at least to some extent moved in favour of broader disclosure obligations.

Given that the right to obtain information under section 7a is based on the Enforcement Directive and that the CJEU in *IT Development* considered the Directive applicable outside pure infringement proceedings, it is possible that courts now would allow for such disclosure orders even in contractual disputes concerning trademarks, provided the alleged breach of contract also constitutes trademark infringement.

6.2.3. Damages

Unlike general contract law damages, IP infringement damages are awarded using a two-tier system in Finland. Under section 69.1 of the Trademarks Act, the infringer may be required to pay full damages if the infringement was negligent or wilful. Under

68. See section 75 of the Trademark Act.
69. Conversely, the Market Court is also competent to hear contract claims when these are related to an infringement claim. See section 1:5 of the Proceedings in the Market Court Act (100/2013).
70. See, e.g., the Finnish Supreme Court in KKO 2019:10
71. HE 26/2006, p. 19.
72. The Finnish Supreme Court in KKO 2019:10

section 69.2 of the Trademarks Act, however, the infringer may in any event be ordered to pay 'reasonable compensation', even if the infringement was innocent (i.e., at a strict liability standard, without even negligence).

The quantum of 'reasonable compensation' pursuant to section 69.2 is generally assessed as a fictitious royalty rate, often set at some percentage of the infringer's turnover generated from the infringement.[73] No proof of actual loss or injury is required. Thus, unlike the general contractual damages scheme, the infringement remedy essentially provides for a system of 'baseline' damages irrespective of proof of quantum.

The quantum of 'full damages' pursuant to section 69.1 must be also be assessed in view of the Enforcement Directive's rules. This has been taken to mean that the infringer's profits, on a case-by-case basis, may be used as a proxy for assessing the loss sustained by the aggrieved party.[74] This provides for neither a true 'account of profits' remedy nor for a discharge of the claimant's obligation to prove its losses, but in some instances this principle may alleviate evidentiary problems (given also the general lack of, e.g., US-style discovery in Finnish law).

While historically the benefits of this IP evidence regime may not in themselves have been attractive enough to opt for infringement proceedings instead of breach of contract proceedings (with, e.g., forum implications), the above-mentioned possibility of potentially using these remedies *in* contracts disputes may increase the relevance of the IP evidence regime even in licensing contexts. There is nevertheless no case law on the issue as of the writing hereof.

7. INFRINGEMENT OF THE TRADEMARK BY A THIRD PARTY

During the term of the licence agreement, the parties may become aware of a third party infringing on the licensed trademark. The parties' general obligations of good faith cooperation (see 4.1) may in such instances require them to notify the other party of the infringement, but it will nevertheless often be advisable to agree more specifically on the issue.[75]

Under section 42.4 of the Trademarks Act, a licensee may initiate legal proceedings against a third-party infringer only with the consent of the rightholder or if the parties have agreed on such a right generally (e.g., in the licence agreement). If, however, the licence is exclusive, the licensee may take legal action unilaterally if it first has notified the rightholder and the latter has failed to take action within a reasonable time. When bringing legal action before the Market Court, the licensee must prove sufficient notice to the rightholder. Failing to provide proper proof of this within a deadline set by the court will lead to rejection of the action.[76] It is not, however, a requirement that the licensee has been recorded before taking action.[77]

73. HE 201/2019, p. 168.
74. The Finnish Market Court in MAO:32/17, *BBS GmbH v. vannetukku.fi Oy*, paragraph 37.
75. See, e.g., Sund-Norrgård, *Lojalitet i licensavtal* (2011), section 7.3.3.3, p. 246.
76. See section 19 of the Proceedings in the Market Court Act (100/2013). Many licensees may fail to notice this additional notice requirement in the relevant procedural statute.
77. HE 201/2018, p. 141.

Should the rightholder instead elect to take legal action itself, the licensee may, pursuant to section 42.4 of the Trademarks Act, join in that action in respect of its own losses. This right arises irrespective of whether the licence has been recorded in the trademark register or not.[78]

8. TRADEMARK LICENCES IN RIGHTHOLDER BANKRUPTCIES

The question of whether trademark licences remain effective in the event of the rightholder's bankruptcy is unclear at best.[79]

Given the possibility of recording the trademark licence (see section 2.3), it seems likely that at least duly recorded licences generally will remain effective against the bankruptcy estate and third parties to whom the estate sells the trademark. Even so, however, edge cases may potentially exist where the estate could force an executive sale of the trademark by auction in a manner that would cause the licence to lapse. Commentators have argued that licences should remain effective in these cases also, subject to certain conditions, but the question is not yet settled.

The question of the continued validity of non-recorded trademark licences is even more unclear. Arguments exist for both conclusions.

Given this highly unclear situation, parties are advised to record important licences to minimise risks in this regard.

9. EXPIRY OF THE LICENCE

Finnish law is also largely silent on the practical implications of trademark licences being terminated or expiring.[80] The parties are thus also advised to agree on such implications and the practicalities to be observed.

9.1. Termination for Convenience

As noted above, in section 6.1.4, Finnish law distinguishes between termination for cause (*purku, hävning*) and termination for convenience (*irtisanominen, uppsägning*). Termination for cause is a remedy that is available in the event of a fundamental or material breach of the agreement by the other party. Termination of convenience, in turn, is a general right to terminate agreements for almost any reason.[81]

In most cases, the parties will have agreed on their specific termination rights in the agreement. The parties would typically have agreed on, e.g., the notice period to be observed and on any limitations and procedures to be observed. In these cases, the specific termination terms will govern.

78. HE 201/2018, p. 142.
79. See generally, Tepora, *Fortsätter licensavtal att gälla vid en licensgivares konkurs?*, JFT 1–2/2014 sections 1-21. This is a brief summation thereof.
80. But see discussion in connection to 6.1.4 regarding the specific case of termination *for cause.*
81. The right to terminate for convenience might, as a matter of mandatory law, be precluded by, e.g., anti-discrimination legislation or competition law rules.

In Finnish law it is, however, also recognised that there in most non-fixed-term agreements will exist an implied right to terminate for convenience, absent specific agreement on termination for convenience. In these cases, the terminating party must observe a 'reasonable notice' period. There are no bright line rules for what the notice period should be.

For very long-running agreements, the notice period might even be years.[82] A very rough rule of thumb, however, is that for many common agreements the notice period should be, e.g., one month for each year the agreement has been effect, with a potential cut off point for a maximum notice period of six months.[83] Ultimately, however, the analysis will be fact-specific and depend on the length of the agreement, the depth of the cooperation, the importance of the agreement for the parties' businesses and so on.[84]

No implied termination right will exist, however, during any fixed term of agreement. Thus, if the parties have agreed that the agreement will be in effect for, e.g., a specific calendar year, there will be no implied right to termination during this time.

The traditionally prevailing view in Finnish law has been to imply a termination right into all, or at least most, agreements without a fixed end date.[85] In recent case law, the Supreme Court has suggested that perpetual contractual undertakings might, however, be possible.[86] Conversely, however, even an agreement that by its express wording purports to be 'perpetual' can be subject to termination for convenience, provided reasonable notice is given if there has been a material change in conditions since the agreement was concluded.[87]

The licence agreement will in any event in most cases end at either the date appointed in the agreement or after the expiry of an agreed, or otherwise 'reasonable', notice period in the event of a termination for convenience.

9.2. Requirement to Cease Use of the Marks

In practice, of course, expiry of the licence agreement will mean that the licensee no longer may 'use' the mark in ways that come within the exclusive right conferred by the mark, i.e., which - absent a valid licence - constitutes trademark infringement.

Under section 6 of the Trademark Act, such infringing acts include, e.g., use of the marks on products and services, offering such products for sale, using the mark for marketing purposes, in business documents and so on. Thus, all such use must cease when the expiry or termination of the agreement becomes effective.

Under section 6, 'stocking' products for the purposes of offering or putting them on the market also comes within the scope of the exclusive right conferred by the

82. The Finnish Supreme Court in KKO 2019:13 on the right to terminate the right to use a mill.
83. See, by way of analogy, section 23 of the Agents Act (417/1992).
84. See, e.g., the Finnish Supreme Court in KKO 2018:37 approving of a four-month notice period for an agreement that had lasted 'more than three and half years' (paragraph 19) but note also the case-specific analysis in terms of, e.g., inventory.
85. See generally, e.g., Norros, *Keskustelua ratkaisusta KKO 2019:13*, Lakimies 1/2020, sections 123–131.
86. The Finnish Supreme Court in KKO 2019:13, paragraph 19.
87. The Finnish Supreme Court in KKO 2019:13, paragraph 21.

trademark. Given, however, that this is limited to stocking 'with intent to distribute', it is possible that mere continued possession of products with the licensed trademark affixed in and of itself would not constitute trademark infringement even after expiry of the licence agreement. Absent agreement or a legal rule to the contrary, the licensee may not be able to sell this stock, however.[88]

During the notice period, the licensee generally may continue to sell off accumulated stock, however. The notice period should thus ideally be tailored to allow a reasonable chance to sell off accumulated stock. Where no specific notice period has been agreed on, the required reasonable notice period may also to some extent be considered against the issue of inventory turnover.[89]

The parties may also agree on various sell-off arrangements that allow, e.g., the selling of accumulated stock even after the expiry of the licence otherwise becomes effective. Absent such agreement, use of the marks should cease upon the expiration date.

9.3. Likely No Buyout Requirements

Parties will occasionally argue that, e.g., general duties of good faith cooperation (see section 4.1 above) will imply a more concrete obligation for the licensor to, e.g., buy accumulated stock that the licensee can no longer sell or enter into some other arrangement to alleviate the implications of the licence agreement ending.

Such a repurchase obligation could – as suggested by the DCFR – exist, e.g., at least in the context of commercial agency, franchise and distributorship agreements,[90] but it is unclear if this truly would be the case under Finnish law.

In the context of a manufacturing agreement, a two-justice Supreme Court minority cited this DCFR proposition in support of the terminating party having a duty to explore a commercial settlement to avoid causing unnecessary losses for the other party in respect of goods it could not sell post-termination. The majority did not approve of this proposition, however, instead seemingly preferring the traditional view that the notice period should serve as a sufficient period during which the licensee may wind down its relevant operations in a way that minimises losses.

While it of course cannot be excluded that the minority opinion ultimately would prevail – at least in the context of agreements closer to agency, franchise or distributorship – in view of present case law, there thus seems to be limited scope for an implied buyout obligation in most trademark licence agreements.

88. Should the products already have been 'put on the market', however, the rightholder would have no right to object to their sale even post-expiration. See section 9 of the Trademarks Act on the doctrine of exhaustion.
89. The Finnish Supreme Court in KKO 2018:37, paragraphs 19-24 considering the relevance of inventory issues.
90. DCFR IV. E. – 2:306: Stock, spare parts and materials.

9.4. Likely No Goodwill Indemnity

The DCFR also suggests that a party upon the expiry of agency, franchise and distributorship agreements will have the right to an indemnity/compensation for the goodwill value it has contributed, where it: (a) has significantly increased the other party's volume of business and the other party continues to derive substantial benefits from that business and (b) the payment of the indemnity is reasonable. This is mirrored by the Finnish Commercial Agents Act (417/1992) providing for a similar indemnification.[91]

As arguably, the Commercial Agents Act may have certain analogous application more broadly, e.g., when considering distributorship arrangements, the question arises whether the recipient of a termination notice in respect of a trademark licence could have the right to seek indemnification for the licensing arrangement ending. A great degree of scepticism is warranted, however.

Some commentators have rejected an indemnification obligation existing even for distributorship agreements,[92] which are close to the subject matter of the Agency Act.[93] As noted above, in section 9.3, the Finnish Supreme Court also does not seem to have endorsed a broad application of the DCFR's propositions on post-termination rights in respect of agency, franchise and distributorship arrangements.

While it thus should not be excluded that a Finnish court could find a right to a goodwill indemnity in connection to some trademark licence arrangements, the scope of such rights will likely be limited. Parties should ideally, however, in any event seek to agree on whether such a right should be applied. Some licensors may of course also prefer to not draw attention to the issue and instead trust that the courts also will not imply such an obligation into the relationship.

91. The Finnish Agents Act is based on Directive 86/653 on commercial agents, that the DCFR's proposition also is largely based on.
92. See, e.g., Rautpalo and Lencioni, *Jälleenmyyntisopimukset* (2016), section 8.1.3, p. 161.
93. As showed by the DCFR lumping agency, franchise and distributorship arrangements under the same rule.

France

Arnaud Michel & Tougane Loumeau

1. INTRODUCTION TO TRADEMARK LICENSING IN FRANCE

1.1. Sources of Legislation on Trademark Licensing in France

There are three types of trademarks enforceable in the French territory: French trademarks, international trademarks designating France (filed internationally through the Madrid filing system) and EU trademarks (EUTMs) (that have equal effect throughout the Union). Since international trademarks ultimately consist in a bundle of national registrations, we will hereunder only distinguish between French trademarks and EUTMs.

French trademarks are mostly governed by French trademark law, which is contained in Part 7 of the French Intellectual Property Code (FCIP). Since France is a Member State of the European Union, French trademark law must comply with the EU Directive on trademarks (Directive).[1] Trademark licensing is dealt with in Article 25 of the Directive and in Articles L714-1 and R714-1 of the FCIP.

EUTMs are mostly governed by the EU Trademark Regulation (EUTMR)[2] which is directly applicable in France. The EUTMR must also comply with the Directive. EUTM licensing is dealt with in Article 25 of the EUTMR.

The provisions on licensing are substantially similar in these three pieces of legislation.

1. Directive (EU) No. 2015/2436 of the European Parliament and of the Council of 16 December 2015.
2. Regulation (EU) No. 2017/1001 of the European Parliament and of the Council of 14 June 2017.

1.2. Trademarks as Objects of Contractual Arrangements

There are not many specific provisions on trademark licensing in French and EU trademark legislation, and they only deal with a small part of the issues that may arise in relation to trademark licensing.

Under French law, a trademark right is regarded as a property right[3] on a movable and intangible good and trademark licences are regarded as a special type of leasing agreement covering such a good. As such, trademark licence agreements are covered by the principles of law applicable to leasing agreements which are contained in Articles 1708 et seq. of the French Civil Code. Since most of these rules date back to the Napoleonian Code of 1804 and have been devised for real estate, they have been adapted by case law when the subject matter of the lease consists in a trademark. Licence agreements are also largely governed by the principles of general contract law which are contained in the French Civil Code and/or, to a lesser extent, in the French code of commerce. Civil contract law underwent a major reform in 2016, applicable to contracts entered into on or after 1 October 2016.

1.3. The Delimitation Between Proprietary Trademark Rules and Contract Law

The question of the delimitation between proprietary trademark rules and contract law is of practical importance since contract litigation is normally heard by commercial courts, while judicial courts (or trademark offices, for nullity and revocation claims raised by way of an action) have exclusive jurisdiction over actions and claims 'relating to trademarks'.[4] According to established case law, an action should be regarded as relating to a trademark when it involves the use of rules specific to trademark law. The distinction between such an action and a simple contractual action involving a trademark may sometimes be difficult to implement.

This is notably the case where contract issues and trademark issues are finely intertwined. An example may be found in the '*Plantation*' case, where a debate on the qualification of the dispute went up to the French Supreme Court. Cognac Ferrand, a company owning the 'Plantation' trademark for alcoholic beverages, had entered into a coexistence agreement (materialized by an exchange of emails) with Grays Inc., a competitor who owned the 'Old Grove Plantation' trademark. Considering that Grays had breached the agreement whereby it had undertaken not to use the 'Plantation' trademark, Cognac Ferrand sued it before the Paris commercial court on the basis of contractual law. Grays pleaded lack of competence and contended that the case should have been brought before the Paris judicial court. The commercial court having dismissed Grays' defence, Grays lodged an appeal. The Paris Court of Appeal reversed the commercial court's decision and declared the judicial court competent. Cognac Ferrand referred the case to the French Supreme Court, where it argued that the dispute concerned the alleged non-performance of the agreement rather than a question of

3. Article L713-1 FCIP.
4. Article L716-5 FCIP.

rights over the 'Plantation' trademark. The Supreme Court held that since the parties disagreed about the trademark rights and since the action was aimed at obtaining the performance of the agreement, it was necessary to determine the content of Grays' obligations and the potential breach thereof, which implied implementing rules specific to trademark law.[5]

Another delicate situation arises when the alleged trademark infringement results from non-performance or improper performance of a contractual obligation. Under French law, there is a general principle ('principle of non-cumulation') which implies that one person cannot hold another person liable in both contract and tort for the same acts, and that in a situation where the same acts could give rise to tortious liability or contractual liability, tortious liability is excluded in favour of contractual liability.[6] However, trademark law specifies that the 'proprietor of a trademark may invoke the rights conferred by that trademark against a licensee who contravenes any provision in his licensing contract with regard to its duration, the form covered by the registration in which the trademark may be used, the scope of the goods or services for which the licence is granted, the territory in which the trademark may be affixed, or the quality of the goods manufactured or of the services provided by the licensee'.[7] This means that, when the licensee uses the trademark in a manner that contravenes a provision in the licence agreement of the type listed above, he is regarded as an infringer against whom the licensor is entitled to enforce his trademark rights. The European Court of Justice (CJEU) has ruled that such list is exhaustive, so that breaches of other contractual provisions may only give rise to contractual liability.[8]

2. TRADEMARK LICENSING AND COMPETITION LAW

As the OECD puts it, 'trademark licenses can stimulate competition, but may also be used for restrictive business practices that harm competition as well as international trade and are not essential to "the legitimate protection of the trademark owner's exclusive right"'.[9] Since the provisions of a trademark licence agreement tend to influence the organization of the concerned market, trademark licensing may sometimes come into conflict with principles of trade and competition policy.

French competition law is mostly contained in the French code of commerce. It generally mirrors similar principles that are contained in the Treaty on the Functioning of the European Union (TFEU) and that apply to competition between EU Member States on the EU internal market.

5. French Supreme Court (Cour de cassation), Commercial Chamber, 5 July 2017, No. 16-14764.
6. French Supreme Court (Cour de cassation), Civil Chamber, 11 January 1922, *GAJC*; Civ. 1, 11 January 1989, No. 86-17323.
7. Article L714-1 §5 FCIP, Article 25(2) of the Directive, Article 25(2) EUTMR.
8. CJEU (1st Chamber), 23 April 2009, C-59/08, *Copad vs Christian Dior Couture.*
9. OECD, *Recommendation of the Council concerning Action against Restrictive Business Practices relating to the Use of Trademarks and Trademark Licences*, OECD/LEGAL/0162 p. 3.

2.1. Antitrust Legislation

2.1.1. Main Principles

- Article L420-1 of the code of commerce prohibits all agreements, decisions and concerted practices which may affect trade, and which have as their object or effect the prevention, restriction, or distortion of competition. A similar principle is laid down in Article 101(1) TFEU regarding the EU Single Market.
- Article L420-2 of the code of commerce prohibits abuse of dominant position (a similar principle is set up in Article 102 TFEU) and abuse of economic dependency.

Any agreement or contractual provision relating to a prohibited practice shall be automatically regarded as invalid. However, a practice which may fall under the prohibitions described above may be declared valid if the author of such practice justifies that it contributes to improving economic progress, while allowing consumers a fair share of the resulting benefit, without affording the undertakings concerned the possibility of eliminating competition in respect of a substantial part of the products in question. To be valid, the restrictions imposed should be indispensable to the attainment of these objectives.[10]

Parties are responsible for conducting their own analysis of their agreement in order not to enter into an anticompetitive contract. Control of the contract validity is made by courts and the French Competition Authority through, for instance, complaints, market watching, or enquiries.

2.1.2. Exemptions

Certain types of agreements that could potentially fall under the scope of Article 101(1) are generally regarded as creating sufficient benefits to outweigh the anticompetitive effects. Therefore, European authorities have issued several so-called Block Exemption Regulations (BER), specifying the conditions under which certain types of agreements are exempted from the prohibition laid down in Article 101(1) TFEU. There does not exist any such BER for agreements where the main purpose is the licensing of a trademark. However, since trademark licences are often entered into within a more general framework (e.g., a distribution system, a franchise agreement, technology transfer, etc.), certain BERs may be of interest regarding trademark licensing, namely:

- The Vertical Block Exemption Regulation (VBER):[11] the VBER applies to vertical agreements, defined as 'an agreement or concerted practice entered into between two or more undertakings each of which operates, for the purposes of the agreement or the concerted practice, at a different level of the

10. Article 101(3) TFUE; Article L420-4 of the French code of commerce.
11. Regulation (EU) No. 330/2010 of 20 April 2010 on the application of Article 101(3) of the Treaty on the Functioning of the European Union to categories of vertical agreements and concerted practices.

production or distribution chain, and relating to the conditions under which the parties may purchase, sell or resell certain goods or services'.[12] It also covers vertical agreements containing ancillary provisions on the assignment or use of intellectual property rights. Distribution agreements between manufacturers and wholesalers or resellers are typical examples of vertical agreements.[13]
- The Technology Transfer Block Exemption Regulation (TTBER):[14] the TTBER applies to technology transfer agreements. Although this regulation does not apply to trademark licences, it may serve as a guideline to assess the compatibility of a licence with competition law.

The functioning of the two Regulations is based on a threshold system (generally a 30% market share).

When the parties' market share is above this threshold, the contract is not exempted and needs to be assessed on an individual basis. When the parties' market share is below this threshold, the contract benefits, in principle, from a safe harbour unless it contains certain suspect contractual provisions, so-called hardcore restrictions or excluded restrictions. The presence of 'hardcore' restrictions has the consequence that the whole agreement is unable to benefit from the block exemption. When a contract contains one or several 'excluded' restrictions, the contract may benefit from the exemption presumption except as regards these restrictions. Assessment of the validity of the concerned clause must be done on a case-by-case basis taking all factors into consideration.

2.2. Other Unfair Competition Legislation

Article L442-1 of the code of commerce provides that persons carrying out production, distribution or service activities engage their responsibility and must compensate the damage they caused when, in the context of commercial negotiations, the conclusion of a contract, or of the execution thereof: (i) they obtain or attempt to obtain from the other party an advantage which does not correspond to any consideration or which is manifestly disproportionate to the value of the consideration granted; or (ii) they subject or attempt to subject the other party to obligations creating a significant imbalance in the rights and obligations of the parties.

2.3. The Principle of Free Movement of Goods Within the EEA

Articles 34 and 35 TFEU prohibit quantitative restrictions on imports and exports and all measures having equivalent effect between EU Member States (principle of free

12. Article 1(1)a) VBER.
13. European Commission, Directorate-General for Competition, *The Competition Rules for Supply and Distribution Agreements*, 25 April 2013.
14. Commission Regulation (EU) No. 311/2014 of 21 March 2014 on the application of Article 101(3) of the Treaty on the Functioning of the European Union to categories of technology transfer agreements.

movement of goods within the EU Single Market). However, Article 36 expressly provides that these provisions do not preclude prohibitions or restrictions on imports, exports or goods in transit justified (among other grounds) on the protection of industrial and commercial property, on condition that they do not constitute a means of arbitrary discrimination or a disguised restriction on trade between Member States.

As regards trademark rights, the CJEU has ruled that 'an obstacle to the free movement of goods may arise out of the existence, within a national legislation concerning industrial and commercial property, of provisions laying down that a trademark owner's right is not exhausted when the product protected by the trademark is marketed in another Member State, with the result that the trademark owner can prevent importation of the product into his own Member State when it has been marketed in another Member State. (...) In fact, if a trademark owner could prevent the import of protected products marketed by him or with his consent in another Member State, he would be able to partition off national markets and thereby restrict trade between Member States, in a situation where no such restriction was necessary to guarantee the essence of the exclusive right flowing from the trademark'.[15]

The principle of trademark exhaustion has been incorporated in Article L713-4 FCIP and in Article 15 EUTMR: under these provisions, a French trademark or an EUTM shall not entitle the owner to prohibit its use in relation to goods which have been put on the market in the European Economic Area[16] (EEA) under that trademark by the owner or with his consent, except where there exist legitimate reasons for the owner to oppose further commercialization of the goods.

This principle has consequences with regard to licensing. The owner of a trademark may not use the licence to prevent free circulation of the branded products between EEA Member States and create an artificial partitioning of the EEA market (see also below section 5.1.2).

The impact of competition law on trademark licensing will be further detailed in this presentation, as we study certain contractual provisions.

3. FORMATION OF TRADEMARK LICENCE AGREEMENTS IN FRANCE

3.1. Pre-contractual Obligations

Article 1112-1 of the French Civil Code provides for a general obligation for a party who has knowledge of information which is crucial for the other party's consent, to disclose such information to that party, when the latter is legitimately unaware of that information or legitimately trusts his co-contractor.

On a more specific level, franchise law contains pre-contractual obligations. Article L330-3 of the code of commerce covers agreements whereby a person makes available to another person a trade name, a trademark or a signboard on condition that

15. CJEU, 31 October 1974, C-16/74, *Centrafarm vs Winthrop.*
16. The European Economic Area consists of the European Union + Iceland, Norway, and Lichtenstein.

the latter performs his activity on an exclusive or quasi-exclusive basis, which is the case in franchise agreements.

It results from Articles L330-3 and R330-3 FCC, that at least twenty days prior to the signature of the franchise agreement, the franchisor/licensor is obliged to provide the other party with a document containing sincere information that enables him to make an informed decision, as well as a draft of the envisaged agreement. Failure to comply with such an obligation may lead to the nullity of the agreement and may render the franchisor/licensor liable for the franchisee's/licensee's loss of the opportunity not to enter into the franchise agreement, or to enter into it on more favourable terms.[17]

3.2. Formal Requirements

Contrary to patent licence agreements, there is no legal requirement for trademark licence agreements to be concluded in written form. However, in practice, a written document will be necessary for registration purposes and almost always necessary for evidencing the existence and scope of the licence.[18]

3.3. Registration Formalities

Unregistered licences are valid and binding on the parties. Registration is only required for opposability purposes vis-à-vis third parties. Thus, both the FCIP[19] and the EUTMR[20] provide that legal acts concerning a trademark shall have effects vis-à-vis third parties only after entry in the corresponding Register. Nevertheless, such an act, before it is so entered, shall have effect vis-à-vis third parties who have acquired rights in the trademark after the date of that act but who knew of the act at the date on which the rights were acquired.

As far as EUTMs are concerned, the CJEU has ruled that the lack of effects, vis-à-vis third parties, of an unregistered licence, is intended to protect a person who has, or may have, rights in an EUTM as an object of property, and that it does not apply to a situation in which a third party, by infringing the mark, infringes the rights conferred by the EUTM. Therefore, a licensee may bring proceedings alleging infringement of an EUTM which is the subject of the licence, although that licence has not been entered in the register.[21] Likewise, opposition against an EUTM may be lodged by a licensee authorized by the owner of the earlier trademark on which the opposition is based, even if the licence has not been published.[22]

17. French Supreme Court (Cour de cassation), Commercial Chamber, 15 March 2017, No. 15-16406.
18. For instance, Paris Court of First Instance (Tribunal de grande instance), 20 June 2019, No. 17-12756; Paris Court of First Instance (Tribunal de grande instance), 24 November 2016, No. 15-17039.
19. Article L714-7 §§1 and 2 FCIP.
20. Article 27(1) EUTMR.
21. CJEU, 4 February 2016, C-163/15, *Hassan / Breiding*.
22. Article 46(1)a) EUTMR.

As regards French trademarks, there is no doubt that an unregistered licensee is entitled to intervene in infringement proceedings brought by the owner of the trademark, for the purpose of obtaining compensation for his own damage[23] (as is also the case for an EUTM[24]). It is however less clear whether an unregistered licensee is entitled to bring trademark infringement proceedings on his own, in the few situations where a registered licensee would be allowed to do so. Therefore, registration of the licence is highly recommended before engaging in trademark infringement proceedings.[25]

The grant or transfer of a trademark licence is entered in the corresponding register (French national trademark register, international trademark register or Register of European Union trademarks) and published at the request of any of the parties. Registration is subject to the payment of a fee. If the agreement is confidential, it is possible to register a redacted version of the licence agreement or to register an iterative agreement which summarizes the main points of the original licence agreement without disclosing confidential elements.

4. SUBJECT MATTER OF THE TRADEMARK LICENCE AGREEMENT

It is a truism to say that the subject matter of a trademark licence is the granting of exploitation rights on a trademark. Nevertheless, the definition of 'trademark' requires a few clarifications.

The licence may cover a trademark or a trademark application.[26]

The licence must cover a trademark or trademark application which has a legal existence. For instance, it has been ruled that the owner of the 'Azzaro' trademark may not grant a licence on the 'Azzaroville' 'trademark', which has no existence yet, even though he would be able to prohibit the use of this latter sign.[27] Neither may the licence cover products or services which are different or similar to the ones covered by the licensed trademark.[28] It is possible to enter into agreements whereby a party who owns a trademark authorizes another party to use similar or different signs (or the same sign on similar or different products or services), where such use would fall under the scope of the trademark's protection. However, these agreements are not regarded as licences but rather as coexistence agreements or non-suing agreements.

23. Article L714-7 § 3 FCIP.
24. Article 25(4) EUTMR.
25. About the actions available to the licensee in case of trademark infringement by a third party, see 6.1.3 below.
26. Article L714-1 § 8 FCIP; Article 28 EUTMR.
27. French Supreme Court (Cour de cassation), Commercial Chamber, 3 March 1987, published in Dalloz 1987, p. 515.
28. Paris Court of First Instance (Tribunal de grande instance), 24 November 2016, No. 15-17039.

5. SCOPE OF THE TRADEMARK LICENCE AGREEMENT

5.1. Delimitation of the Licence

5.1.1. Products and Services

A trademark may be licensed for some or all of the goods or services for which it is registered.[29]

5.1.2. Territory

A trademark may be licensed for the whole or part of the territory for which it is registered.[30] This is not the case for the assignment of a trademark.

For the licensee, using the trademark on a territory outside the licensed territory may amount to infringement of the trademark rights which the licensor may own in that outside territory or to contractual breach. However, account must be taken of how this articulates with the principle of free movement of goods within the EU market.

As explained above (see section 2.3), the owner of a trademark may not use the licence to prevent the free circulation of the branded products between EEA Member States and to create an artificial partitioning of the EEA market.

Thus, on 25 March 2019, the European Commission fined Nike Inc. and some Nike European subsidiaries EUR 12.5 million for using licensing to ban traders from selling licensed merchandise to other countries within the EEA. The case concerned products featuring the brands of some of Europe's best-known football clubs or federations (including the French Football Federation). Through sponsorship agreements, Nike had obtained licences from these clubs and federations and acted as a licensor that grants licences to third parties, for the manufacture and distribution of those products. The Commission concluded that, in this role as a licensor, Nike included clauses that partitioned the Single Market and prevented licensees in Europe from selling products cross-border. The Commission granted Nike a 40% fine reduction in return for its cooperation.[31]

Contractual restrictions that relate to market partitioning are regarded as hardcore restrictions by both the VBER and the TTBER (see above section 2). However, a distinction must be made between active sales (i.e., initiatives to approach or target customers) and passive sales (i.e., sales in response to unsolicited order). Clauses that restrict active sales by the licensee into the exclusive territory allocated by the licensor to himself or to another licensee are not regarded as anticompetitive. On the contrary, restrictions on passive sales are generally regarded as severely anticompetitive.[32]

29. Article L714-1 § 4 FCIP; Article 25(1) EUTMR.
30. Article L714-1 § 4 FCIP; Article 25(1) EUTMR.
31. European Commission (Competition DG), 25 March 2019, No. AT 40436, *Ancillary Sports Merchandise.*
32. Article 4 VBER; Articles 4(1)c) and 4(2)b) TTBER.

5.1.3. *Duration*

A trademark is renewable on an unlimited basis and may theoretically be perpetual. However, under French law, perpetual commitments are prohibited.[33] This principle is based on the constitutional principle of individual freedom.[34]

Therefore, a trademark licence may be granted either for a fixed duration or for an indeterminate duration. In the latter case, the agreement may be terminated at any time by either party subject to observing the contractually agreed period of notice or, failing that, a reasonable period of time.[35] If the parties have provided that the agreement is perpetual, the agreement is not invalid; it shall be regarded as an agreement with an indeterminate duration.[36]

5.2. Modalities of the Licence

5.2.1. *Exclusivity*

Article L714-1 §4 of the FCIP and Article 25(1) EUTMR provide that trademark licences may be exclusive or non-exclusive, but do not give any definition of the notion of exclusivity.

Exclusivity granted by the licensor to the licensee. It is generally understood that in the case of a non-exclusive licence, a licensor is free to grant further licences to other persons in relation to the rights granted to a licensee, and consequently to exercise these rights himself. The generally understood meaning of 'exclusive licence' is a licence that does not leave a licensor free to grant further licences to other persons in relation to the rights granted to a licensee.

French law does not make a distinction between exclusive licences and sole licences. The French Supreme Court has ruled that when the licence agreement does not contain any exclusivity clause, the licensor is free to exploit the trademark himself and to sell branded products to his licensee's clients and/or at a lower price, unless there is a clause to the contrary or the licensor has engaged in specific disloyal actions.[37] Reversely, it has been ruled that 'unless otherwise stipulated in the exclusive licence agreement, the trademark owner shall refrain from using the trademark during the period of performance of the agreement, irrespective of the duration of the agreement and the amount of the royalty'.[38] However, it is not certain that this would apply if the licensor already exploited the trademark at the time the licence was concluded, with the knowledge of the licensee. It would in any case be safer to provide for this question in the contract.

'Most favoured licensee' clauses are not invalid under French law.

---

33. Article 1210 French Civil Code.
34. Constitutional Council, 9 November 1999, No. 99-419, Law on civil union.
35. Article 1211 French Civil Code; see also French Supreme Court (Cour de cassation), Commercial Chamber, 8 February 2017, No. 14-28232.
36. Article 1210 French Civil Code.
37. French Supreme Court (Cour de cassation), Commercial Chamber, 14 November 2006, No. 04-16338.
38. French Supreme Court (Cour de cassation), Commercial Chamber, 10 January 1995, No. 92-18923.

The status of 'exclusive licensee' provides a licensee specific rights in relation to infringement proceedings, as explained below in section 6.1.3.

Exclusivity granted by the licensee to the licensor. When the licensee grants exclusivity to the licensor, the latter is obliged to provide the licensee with pre-contractual information[39] (see above section 3.1).

Besides, Article L330-1 of the code of commerce provides that the period of validity of any exclusivity clause by which the lessee of movable property undertakes vis-à-vis its lessor not to use similar or complementary objects from another supplier is limited to a maximum of ten years. This may apply to trademark licences.

5.2.2. Selective Distribution Network and the Internet

When the licensor operates a selective distribution network, he generally imposes specific requirements on the licensee as regards the distribution of the branded products. These clauses are generally regarded as valid if they are not unjustified.

In 2011, the CJEU issued a decision where it held that a clause in a selective distribution contract prohibiting de facto the internet as a method of marketing the contractual products may not benefit from the block exemption provided for in the VBER, even though it could be exempted on an individual basis. More specifically, it held that in the context of a selective distribution system, a contractual clause requiring sales of cosmetics and personal care products to be made in a physical space where a qualified pharmacist must be present, resulting in a ban on the use of the internet for those sales, amounts to a restriction by object where, following an individual and specific examination of the content and objective of that contractual clause and the legal and economic context of which it forms a part, it is apparent that, having regard to the properties of the products at issue, that clause is not objectively justified.[40] Later on, the French courts declared that the contractual clause at stake was indeed disproportionate and illegal.[41]

Bang & Olufsen was similarly fined EUR 900,000 by the French Competition Authority for having prohibited de facto its distributors from selling the branded products on the internet. This amount was later reduced to EUR 10,000 by the Paris Court of appeal, which took mitigating circumstances into consideration.[42]

In view of this case law, a clause in a trademark licence that prohibits the licensee from using the trademark on the internet may be regarded as illegal if it unduly restricts competition.

39. French Supreme Court (Cour de cassation), Commercial Chamber, 4 May 2010, No. 09-15139.
40. CJEU, 13 October 2011, C-439/09, *Pierre Fabre.*
41. French Supreme Court (Cour de cassation), Commercial Chamber, 24 September 2013, No. 12-14344.
42. French Competition Authority, 12 December 2012, No. 12-D-23; Paris Court of Appeal, 13 March 2014, No. 2013/00714.

6. THE PARTIES' RIGHTS AND OBLIGATIONS IN A TRADEMARK LICENCE AGREEMENT

Hereunder, we will detail a few obligations which are of particular interest with regard to trademark licences.

6.1. The Licensor's Obligations

6.1.1. Maintenance of the Trademark

The licensor must maintain the licensed trademark. This is derived from the general obligation of the lessor to deliver and maintain the leased property.[43] A licence agreement lapses if the trademark on which it is based disappears.[44] This means notably that the licensor has an obligation to renew the trademark as long as the licence agreement remains in force.

6.1.2. Undisturbed Enjoyment of the Trademark by the Licensee

The licensor is obliged to ensure that the licensee enjoys the trademark undisturbed. This is derived from a general obligation of the lessor with regard to the leased property.[45]

This obligation entails that the licensor must refrain from attempting to evict the licensee from the enjoyment of the trademark.

The licensor is also obliged to guarantee the licensee against eviction by a third party when that eviction is based on a legal claim. This may be the case, for instance, if the property of the trademark is challenged[46] or if the trademark is invalidated or revoked following an action from a third party. Since the disappearance of a trademark has an absolute effect, the licence agreement will lapse, even when the licensee was not part of the legal proceedings that have caused it.[47] The licensee will have to indemnify the licensee if the latter is sued for infringement by a third party unless the latter has committed a personal fault. Organization of the defence of the trademark in the event of an action lodged by a third party is an important clause in trademark agreements.

On the opposite, the licensor is not obliged to guarantee the licensee against factual disturbances caused by third parties, for instance, acts of infringement of the trademark.

43. Articles 1719-1° and 2° and 1720 of the French Civil Code.
44. French Supreme Court (Cour de cassation), Commercial Chamber, 28 January 2003, No. 00-12149.
45. Articles 1719-3° and 1725 to 1727 of the French Civil Code.
46. For instance, French Supreme Court (Cour de cassation), Commercial Chamber, 17 January 2018, No. 15-25894.
47. French Supreme Court (Cour de cassation), Commercial Chamber, 1 June 1999, No. 97-12.853; 15 January 2008, No. 06-15889.

The licensor may not limit or exclude his liability as regards the existence of the trademark and the eviction of the licensee caused by the licensor's own actions. All other potential grounds of liability may be contractually excluded.[48]

6.1.3. Organization of the Defence of the Trademark in Case of an Infringement by a Third Party

The law provides that trademark infringement actions are brought by the owner of the trademark or by the licensee with the consent of the owner, unless otherwise stipulated in the contract.[49]

Until recently, the holder of a non-exclusive licence was not entitled to initiate trademark infringement proceedings, even with the authorization of the owner. This change was brought following a trademark law reform which entered into force in December 2019.[50] However, only the holder of an exclusive licence may bring such proceedings if the owner of the trademark, after formal notice, does not himself bring infringement proceedings within an appropriate period.[51]

Any party to a licence agreement is entitled to intervene in infringement proceedings brought by another party in order to obtain compensation for its own damage.

Since this mechanism only applies when it is not otherwise provided in the contract, it is advisable for a licensor in an exclusive licence agreement to provide for a system that gives him or her more control on the infringement proceedings by prohibiting a licensee to commence infringement proceedings unless express authorization is granted by a licensor on a case-by-case basis.

6.2. The Licensee's Obligations

6.2.1. The Payment of the Price

The parties enjoy large freedom to fix the nature, amount and form of the consideration furnished by the licensee. This choice must be assessed from a taxation perspective (national or international), a subject which is outside the scope of this overview.

In France, the payment of a sum of money is the most common type of consideration in trademark licence agreements, generally under the form of royalties based on the output or the turnover of the licensee, with or without the provision of a minimum royalty. The calculation method must be clearly indicated to avoid situations where the price would be regarded as undetermined (which is a cause for invalidity of the contract).

A licence granted on a free basis is not invalid, but it may be a potential source of difficulty. A contract may be regarded as invalid if, at the time of execution, the

48. For instance, French Supreme Court (Cour de cassation), Commercial Chamber, 11 March 1986, No. 84-11231.
49. Articles L716-4-2 §1, 1st sentence FCIP and 25(3) 1st sentence EUTMR.
50. Government Order No. 2019-1169 of 13 November 2019, Article 8.
51. Article L716-4-2 §1 2nd sentence FCIP and 25(3) 2nd sentence EUTMR.

compensation was paltry or illusory.[52] A licensor may have a good reason to grant a licence for a low price or for free, but depending on the circumstances, tax authorities may consider that such a licence constitutes an abnormal management decision, and that the licensor should be taxed as if he had received consideration.

The official currency in France is the Euro.[53] The choice of another currency is legal for international agreements but is forbidden in purely internal agreements, unless the parties are professionals and the use of a foreign currency is common for the operation at stake.[54] Unless otherwise agreed, payment costs are borne by the debtor.[55] Payments cannot be made in cash for sums above EUR 1,000 (or in electronic money for sums above EUR 3,000) if the debtor is domiciled in France and/or if the payment is made for professional reasons.[56] There are customs declaration obligations for the importation or exportation (physically or by mail) of funds of EUR 10,000 or more in cash money to or from France.[57]

The licensor is generally not entitled to control the prices charged by the licensee to his own customers for the branded products. Both the VBER and the TTBER regard clauses by which the licensor/supplier fixes the price at which licensees/distributors can sell/resell their products as anticompetitive. However, the imposition of maximum resale prices or the recommendation of resale prices is much less likely to be regarded as anticompetitive than the imposition of minimum prices.[58]

6.2.2. The Use of the Trademark

The licensee is generally regarded as having an obligation to use the trademark to its best capacities and in compliance with the functions of that trademark. This is derived from the general good faith principle and from the obligation of the lessee to use the leased property according to its destination.[59] 'Best' should be understood as remaining within reasonable bounds. Judges will generally not expect a licensee to go beyond the unreasonable. The assessment of 'best' or 'reasonable' endeavours will depend on the circumstances of the case.

This obligation to use the trademark undoubtedly applies when the licence has been granted on an exclusive basis or when the licensor's revenue is based on the trademark-related activity. In such situations, indeed, the lack of use could lead to the revocation of the trademark for lack of use and the licensor would be deprived of his revenues. It is more questionable whether such an obligation applies when the licensee's revenues are based on a lump sum or even when there is a minimum royalty

52. Article 1169 of the French Civil Code.
53. Article L111-1 of the French Financial and Monetary Code.
54. Article 1343-3 of the French Civil Code.
55. Article 1342-7 of the French Civil Code.
56. Article L112-6 and D112-3 (as modified as of 18 April 2018) of the Financial and Monetary Code.
57. Article L152-1 (as modified as of 3 December 2020 and applicable as of 3 June 2021) of the Financial and Monetary Code and Article 464 of the Customs Code for transfers between France and the European Union; EU Regulation 2018/1672 for transfers between an EU country and a third country.
58. Article 4 a) VBER; Articles 4(1)a) and 4(2)a) TTBER.
59. Article 1728 of the French Civil Code.

clause. In any case, it is safer for a licensor to expressly provide for a general performance obligation in the agreement.

Under French law, there is no obligation for the licensor to control the quality of the products or services marketed under the trademark. However, in practice, the licensor is generally attached to his trademark's goodwill and reputation. Besides, legislation on the protection of the consumer requires that all producers involved in the production process should be made liable, in so far as their finished product, component part or any raw material supplied by them was defective. 'Producer' means the manufacturer of a finished product, the producer of any raw material or the manufacturer of a component part and any person who, by putting his name, trademark or other distinguishing feature on the product, presents himself as its producer. A licensor may therefore be held liable within this context and this risk is all the higher if his role is made apparent on the product. These considerations make quality control clauses in trademark licence agreements particularly important. The restrictions that tend to preserve the quality or the aura of luxury of the products and services concerned are generally regarded as not anticompetitive, provided they are justified and proportionate.

6.2.3. Non-challenge Clauses

The TTBER considers that any direct or indirect obligation on a party not to challenge the validity of the licensed intellectual property rights which the licensor holds in the EU is prima facie anticompetitive. However, it reserves the possibility for the licensor, in the case of an exclusive licence, of providing for termination of the licence agreement in the event that the licensee challenges the validity of any of the licensed rights.[60]

6.3. Sublicence and Assignment of the Licence

Under general leasing law, the lessee is entitled to sublet or assign his leasing agreement unless otherwise stipulated in the agreement.[61] However, under general contract law, the creditor may refuse that the performance be carried out by a different person than the intended debtor when the creditor has a legitimate reason for personal performance by such debtor (*'intuitu personae'*).[62] A trademark licence tends to be generally regarded as an *'intuitu personae'* contract with regard to the licensee, which means that if the licence agreement is silent, a licensee is not entitled to grant sublicences or to assign the contract. Therefore, if a sub-licensing right is requested by a licensee, it must be expressly provided for. In any case, if the right is not required, it is safer for a licensor to specify expressly that sublicences are excluded.

A pure trademark licence agreement is generally regarded as not being *'intuitu personae'* with regard to the licensor. This means that the licensor may transfer the

60. Article 5(1)b) TTBER.
61. Article 1717 of the French Civil Code.
62. Article 1342-2 of the French Civil Code.

trademark and the licence agreement without the licensee's consent.[63] However, when the licence agreement is part of a contractual relationship, the scope of which is broader than the trademark licence and where the identity of the licensor is important for the licensee (for instance, a franchise agreement), the licence agreement may be regarded as '*intuitu personae*' including with regard to the licensor.[64]

7. PRINCIPLES OF INTERPRETATION AND AMENDMENT OF THE LICENCE AGREEMENT

Under French law, the essential principle of contract interpretation is that a contract is to be interpreted according to the common intention of the parties rather than to the literal meaning of the words. If that intention cannot be established, the contract is to be interpreted according to the meaning that reasonable persons would give to it in the same circumstances.[65] On the other hand, a clear and precise contractual provision cannot be interpreted under pain of distortion.[66]

Under French law, there are no formal requirements for amending contracts. Clauses according to which a variation of any term of the agreement must be in writing and signed by the parties are common.

8. BREACH AND TERMINATION OF TRADEMARK LICENCE AGREEMENTS

8.1. Non-performance or Defective Performance

8.1.1. Breach of the Trademark Licence Agreement by the Licensee

As explained above (section 1.3), breach of the trademark licence agreement may in principle only give rise to contractual liability. However, trademark law specifies that the 'proprietor of a trademark may invoke the rights conferred by that trademark against a licensee who contravenes any provision in his licensing contract with regard to its duration, the form covered by the registration in which the trademark may be used, the scope of the goods or services for which the licence is granted, the territory in which the trademark may be affixed, or the quality of the goods manufactured or of the services provided by the licensee'.[67] Therefore, when the licensee contravenes any of the listed provisions, he may be sued on tort law for trademark infringement.

This legal provision gave rise in France to a debate in relation to luxury products: can the violation by the licensee of contractual provisions prohibiting the sale of luxury products through distribution channels that may be detrimental to the trademark's prestige (such as discount stores that are not part of the selective distribution network) give rise to a trademark infringement tort action? The CJEU, to which the question was

63. Article 1743 of the French Civil Code.
64. French Supreme Court (Cour de cassation), Commercial Chamber, 31 January 2012, No. 10-27603.
65. Article 1188 of the French Civil Code.
66. Article 1192 of the French Civil Code.
67. Article L714-1 §5 FCIP, Article 25(2) of the Directive, Article 25(2) EUTMR.

referred, ruled that the quality of luxury goods is 'not just the result of their material characteristics, but also of the allure and prestigious image which bestows on them an aura of luxury' so that 'an impairment to that aura of luxury is likely to affect the actual quality of those goods'.[68] It results therefrom that the licensee who damages the trademark's aura of luxury by violating such a provision may be sued on the ground of trademark infringement on account of his having contravened a provision regarding the quality of the goods.

In the same case, the CJEU further ruled that when a licensee puts branded goods on the market in disregard of a provision in the licence agreement, the licensor's rights on the trademark are exhausted unless the provision in question is included in those listed above. Therefore, if the breach committed by the licensee is one of those on the list, the trademark owner is entitled to oppose further commercialization of the branded goods by the third party to whom they were sold. Otherwise, the trademark owner will only be able to do so if he has legitimate reasons (other than the fact that the licence agreement was violated) to oppose such further commercialization.

8.1.2. Remedies for Non-performance

In the event of a breach of the trademark licence agreement, the aggrieved party may resort to a certain number of contractual remedies, including the right to terminate the agreement and a right to damages.[69]

Termination of the agreement is generally governed by termination clauses whereby the parties provide which breach will entail the termination of the agreement. Termination takes place after formal notice if the non-performing party has not remedied the breach in the meantime, unless the agreement provides that the termination will take place automatically.[70] In the absence of a termination clause, and provided the breach is fundamental, the agreement may be terminated by notice of the aggrieved party (at the latter's own risks) or by court decision.[71]

Damages for contractual non-performance cover the loss which the aggrieved party has suffered and the gain of which it has been deprived.[72] However, the non-performing party is liable only for loss which it foresaw or could reasonably have foreseen at the time of conclusion of the contract as a likely result of its non-performance, unless the non-performance was intentional or grossly negligent.[73] Even in the case of intentional or grossly negligent non-performance, the damages may only cover direct and immediate consequences.[74] The licence agreement may provide that a party who fails to perform is to pay a specified sum to the aggrieved party for such non-performance. In that case, a court may not award the aggrieved party a higher or

68. CJEU (1st Chamber), 23 April 2009, C-59/08, *Copad vs. Christian Dior Couture.*
69. Article 1217 of the French Civil Code.
70. Article 1225 of the French Civil Code.
71. Articles 1224 and 1226 of the French Civil Code.
72. Article 1231-2 of the French Civil Code.
73. Article 1231-3 of the French Civil Code.
74. Article 1231-4 of the French Civil Code.

lower sum. However, where the specified sum is grossly excessive or paltry, a court may reduce or increase it.[75]

When the licensee's breach amounts to trademark infringement, the licensor is entitled to the remedies available under trademark law. Damages for trademark infringement are assessed as set forth in the Intellectual Property Rights (IPR) Enforcement Directive of 29 April 2004.[76] Damages must be appropriate to the actual prejudice suffered and should take into account the following elements: (i) the negative economic consequences, including losses and lost profits, which the injured party has suffered; (ii) any unfair profits made by the infringer (including the savings made by the infringer on intellectual, material and promotional investments); and (iii) the moral prejudice caused to the right holder by the infringement. However, they may, as an alternative and on the injured party's request, be set as a lump sum that must be higher than the amount of royalties or fees that would have been due if the infringer had requested authorization to use the right. The grant of such a lump sum does not preclude the owner from receiving compensation for the moral prejudice suffered.[77] French courts do not apply one specific method to assess such amount of royalties. The assessment will vary depending on the circumstances of the case. Other available remedies include prohibition injunctions with a daily fine (or a fine per infringing product) for non-compliance, withdrawal measures, publication of the court judgment and lawyer's fees reimbursement.

8.1.3. *Insolvency*

Under French law, a party may not terminate an agreement on the sole ground of the other party being the subject of insolvency proceedings. The party who wishes to terminate the agreement on account of the other party's insolvency will need to follow a specific procedure by which he formally requests the representative of that party to agree to the termination. Termination will take place if the representative accepts or remains silent after a certain period. Any contractual stipulation to the contrary shall be regarded null and void.[78]

8.2. Effects of Termination

When the licence agreement is terminated for whatever reason, the licensee must cease the use of the trademark. The treatment of the inventories of branded goods should be dealt with in the licence agreement.

The sublicence agreements will also terminate unless the agreement provides otherwise.

When the agreement is declared invalid, it is regarded as if it had never existed and should therefore give rise to the restitution of the performance already made.[79] The

75. Article 1231-5 of the French Civil Code.
76. Directive (EU) No. 2004/48 of the European Parliament and of the Council of 29 April 2004.
77. Article L716-4-10 FCIP.
78. Article L622-13 FCC.
79. Article 1178 of the French Civil Code.

consequence is that the royalties paid by the licensee should in principle be paid back by the licensor. However, in leasing law, when a leasing agreement is invalidated, the lessor is entitled to an occupancy allowance in return for the use of the leased property.[80] In the same manner, it has been ruled that 'the invalidity of a licence agreement resulting from the invalidity of the patent to which it relates does not, whatever the grounds for such invalidity, have the consequence of retroactively depriving the licensee of all grounds for the remuneration charged to him in return for the prerogatives which he actually enjoyed'.[81] This solution may be transposed to a trademark licence agreement. Based on such principle, courts generally decide that the royalties paid before the invalidation do not have to be paid back by the licensor.[82]

8.3. Governing Law and Jurisdiction

The parties may choose the law governing the agreement, as well as the courts where they want their potential disputes to be heard. However, if the dispute involves the application of trademark law, the choice will be limited since the trademark shall be governed by its own legal regime (French law for a French trademark and the EUTMR for an EUTM) and may be submitted to specific jurisdiction rules. For instance, validity issues must be heard by the courts of France.[83] Jurisdiction regarding an EUTM is governed by the EUTMR.[84]

80. French Supreme Court (Cour de cassation), Commercial Chamber, 9 November 2007, No. 06-19508.
81. French Supreme Court (Cour de cassation), Commercial Chamber, 28 January 2003, No. 00-12149.
82. Douai Court of Appeal, 29 September 2005, No. 03/00940.
83. Regulation (EU) No. 1215/2012 of 12 December 2012 on jurisdiction and the recognition and enforcement of judgments in civil and commercial matters.
84. Articles 63 and 122 et seq. EUTMR.

Germany

Christoph Rieken & Stefanie Weidner

1. INTRODUCTION TO TRADEMARK LICENSING IN GERMANY

1.1. Licensable Subject Matter under German Trademark Law

Licence agreements can be freely designed under German law, i.e., with no formal and only few mandatory requirements to apply.

The trademark law regime in Germany comprises not only: (1) registered European Union trademarks (EUTMs) but via the German Act on the Protection of Trademarks and other Signs (**German Trademark Act**) also (2) registered or (3) unregistered German national trademarks and (4) commercial designations (*Geschäftliche Bezeichnungen*), i.e.: (i) signs used in trade as a name, company name or company logo (*Unternehmenskennzeichen*) and (ii) titles of works (*Werktitel*), such as books and movies, music works, stage works or other comparable works. The acquisition of trademark protection and/or protection for a commercial designation grants to the owner of the trademark and/or commercial designation an exclusive right which forms the basis for any licensing.

1.2. Legal Framework

Unlike other types of contracts, like rental or lease agreement, licence agreements are not specifically regulated in the German Civil Code (*Bürgerliches Gesetzbuch*) but are regarded as contracts sui generis.[1] Therefore, the rules of general contract law apply[2] which are complemented by sections 30[3] and 31 of the German Trademark Act. Section 30(1) of the German Trademark Act reads:

---

1. Cf. Hildebrandt, Marken und andere Kennzeichen, § 24 paragraph 19.
2. Cf. Pahlow in: Ekey/Bender/Fuchs-Wissemann, MarkenR, § 30 paragraph 20.
3. Section 30(1), (2), (3), (4) and (6) of the German Trademark Act transposes Article 25 of the Directive of the European Parliament and of the Council of 16 December 2015 to approximate the laws of the Member States relating to trademarks (Trademark Directive (EU) 2015/2436). Insofar

(1) The right arising from the registration of a trademark, the use of a trademark or the fact of being a well-known mark may for all or for a part of the goods or services for which the trademark enjoys protection to form the subject-matter of exclusive or non-exclusive licences for the territory of the Federal Republic of Germany as a whole or part of this territory.

(2) The owner of a trademark may assert the rights from the trademark against a licensee who acts contrary to a provision of the licence agreement with regard to

1. the term of the licence,
2. the manner in which the trademark may be used, as covered by the registration,
3. the nature of the goods or services for which the licence was issued,
4. the territory in which the trademark may be affixed, or
5. the quality of the goods manufactured by them or of the services provided by them.

(3) The licensee may lodge an infringement action of a trademark only with the consent of its owner.

(4) A licensee may, for the purpose of claiming compensation for damage suffered by him, intervene in an infringement action brought by the owner of the trademark.

(5) A transfer of rights in accordance with section 27 or the grant of a licence in accordance with subsection (1) shall not affect licences previously granted to third parties.

Section 31 of the German Trademark Act reads:

> Sections 27 to 30 shall apply mutatis mutandis to rights established by virtue of application for trademarks.

Thus, already a trademark application can be subject matter of a licence agreement. Please note that section 30 of the German Trademark Act does not directly apply to licences for commercial designations or work titles. Whereas also commercial designations and work titles can be subject to licence agreements under German law, the following overview shall focus on licences for registered and unregistered trademarks:

2. FORMALITIES

2.1. No Form Requirements

There are no form requirements for granting a trademark licence under German law. No written agreement is required. Thus, a licence agreement can be established orally. Also the grant of an implied licence is possible.[4] For the purpose of documentation and proof, it is, however, advisable to conclude a written agreement.[5]

---

since January 2019 section 30 of the German Trademark Act has to be interpreted in conformity with Trademark Directive (EU) 2015/2436, cf. Ekey in: Ekey/Bender/Fuchs-Wissemann, MarkenR, E 2, paragraph 20.

4. Cf. Federal Court of Justice GRUR 2018, 297, 299, paragraph 29.
5. Cf. Federal Court of Justice GRUR 2020, 57, 58 et seq., paragraphs 21–24; Federal Court of Justice GRUR 2016, 965, 968 et seqq., paragraphs 37, 51 et seq.; Federal Court of Justice GRUR 2016, 201, 203, paragraphs 31 et seqq.; Federal Court of Justice GRUR 2013, 1150, 1154, paragraph 50.

2.2. Optional Registration of Licence

It is not required under German law to register the grant of a trademark licence in the register of the German Patent and Trademark Office (*GPTO*). However, it is possible to do so according to section 30(6) of the German Trademark Act. Pursuant to section 30(6) sentence 1 of the German Trademark Act, the GPTO shall, upon request of the owner or the licensee, enter the grant of a licence in the register if the consent of the other party is proven. The same applies to the amendment of a registered licence (section 30(6) sentence 2 of the German Trademark Act). The entry will be cancelled at the request of the owner of the trademark or the licensee (section 30(6) sentence 3 of the German Trademark Act). However, the request for cancellation by the owner of the trademark must be accompanied by evidence of the consent of the licensee or his legal successor designated at the time of registration (section 30(6) sentence 4 of the German Trademark Act).

Since the registration of the grant of a licence is optional, the registration only has a declaratory effect, but it does not trigger legal consequences.[6]

2.3. Trademark-Specific Provisions

The German Trademark Act does not limit the content of a licence agreement. Therefore, the parties are generally free to agree on the content and scope of a licence agreement except for mandatory German and European Law. Relevant limitations to the content of trademark agreements are found in antitrust law (*see* section 3.1. Antitrust), German unfair competition law (*see* section 3.3. Unfair Competition) and general German contract law (*see*, e.g., section 3.4 Standard Terms and Conditions). The following shall provide an overview of the essential licence terms and potential restrictions that might apply under German law.

2.4. Exclusivity

According to section 30(1) of the German Trademark Act, the licence can be exclusive or non-exclusive. In case of an exclusive licence, the licensor is not allowed to grant a licence with the same content to a third party and he is also not allowed to use his trademark within the scope of the exclusive licence[7]. However, it is of course possible to regulate that the licensor shall be allowed to use his trademark which is referred to as a 'sole license' (*Alleinlizenz*). For the sake of clarity, it is recommended to explicitly regulate the entitlement or restriction respectively of the licensor to use the trademark in the licence agreement.

6. Cf. Hacker, GRUR 2019, 235, 243; Pahlow in: Ekey/Bender/Fuchs-Wissemann, MarkenR, § 30 paragraph 105.
7. In Germany, it is predominantly assumed that an exclusive licence to a trademark is a right in rem, cf. Federal Court of Justice GRUR 2007, 877, 879, paragraph 29; Higher Regional Court of Hamburg GRUR-RR 2005, 181, 182; Higher Regional Court of Munich NJW-RR 1997, 1266, 1267; Fezer, MarkenR, § 30 paragraph 8; Ingerl/Rohnke in: Ingerl/Rohnke, MarkenG, § 30 paragraph 12; Taxhet in: Kur/v. Bomhard/Albrecht, BeckOK MarkenR, § 30 paragraph 10.

Please note that under exceptional circumstances, exclusive licence agreements may (other than non-exclusive ones) have the potential to restrain competition. Thus, antitrust law needs to be kept in mind, if a trademark is an essential prerequisite for market success and if the trademark licence agreement shall include clauses regarding competition bans, territorial restrictions within the EU and restrictions of the licensee to certain groups of customers as well as non-challenge clauses.[8]

2.5. Assignability

Under German law, the licence agreement as such (i.e., as a whole agreement with all rights and all obligations) can only be assigned/transferred to a third party with the consent of all three parties, i.e., licensor, licensee and the assignee. As the transfer of the whole licence agreement would replace the licensee as debtor with a third party, the licensor's upfront consent to such transfer is rarely found in any (German) trademark licence agreement. Moreover, the parties can agree that the licensee shall be entitled to assign his licence rights to a third party (i.e., not the obligations, for which the licensee remains responsible) in the licence agreement.[9] Such right to assign will often be limited to the assignment to affiliates in order to maintain (indirect) control over the trademark use. The regulation on assignability of any rights under a trademark licence should be explicitly regulated because, in case of doubt, the licensor's consent to assign the licence will not be deemed to have been granted. The above applies irrespective of the nature of the licence as exclusive or non-exclusive.

2.6. Sublicence

The licensee also requires the licensor's consent to grant sublicences under German trademark law. This applies irrespective of the nature of the licence as exclusive or non-exclusive. Thus, if the licensee shall be entitled to grant sublicences, it should be clearly regulated in the licence agreement.

2.7. Obligation to Use

As in many jurisdictions, the owner of a German trademark has the obligation to genuinely use the (licensed) trademark after a five years grace period in order to maintain his trademark rights. According to section 25(1) of the German Trademark Act, the owner of a trademark is obliged to use his trademark in accordance with section 26 of the German Trademark Act within the last five years prior to the assertion of the right for the relevant goods or services. If a trademark is not used in accordance with section 26 of the German Trademark Act, the owner may not assert his trademark rights vis-à-vis third parties within the meaning of sections 14 and 18–19c of the German Trademark Act (section 25(1) of the German Trademark Act). According to

8. Cf. Ingerl/Rohnke in: Ingerl/Rohnke, MarkenG, § 30 paragraph 122.
9. Cf. Ingerl/Rohnke in: Ingerl/Rohnke, MarkenG, § 30 paragraph 49; Pahlow in: Ekey/Bender/Fuchs-Wissemann, MarkenR, § 30 paragraph 51.

section 26(2) of the German Trademark Act, the use of the trademark with the consent of the owner is deemed as use by the owner. Therefore, the use of the trademark by the licensee maintains the trademark rights of the owner. Against this background, the licensee should be obliged under the licence agreement to use the trademark.

2.8. Quality Control and Goodwill

The main commercial value of a trademark is the goodwill it conveys. It is therefore essential for any trademark owner to protect the goodwill of the trademark and the goods and services marketed under the trademark. Therefore, in case of significant defects which are able to damage the goodwill of the trademark, the owner of a trademark might be entitled to take legal action against the licensee.[10] However, quality control should prevent such a scenario, and thus, the owner of a trademark should, by inclusion of a provision in the licence agreement, ensure the quality of the goods and/or services offered by the licensee under the licensed trademark. Therefore, it is usual to stipulate quality criteria and to entitle the licensor to inspect the products sold under the licensed trademark.[11] Moreover, the licensee can be obliged to add an appropriate notice on the product or the packaging of the product which clarifies the origin of the product.

2.9. Audit Right

As the trademark use by the licensee is not evident to the licensor, an audit right should be included in the licensee agreement. Usually, the parties agree on an audit by a professional auditor and on a cost allocation whereby the licensor pays for the audit unless the audit reveals that the reported use deviates by a certain percentage (usually between 1% and 5%) from the actual use of the licensed trademark to the detriment of the licensor, in which case the licensee has to pay for the auditing.

2.10. Trademark Infringement

2.10.1. Right to Sue of Licensor

Under German law, the trademark owner/licensor remains entitled to take legal actions against third parties in case of an infringement of his trademark, even in case he granted an exclusive licence for his trademark and is thus not entitled to use the licensed trademark. In addition to any contractual rights, the owner of a trademark remains entitled to asserting the rights from his trademark against any licensee who acts contrary to a provision of the licence agreement. Pursuant to section 30(2) of the German Trademark Act, the owner of a trademark may assert claims against a licensee

10. Cf. Pahlow in: Ekey/Bender/Fuchs-Wissemann, MarkenR, § 30 paragraph 70.
11. Cf. Ingerl/Rohnke in: Ingerl/Rohnke, MarkenG, § 30 paragraph 134; regarding option number two, cf. CJEU GRUR 2009, 593, 596, paragraphs 44 et seq.; Federal Court of Justice GRUR 1984, 737, 738 et seq.; Federal Court of Justice GRUR 1970, 528, 532; Federal Court of Justice GRUR 1965, 676, 678 et seq.

if the licensee acts contrary to provisions with regard to: (1) the term of the licence; (2) the manner in which the trademark may be used, as covered by the registration; (3) the nature of the goods or services for which the licence was issued; (4) the territory in which the trademark may be affixed; or (5) the quality of the goods manufactured by it or of the services provided by it.

2.10.2. Right to Sue of Licensee

Consent of licensor required. Irrespective of the nature as a non-exclusive or exclusive licence, the licensee can only bring an action against a third party for infringement of the licensed trademark with the consent of the trademark owner/licensor (section 30(3) sentence 1 of the German Trademark Act). According to section 30(3) sentence 2 of the German Trademark Act, the owner of an exclusive licence may only lodge an infringement action without the consent of the owner of the trademark if the owner, after having been formally requested to do so, has not brought an action for infringement himself within a reasonable period of time. Please note that the licensee requires the consent of the trademark owner even for sending a warning letter to a third party when asserting trademark infringement. The contracting parties can, however, deviate from the regulations in section 30(3) of the German Trademark Act by individual agreement. The consent may even be given impliedly. For an implied consent of the owner of the trademark, the grant of an exclusive licence is not sufficient, but additional indications for his implied consent are in fact necessary. To have a clear regulation and taking into account that time is of essence if the trademark infringements shall be subject of an interim injunction, it is highly recommendable to clearly regulate the licensee's rights to sue for infringement of the licensed trademarks in the licence agreement.

Damages. The German Federal Court of Justice (BGH) stated in several decisions that the licensee does not have own claims for damages due to the wording of section 14(6) of the German Trademark Act ('Any person who performs the act of infringement intentionally or negligently shall be obliged to compensate the owner of the trademark [...]'). Further, the licensee also does not have own claims for injunctive relief against third parties according to section 14(5) of the German Trademark Act ('Any person who uses a sign contrary to subsections (2) to (4) may, in the event of the risk of recurrent infringement, be sued by the owner of the trademark'). However, the licensee can claim injunctive relief in his own name as a nominal plaintiff (*gewillkürte Prozessstandschaft*), if the requirements according to section 30(3) sentence 1 of the German Trademark Act (especially the consent of the owner of the trademark) are fulfilled and if the licensee has a legitimate interest of his own in independently asserting claims against the infringer by way of a lawsuit. Such a legitimate interest of the licensee is usually given.

Joint action. The licensee may also take part in an infringement action of the owner of the licensed trademark as a 'joinder of parties' (*einfache Streitgenossen*, section 59 of the German Code of Civil Procedure, section 30(4) of the German Trademark Act), in order to claim compensation for damages. However, the licensee can only sue for payment of damages to the trademark owner and not to himself, *unless* the trademark owner has also substantively entitled him to collect his damage claims (*materiell-rechtliche Einziehungsermächtigung*, sections 362(2), 185(1) of the German Civil Code) or has assigned his claims to the licensee. If the licensee sues for payment of damages to the trademark owner, the licensee can claim compensation for his damages from the licensor afterwards ('concept of third party liquidation'/ '*Drittschadensliquidation*').

Right to information. The licensee does not have own rights to request information according to section 19(1) of the German Trademark Act and section 242 of the German Civil Code against the infringer of the trademark. However, with the consent of the trademark owner, the licensee may assert the right to information in his own name as a nominal plaintiff ('*gewillkürte Prozessstandschaft*') against the trademark infringer and also with regard to third-party information (section 19(1) and (3) of the German Trademark Act, '*Drittauskunft*') in order to be able to take legal actions against other infringers.

2.11. Termination

2.11.1. Ordinary Termination

The parties are free to agree on the duration of the licence agreement and the conditions for a termination or even to exclude ordinary termination rights. However, please note that the exclusion of ordinary termination rights will not make a licence truly perpetual under German law. In any case, the licence agreement can be terminated after thirty years (analogous to sections 581(2), 544 of the German Civil Code). If the licence agreement contains a termination period, this period will apply. If the notice period for an ordinary termination is not regulated in the licence agreement, the notice period has to be determined by interpretation of the contract. In the absence of any indication to the contrary, a notice period of six months will be assumed (analogous to sections 624(1) sentence 2, 584(1) of the German Civil Code).

2.11.2. Extraordinary Termination

Extraordinary termination rights for certain cases can be specified in the licence agreement. However, the extraordinary termination of the licence agreement cannot be validly excluded. Thus, if regulations with regard to an extraordinary termination are missing in the licence agreement, statutory law on extraordinary termination will apply (i.e., section 314 and sections 581(2), 543 of the German Civil Code). Therefore, any party may terminate the licence agreement if the terminating party can no longer be reasonably expected to continue the contractual relationship, taking into account all circumstances and weighing up the interests of both parties. In most cases, a previous notification in the form of a formal warning letter is necessary before terminating the licence agreement extraordinarily (sections 314(2), 543(3) of the German Civil Code). However, by exception, a previous notification is disposable if the further proper functioning of the agreement (e.g., breach of trust) is not given anymore. Examples for extraordinary termination grounds of a licence agreement are: (i) the repeated default in payment of royalties, (ii) serious deviations from quality specifications and (iii) the use of the trademark outside the licensed territory or (iv) for products other than the licensed products.

2.11.3. Consequences of Termination

Acquired trademark rights via use and goodwill. After termination of the licence agreement, the licensee is not allowed to use the trademark anymore. In case the licensee acquired a trademark right in the licensed trademark via use, he is obliged to transfer the trademark to the licensor after the termination of the licence agreement. Also any goodwill belongs completely to the owner of the trademark. However, both points should be included in the trademark licence agreement for the sake of clarification.

Damages for extraordinary termination. The party who has reason to terminate the licence agreement extraordinarily due to an infringement of the licence agreement by the other party is entitled to claim damages (see section 280 of the German Civil Code), provided the terminating has suffered a loss and the other party has acted culpably (i.e., with intent or negligence).

Compensation for Termination. The licensee is not generally entitled to claim any form of compensation/indemnity for the investment he made into the brand when the licence agreement is terminated. Only in the exceptional case that the licensee is part of the sales organisation of the owner of the trademark like a commercial agent (see section 84(1) of the German Commercial Code) and if he is additionally under a contractual obligation to transfer his customer base to the owner of the trademark after the termination of the licence agreement, he might be entitled to request a compensation for such obligation.

Termination of sublicence agreements. Neither the German Trademark Act nor Trademark Directive (EU) 2015/2436 contains any rule regarding the legal standing of sublicence agreements in case of termination of the main licence agreement. Please note that the termination of the main licence agreement will not per se terminate the sublicence agreement. For trademark cases, this has not been decided by the German Federal Court of Justice (*BGH*) yet, but in copyright cases, the BGH held that sublicences persisted even when the main licence agreement had terminated. Prerequisite for such persistence was that the interests of the sublicensee to keep the sublicence prevail over those of the rights owner to have it terminated which was found to be the regular case. The interest of the licensor for termination of the sublicence agreement might however prevail if, for example, the sublicensee is (co-)responsible for the termination of the main licence agreement. If the main licence agreement was terminated but the sublicence agreement is still in force, the owner of the trademark will however be entitled to the licence fees owed by the sublicensee to the licensee (and sublicensor). Thus, in case sublicensing is allowed under the licence agreement, it is recommended to also include a provision on the termination of any sublicence.

3. LEGAL RESTRICTIONS TO TRADEMARK LICENCE AGREEMENTS

3.1. Antitrust

As far as the internal market of the EU is concerned, Article 101 of the Treaty on the Functioning of the European Union (**TFEU**) applies. Article 101(1) TFEU prohibits three types of coordinated market behaviour which lead to a distortion of competition: (1) horizontal restrictive agreements as well as (2) vertical restrictive agreements and (3) corresponding concerted practices. Such agreements are void according to Article 101(2) TFEU. Please note that trademark use-related restrictions in a trademark licence agreement are not regarded as illegal distortion of competition: The owner of the trademark is, for example, free to decide about the duration of the grant of the licence, whether it encompasses all of the goods or services for which the trademark enjoys protection and if the licensee is entitled to grant sublicences.[12] Further, provisions in licence agreements that ensure the quality of the goods or services for which the trademark enjoys protection or the protection of the goodwill of the trademark do not violate antitrust law.[13] The owner of the trademark can, for example, oblige the licensee to design the packaging of the goods in a special way or to promote the products in a certain way, in order to maintain the image of the trademark.[14] The obligation to use a licence notice on the packaging of the goods to indicate the origin of the goods is permitted too.[15] Thus, antitrust law becomes relevant when the trademark licence agreement includes restricting clauses that reach beyond the subject matter of the trademark monopoly.

3.2. Exclusivity & Territory Restrictions

Exclusive licences as such are not regarded as restricting competition since the scope of the licence is within the boundaries of the trademark as a legal monopoly right as stipulated in section 30 (1) of the German Trademark Act.[16] The exclusivity of a

12. Cf. Kreutzmann, WRP 2006, 453, 454; Nordemann in: Loewenheim et al., KartellR, EU-Recht, 3. Teil. Gewerblicher Rechtsschutz und Urheberrecht, paragraph 61.
13. Cf. CJEU GRUR 2009, 593, 594 et seq., paragraphs 23–30; CJEU GRUR Int 1996, 1144, 1147 et seqq., paragraphs 43, 75 et seq.; CJEU GRUR Int 1981, 315, 316 et seq., paragraphs 16 et seq.; EU Commission, ABl. EG Nr. L 70/69 of 13 March 1978; Higher Regional Court of Frankfurt a. M. WRP 2013, 1662, 1664, paragraph 29; Hacker in: Ströbele/Hacker, MarkenG, § 30 paragraph 118; Pahlow in: Ekey/Bender/Fuchs-Wissemann, MarkenR, § 30 paragraph 70; Obergfell/Hauck in: Dauses/Ludwigs, HB EU WirtschaftsR, Vol. 1, C. III. Geistiges Eigentum, paragraph 138.
14. Cf. EU Commission, ABl. EG Nr. L 70/69 of 13 March 1978; Nordemann in: Loewenheim et al., KartellR, EU-Recht, 3. Teil. Gewerblicher Rechtsschutz und Urheberrecht, paragraph 61; Kreutzmann, WRP 2006, 453, 455; Obergfell/Hauck in: Dauses/Ludwigs, HB EU WirtschaftsR, Vo. 1, C. III. Geistiges Eigentum, paragraph 138.
15. Cf. CJEU GRUR Int 1986, 635, 640, paragraph 72; Fuchs in: Immenga et al., WettbewerbsR, Vol. 1, GVO, Verordnung (EG) Nr. 316/2014, I. Allgemeines, paragraph 84. Such a notice might even be necessary in order to avoid claims according to unfair competition law, *see* section 3.3. Unfair Competition below.
16. Cf. EU Commission GRUR Int 1978, 371, 374; EU Commission GRUR Int 1990, 626, 628; Fezer, MarkenR, § 30 paragraph 74.

trademark licence does therefore not constitute a restriction of competition as such.[17] However, the combination of territorial exclusivity with export and import restrictions may have the effect of creating an absolute territorial protection capable of dividing the common market of the EU on a territorial basis.[18] Such clauses are contrary to antitrust law and cannot be exempted according to Article 101(3) TFEU.[19] The same would apply to clauses which restrict competition outside of the territories for which the trademarks of the licensor enjoy protection.

3.2.1. *Non-challenge Clauses*

Non-challenge clauses are rather common in German trademark licence agreements and are in general[20] admissible with regard to competition law, like the following:

- The licensee undertakes not to attack the licensed trademark itself or to support third parties in attacking the licensed trademark of the licensor.[21]

However, the European Commission has pointed out that in exceptional cases, non-challenge clauses in trademark licence agreements can violate Article 101(1) TFEU.[22] Thus, according to the European Commission, an obligation not to attack the legal status of a trademark can constitute a restriction of competition under Article 101(1) TFEU if the use of a well-known trademark gives a company a significant competitive advantage and if the lack of a licence would be a noticeable barrier to enter into the market.[23] Such clauses can, however, be exempted in accordance with Article 101(3) TFEU.

3.2.2. *Selective Distribution Systems*

Trademark licences form often part of selective distribution systems. The latter are compatible with Article 101(1) TFEU on the condition that the following criteria are met: 'resellers are chosen on the basis of objective criteria of a qualitative nature, laid down uniformly for all potential resellers and not applied in a discriminatory fashion, [...] the characteristics of the product in question necessitate such a network in order to preserve its quality and ensure its proper use and, finally, [...] the criteria laid down

17. Cf. Fezer, MarkenR, § 30 paragraph 74.
18. Cf. EU Commission, Press Release of 9 July 2019, https://ec.europa.eu/commission/presscorner/detail/en/IP_19_3950; EU Commission, Press Release of 25 March 2019, https://ec.europa.eu/commission/presscorner/detail/en/IP_19_1828; Fezer, MarkenR, § 30 paragraph 75.
19. Cf. EU Commission, Press Release of 9 July 2019, https://ec.europa.eu/commission/presscorner/detail/en/IP_19_3950; EU Commission, Press Release of 25 March 2019, https://ec.europa.eu/commission/presscorner/detail/en/IP_19_1828; EU Commission, ABl. EG Nr. L 6/8 of 13 January 1976; EU Commission, ABl. EG Nr. L 233/22 of 12 July 1985; EU Commission, ABl. EG Nr. L 100/32 of 20 April 1990; Fezer, MarkenR, § 30 paragraph 75.
20. In individual cases these clauses can, however, still be void due to competition law.
21. Koch in: Walz, BeckFormB ZivilR, R. Gewerblicher Rechtsschutz, 1. Markenlizenzvertrag: Trademark License Agreement, § 17 No-contest clause.
22. Cf. EU Commission GRUR Int 1990, 626.
23. Cf. Loew in: Krauß/Weise, BeckOF Vertrag, 14.2 Markenlizenzvertrag, paragraph 15.

do not go beyond what is necessary'.[24] Thus, selected distribution systems that are designed to preserve the luxury image of the (trademarked) goods are not prohibited by Article 101(1) TFEU.[25] In this context, for example, a contractual clause that prohibits authorised distributors in a selective distribution system from using, in a discernible manner, third-party platforms for the online sale of the (trademarked) contract goods is legally permitted if all the above-mentioned conditions are met.[26]

3.3. Unfair Competition

A trademark licence agreement can be invalid according to the German Act against Unfair Competition (German Unfair Competition Act).[27] Such was assumed when the licence misleads the consumers about the quality of the product[28]. However, a relevant risk of misleading might only be given if the goods offered by the licensee under the licensed trademark have a lower quality or do not have the same important characteristics as the goods offered by the licensor under the same trademark.[29] Not considered unfair is a potential confusion with regard to the origin of the goods or services as such, since that risk is immanent to all licences.[30] Any use of a licenced trademark carries a risk that the relevant public may be mistaken as to the commercial origin of the product for which the trademark is used.[31] However, section 30 of the German Trademark Act expressly permits the granting of licences to a trademark. Therefore, German courts do not assume a relevant risk of confusion if the use of the trademark is merely accompanied by a likelihood of confusion with regard to the origin of the product.[32]

3.4. Standard Terms and Conditions

If standard terms and conditions (*STC*) are used, these provisions must comply with the statutory rules (sections 305 et seqq. of the German Civil Code). Please note that all pre-formulated contract terms for more than two contracts are considered STC under German law. According to section 307(1) of the German Civil Code, provisions in STC

24. CJEU GRUR Int 2011, 1077, 1080, paragraph 41; CJEU GRUR Int 1981, 315, 316, paragraphs 15 et seq.
25. Cf. CJEU MMR 2018, 77, 78, paragraphs 29, 36.
26. Cf. CJEU MMR 2018, 77, 78 et seqq., paragraphs 40 et seqq., paragraph 68.
27. *See* for further details: Fezer in: Fezer/Büscher/Obergfell, LauterkeitsR, Vol. 1, § 2, B. Geschäftliche Handlung, paragraphs 129–132; Hacker in: Ströbele/Hacker, MarkenG, § 30 paragraphs 109 et seq.
28. Cf. Federal Court of Justice GRUR 1966, 375 (377) – Meßmer Tee II.
29. Cf. Federal Court of Justice GRUR 2002, 703, 705; Federal Court of Justice GRUR 1984, 737, 738 et seq.; Federal Court of Justice GRUR 1970, 528, 531 et seq.; Federal Court of Justice GRUR 1965, 676, 677 et seq.; Taxhet in: Kur/v. Bomhard/Albrecht, BeckOK MarkenR, § 30 paragraph 133.
30. Cf. Federal Court of Justice GRUR 2016, 965, 966, paragraph 23; Federal Court of Justice GRUR 2002, 703, 705; Higher Regional Court of Frankfurt a. M. BeckRS 2018, 10734, paragraph 6; Hacker in: Ströbele/Hacker, MarkenG, § 30 paragraph 109; Ingerl/Rohnke in: Ingerl/Rohnke, MarkenG, § 30 paragraphs 133–136.
31. Cf. Taxhet in: Kur/v. Bomhard/Albrecht, BeckOK MarkenR, § 30 paragraph 133.
32. Cf. Federal Court of Justice GRUR 2016, 965, 966, paragraph 23; Federal Court of Justice GRUR 2002, 703, 705; Higher Regional Court of Frankfurt a. M. BeckRS 2018, 10734, paragraph 6; Taxhet in: Kur/v. Bomhard/Albrecht, BeckOK MarkenR, § 30 paragraph 133.

are invalid if they unreasonably disadvantage the other party. This might, for example, be the case if the licensor prohibits the licensee from advertising its products when every other competitor is allowed to such use.[33] Further, a provision in STC may not oblige the licensee to refrain from actions of use of the trademark which are actually permitted pursuant to section 24 of the German Trademark Act.[34] Any invalidity due to STC is closely linked to German unfair competition law, as the use of clauses that do not comply with STC requirements is generally considered unfair.

4. TRANSFER OF LICENSED TRADEMARKS

Registered and unregistered trademarks are transferable under German law. Such transfer does not affect licences previously granted to third parties (cf. section 30(5) of the German Trademark Act). According to the Federal Court of Justice, the transfer of a trademark to another person or entity has no impact on pre-existing licence agreements.[35] Previously granted licences are therefore still effective, even if the trademark was transferred to a third party or if another licence was granted to a third party.[36] The new owner of the trademark needs the consent of the licensee in order to enter into the existing licence agreement.[37] Otherwise, the licence agreement will persist between the original parties.[38] The licensee retains his right to use the trademark according to the conditions in the licence agreement.[39] However, the new owner of the trademark can obtain the right of termination by assignment from the former owner of the trademark.[40]

5. EXHAUSTION OF TRADEMARK RIGHTS

With the conclusion of the licence agreement, the owner of the trademark usually consents to the sale of the trademarked goods which might lead to the exhaustion of the licensor's trademark rights in accordance to section 24(1) of the German Trademark Act.[41] Such exhaustion shall prevent the owner of a trademark to prohibit a third party from using the trademark for goods which have been put on the market under this trademark by the trademark owner or with his consent in Germany, in one of the other Member States of the European Union or in another Contracting Party to the Agreement

33. Cf. Higher Regional Court of Munich ZVertriebsR 2015, 256, 257 et seq.; *see* [5.1.3. Consequences of a Termination] below, for another example.
34. Cf. Higher Regional Court of Munich GRUR-RR 2006, 363, 366.
35. Cf. Federal Court of Justice GRUR 2020, 57, 62, paragraph 56.
36. Cf. Ingerl/Rohnke in: Ingerl/Rohnke, MarkenG, § 30 paragraph 113; Pahlow in: Ekey/Bender/Fuchs-Wissemann, MarkenR, § 30 paragraph 81; Taxhet in: Kur/v. Bomhard/Albrecht, BeckOK MarkenR, § 30 paragraph 169; Hildebrandt, Marken und andere Kennzeichen, § 24 paragraph 36; Lange, Marken- und Kennzeichenrecht, § 4 paragraph 2101.
37. Cf. Federal Court of Justice GRUR 2016, 201, 205, paragraph 53.
38. Cf. Federal Court of Justice GRUR 2020, 57, 62, paragraph 56; Federal Court of Justice GRUR 2016, 201, 205, paragraph 53.
39. Cf. Ingerl/Rohnke in: Ingerl/Rohnke, MarkenG, § 30 paragraph 113.
40. Cf. Federal Court of Justice GRUR 2020, 57, 62, paragraphs 58 et seqq.
41. Cf. CJEU GRUR 2009, 1159, 1161; CJEU GRUR Int 2002, 147, 151, paragraphs 46 et seq.; Regional Court of Düsseldorf GRUR-RS 2016, 120584, paragraph 26; Ekey in: Ekey/Bender/Fuchs-Wissemann, MarkenR, § 24 paragraph 39.

on the European Economic Area. The rule of exhaustion shall prevent the trademark owner from being able to control the further distribution channels of the trademarked goods once these goods are in the market with the trademark owner's consent. However, the owner of the trademark does not give his consent to sell goods or services which are, for example, of a lower quality as agreed on in the licence agreement, see section 30(2) no. 5 of the German Trademark Act. In such case, the licensee would put the trademarked goods on the market without the consent of the owner of the trademark.[42] Thus, in cases where the products do not meet the quality criteria, have been altered, or are sold via distribution channels that are detrimental to the image of the trademark, the owner of the trademark may take legal actions against the licensee and even against third parties (e.g., distributors).[43]

6. TRADEMARK LICENCES AND INSOLVENCY

Insolvency law becomes relevant when the licensor or licensee becomes insolvent and gets under administration. As mandatory law, the regulations of the German Insolvency Statue cannot be excluded or limited in the trademark licence agreement.

6.1. Position and Options of the Insolvency Administrator

In German insolvency proceedings, the insolvency administrator (legally) steps into the position of the insolvent party upon the opening of the insolvency proceedings (section 80 of the Insolvency Statute). According to section 103(1) of the German Insolvency Statute, the insolvency administrator can choose between performance and non-performance of a mutual contract of the debtor if the mutual contract was not completely fulfilled by the debtor and its other party at the date when the insolvency proceedings were opened.

6.2. Insolvency of Licensor

Thus, if the licensor is insolvent and the administrator figures he might get a higher licence fee, he will choose non-performance. In such case, the claims of the licensee will not lapse, but they will be unenforceable.[44] The licensee loses the right to use the licensed trademark.[45] If the insolvency administrator chooses non-performance of the contract, the licensee can only assert claims (for non-performance) as an insolvency

42. Cf. CJEU GRUR 2009, 593, 596, paragraphs 50 et seq.; Schulte-Beckhausen, Markenlizenzverträge, paragraph 134.
43. For further exceptions to exhaustion according to section 24(2) German Trademark Act, *see* [4.1. Legal Actions by Licensor Against Third Parties] below and Steudtner in: Kur/v. Bomhard/Albrecht, BeckOK MarkenR, § 24 paragraphs 35–81.
44. Cf. Federal Court of Justice GRUR 2016, 201, 204, paragraph 43; Federal Court of Justice GRUR 2006, 435, 437, paragraph 22.
45. Cf. Pahlow in: Ekey/Bender/Fuchs-Wissemann, MarkenR, § 30 paragraph 86; Berger, GRUR 2013, 321, 323; Hombrecher, WRP 2006, 219; Slopek, WRP 2010, 616, 618.

creditor (section 103(2) sentence 1 of the Insolvency Statute). Thus, German insolvency law does not generally protect a trademark licensee which is a relevant risk to bear in mind when choosing a licensor.

However, the administrator may not choose non-performance if both parties have already fulfilled their main contractual obligations (payment of the licence fees and the granting of the licence) and if there are no remaining secondary obligations (e.g., use of trademark) at the time of the opening of the insolvency proceedings.[46] Such insolvency-proof licences will however be the exception rather than the rule. Against this background, licensees can try to minimise insolvency risks by legal workarounds.[47] However, it is not entirely clear to which extent contractual constructions in licence agreements trying to make the licence 'insolvency-proof' are valid. Moreover, the owner of the trademark will often not be keen to agree to any unfavourable workarounds.

6.3. Insolvency of Licensee

In case of insolvency of the licensee, the licensor will generally try to terminate the trademark licence agreement. However, after the opening of the insolvency proceedings was requested, the owner of the trademark may, however, not terminate the licence agreement because of default in the payment of licence fees arising before the opening of the insolvency proceedings was requested (section 112 no. 1 of the Insolvency Statute analogously) or because of degradation of the debtor's financial situation (section 112 no. 2 of the Insolvency Statute analogously).[48] Thus, the licensor should include a termination right in case of the degradation of the licensee's financial situation irrespective of the opening of insolvency proceedings, which must however be executed before the opening.[49] Moreover, the licensor may terminate the licence

46. Cf. Federal Court of Justice GRUR 2016, 201, 204 et seq., paragraph 45; Federal Court of Justice GRUR 2006, 435, 437, paragraph 21; Regional Court of Munich I ZIP 2014, 2406, 2407 et seq., 2410; Regional Court of Munich I GRUR-RR 2012, 142, 145; Haedicke, WRP 2013, 1534 et seq.; According to Pahlow in: Ekey/Bender/Fuchs-Wissemann, MarkenR, § 30 paragraph 100, such legal situations will be unusual because in most cases, there will be important additional duties of the parties; *see* Rieken/Conraths, MarkenR 2013, 63, 64 et seq. for difficulties concerning this kind of legal construction.
47. Cf. Berger, GRUR 2013, 321, 327 et seq.; Hombrecher, WRP 2006, 219, 220 et seq.; Koehler/Ludwig, WRP 2006, 1342, 1343 et seqq.; Rieken/Conraths, MarkenR 2013, 63, 64 et seq., Slopek, WRP 2010, 616, 619 et seqq.; Wimmer, ZIP 2012, 545, 548 et seq.; Ganter, NZI 2011, 833, 837 et seq. (regarding patent licence agreements); Pahlow in: Ekey/Bender/Fuchs-Wissemann, MarkenR, § 30 paragraph 90; Federal Court of Justice GRUR 2006, 435, 436 et seq. (regarding software licences).
48. Cf. Hacker in: Ströbele/Hacker, MarkenG, § 30 paragraph 108; Pahlow in: Ekey/Bender/Fuchs-Wissemann, MarkenR, § 30 paragraph 102; Groß, Der Lizenzvertrag, paragraph 495; Schmoll/Hölder, GRUR 2004, 743, 744 et seq. (regarding patent and know-how licence agreements).
49. Cf. Schmoll/Hölder, GRUR 2004, 743, 744 (regarding patent and know-how licence agreements).

agreement if the (insolvent) licensee does not fulfil his obligation to use the trademark (*see* section 2.7. Obligation to Use above).[50]

6.4. Sublicence Agreements and Insolvency

In case of insolvency of the licensor, the non-performance of the main licence agreement by the insolvency administrator might lead to the termination of the sublicence agreement.[51] However, in case of the insolvency of the licensee, the insolvency administrator may not perform the main licence agreement, but fulfil the sublicence agreement or vice versa (section 103 of the Insolvency Statute).[52] If the insolvency administrator decides for non-performance of the main licence agreement and performance of the sublicence agreement according to section 103(1) of the Insolvency Statute, the owner of the trademark has the above-mentioned claims against his former licensee, who sublicensed the trademark (*see* section 2.11.3. Termination of sublicence agreements above).[53]

50. Cf. Hacker in: Ströbele/Hacker, MarkenG, § 30 paragraph 108; Schmoll/Hölder, GRUR 2004, 743, 746 (regarding patent and know-how licence agreements).
51. Cf. Seegel, CR 2013, 205, 210 et seq.
52. Cf. Federal Court of Justice GRUR 2012, 916, 918, paragraph 26; criticising the judgment of the Federal Court of Justice: Pahlow in: Ekey/Bender/Fuchs-Wissemann, MarkenR, § 30 paragraphs 92 et seq.
53. Cf. Federal Court of Justice GRUR 2012, 916, 918, paragraph 26.

Japan

Seiro Hatano, Masakatsu Nagashima & Kenji Marusumi

1. INTRODUCTION TO TRADEMARK LICENSING IN JAPAN

In Japan, a trademark right is a property right granted under the Trademark Act and a trademark owner has the exclusive right to use the trademark (Article 25 of the Trademark Act). Based on this exclusive right, the trademark owner has the right to grant a trademark licence to a third party. While the Trademark Act does not provide detailed provisions applicable to a trademark licence agreement, there are some provisions in relation to the basic rules of trademark licences. The Civil Code governs contractual relationships and also applies to trademark agreements, but the Civil Code only provides for general contractual principles and does not set forth any specific provisions applicable for licence agreements themselves. Therefore, this chapter provides an overview of trademark licences and certain major legal issues associated with trademark licences in light of Japanese law.

2. LICENCE REGULATION UNDER THE TRADEMARK ACT

2.1. Overview of Licence System in Japan

Upon a trademark owner granting a licence, the trademark licence immediately becomes effective between the licensor and the licensee in accordance with general contractual principles under the Civil Code. While it is common for a trademark licence to be granted by a written agreement, there is no requirement for a formal agreement and it can instead be made orally, and the court may even find an implied licence under certain circumstances. Although registration is not mandatory in order for the licence to be valid, registration is required in order to assert such licence against a third party and to claim the exclusivity of the exclusive licence against a third party (Registered Exclusive License '*Senyo-Shiyo-Ken*', see section 2.2).

The scope of a trademark licence is largely dependent on the agreement between the trademark owner and licensee and any provisions may be included in the trademark licence agreement, although certain provisions may be invalid or unenforceable if they are not in compliance with the other applicable laws such as competition laws. It should also be borne in mind that a trademark licence is a contractual right, and if the licensee wishes to claim its rights under the licence against a third party, registration of the licence is required as mentioned above.

The licence will continue until terminated or expired according to the licence agreement. Even if the registration of the subject trademark is expired, this will not directly cause the termination of the licence unless it is specifically provided in the licence agreement.

2.1.1. Subject of Licence Agreement

The trademark right holder may establish a registered exclusive licence and non-exclusive licence to the trademark right (Articles 30 and 31). Although the provisions of the Trademark Act assume that the subject of the licence agreement is a registered trademark, it is commonplace for non-registered marks, including those applied for registration but not yet registered, to be the subject of the licence agreement.

It should be noted that such a licence agreement for non-registered marks encompasses only a contractual right, which means that the licensee cannot be protected by the provisions of the Trademark Act.

On the other hand, regardless of trademark registration, if the mark is well known among consumers, such a mark may be protected under the Unfair Competition Prevention Act and the licensee may be able to rely on the precedents under such Act in certain circumstances.

2.2. Registered Exclusive Licence (*Senyo-Shiyo-Ken*)

2.2.1. Requirements for Establishing a Registered Exclusive Licence

The trademark right holder may establish an exclusive right to use the trademark to which he/she holds the right (Article 30). A registration with the Japan Patent Office (JPO) is required in order for a registered exclusive licence to take effect (Article 30 (4) of the Trademark Act, Article 98 (1)(ii) of the Patent Act).

Where a trademark is jointly owned, approval from all joint owners is required in order to establish an effective licence agreement (Article 30 (4) of the Trademark Act, Articles 77(5) and 73(3) of the Patent Act).

Note that it is possible to grant exclusivity rights to the licensee in a licence agreement without registration of a registered exclusive licence ('*Senyo-Shiyo-Ken*'). In that case, however, such licence only encompasses a contractual right and is effective only between the parties of the licence agreement, and it is therefore not possible to enjoy the legal effect provided under the Trademark Act for the registered exclusive licence ('*Senyo-Shiyo-Ken*') (*see* 2.3.5).

2.2.2. *Effect of a Registered Exclusive Licence*

A registered exclusive licence holder (i.e., the registered exclusive licensee) shall have an exclusive right to use a registered trademark in connection with the designated goods or designated services to the extent provided by the agreement under which such right is granted (Article 30 (2)). Once an exclusive licence is registered, the trademark owner (i.e., licensor) is prohibited from using the trademark without authorization from the exclusive licensee (proviso to Article 25).

A holder of the registered exclusive licence is entitled to enforce its exclusive rights as the trademark owner; i.e., the exclusive registered licensee can claim an injunction against those who use the registered trademark without permission from the registered exclusive licensee (Article 36 (1)) and also bring a claim for damages caused by the infringement. An infringer of a registered exclusive licence is also subject to criminal penalty (Articles 78 and 78-2).

When the exclusive licence is registered, it is not clear under the Trademark Act whether the trademark right holder who has granted a registered exclusive licence ('*Senyo-Shiyo-Ken*') to a licensee may file a lawsuit for injunctive relief against an infringer by its own. While the trademark right holder is prohibited from using the trademark by himself/herself without authorization from the licensee of the exclusive licence (the proviso to Article 25), nothing otherwise is stipulated in the Trademark Act.

In this regard, while this was a case relating to patents, the Japanese Supreme Court has ruled that a patent holder can demand injunctive relief even after it has granted a registered exclusive licence to a licensee. The Supreme Court explained that the Patent Act does not explicitly limit the right of a licensor of the registered exclusive licence and a patent holder in this regard, and the interest of the patent holder could be unreasonably jeopardized by the infringement if the licence royalties were based on the revenue of the licensee (given that such infringing goods may be substitutions of patented products, which cause the revenue of the licensee to be decreased) or if a patent right holder restarts using the patent after termination of the registered exclusive licence. Since these reasons could also, in theory, be adapted to trademark cases, this rule of the Supreme Court is likely considered a persuasive precedent even for trademark cases.

2.2.3. *Disposal of a Registered Exclusive Licence*

A registered exclusive licence may be transferred only where the consent of the trademark right holder is obtained or where the transfer falls under general succession, including inheritance (Article 30 (3)). In addition, the consent of the trademark right holder is necessary where a licensee of a registered exclusive licence may establish a right of pledge or grant a non-exclusive licence on its exclusive licence to a third party (Article 30 (4) of the Trademark Act, Article 77 (4) of the Patent Act).

The duration of a trademark right is basically ten years, and only the trademark right holder may renew it by filing an application for registration of renewal (Article 19 (2)). Therefore, a licensee of a registered exclusive licence may not renew the trademark right by itself (it should be noted that the owner may pay the registration fee (excluding the registration fee due and payable at the time of filing a request for renewal of registration) even if this goes against the intention of the person by whom the said fee is to be paid (Article 41-3 (1))).

2.3. Non-exclusive Licence (*Tsujo-Shiyo-Ken*)

2.3.1. Requirements for Establishing a Non-exclusive Licence

It is not mandatory to register a non-exclusive licence under the Japanese Trademark Act in order for such licence to take effect. Where a trademark is jointly owned, approval of all other joint owners is required in order to establish an effective licence agreement (Article 31 (6) of the Trademark Act, Article 73 (3) of the Patent Act).

2.3.2. Effect of a Non-exclusive Licence

The holder of a non-exclusive licence shall have the right to use the registered trademark for the designated goods or designated services to the extent provided by the agreement under which such right is granted (Article 31 (2)).

The non-exclusive licence merely encompasses a contractual right; however, once it is registered with the JPO, the licensee may assert the effect of its licence against a third party who acquires the trademark subsequent to the registration (Article 31 (4)).

2.3.3. Disposal of a Non-exclusive Licence

A non-exclusive licence may be transferred only where the consent of the trademark right holder (the holder of the trademark right and of the exclusive right licence in the case of a non-exclusive licence granted in connection with an exclusive licence) is obtained or where the transfer falls under general succession, including inheritance (Article 31 (3)).

A licensee of a non-exclusive licence may establish a right of pledge or grant a sublicence thereof only where the consent of the trademark right holder is obtained (Article 31 (6) of the Trademark Act and Article 94 (2) of the Patent Act). It should be noted that registration is required in order for the right of pledge to be asserted against third parties (Article 34 (2)).

2.3.4. Treatment of a Non-exclusive Licence in the Case of Licensor's Bankruptcy

If both the bankrupt and its counterparty under a bilateral contract have not yet fulfilled their obligations by the time the bankruptcy proceedings commence, a bankruptcy trustee may cancel the contract or perform the bankrupt's obligations and request the counterparty to perform its obligations (Article 53 (1) of the Bankruptcy Act). Should a non-exclusive licence agreement be considered to fall under this bilateral contract under this provision, the bankruptcy trustee may unilaterally terminate the agreement for the non-exclusive licence at its discretion. However, registration of a non-exclusive licence can prevent the bankruptcy trustee from being able to terminate the agreement for the non-exclusive licence (Article 56 (1) of the Bankruptcy Act).

Therefore, registration of the non-exclusive licence is effective to secure the licensee's rights from not only the transfer of the trademark right but also the bankruptcy of the trademark right holder. Nevertheless, registration of a non-exclusive licence is not common in practice. In the case where such licence is not registered and the licensor goes bankrupt, the licensee under a non-exclusive licence runs the risk of losing such non-exclusive licence, which may cause significant and detrimental damage for the licensee. This issue has been taken quite seriously in patent licensing practice and resulted in the amendment of the Patent Act.

By way of the amendments to the Japanese Patent Act which took effect on 1 April 2012, registration of a non-exclusive licence was abolished, and non-exclusive licences now have effect on any person who subsequently acquired the patent or the exclusive licence without any registration, as regulated by Article 99 of the amended Patent Act. At that time, there was an argument as to whether the Trademark Act should also be revised to stipulate the same regulation as the Patent Act; however, this amendment was subsequently not made in reference to trademark licence.

2.3.5. *Non-registered Exclusive Licence*

In Japanese licensing practice, some licensees may wish to possess exclusive rights but prefer not to register the licence as a registered exclusive licence ('*Senyo-Shiyo-Ken*'). This may simply be because of the burdensome nature of registration, but some licensees tend to avoid registration of the licence as it could make the licensee's licensing strategy visible to the public. In that case, even if the exclusivity right is set forth in the licence agreement, such a licence should technically be treated as a non-exclusive licence ('*Tsujo-Shiyo-Ken*') under the Trademark Act. Such non-registered exclusive licence is valid and binding between the parties, but the licensee cannot exert its exclusivity rights against a third party.

2.3.6. *Injunction by a Licensee of Non-registered Exclusive Licence*

With regard to injunctions, it is generally considered that a licensee of a non-exclusive licence is not entitled to bring a claim for an injunction because Article 36 (1) stipulates only a trademark right holder and licensee of a registered exclusive licence, not a licensee of a non-exclusive licence, as the subject who can file a lawsuit for injunction; however, the issue here is whether a licensee of a non-registered exclusive licence may initiate an action for injunction since such a licensee may have a substantially similar interest to that of a licensee of an exclusive licence.

In this regard, the courts have denied that a licensee of a non-registered exclusive licence can be a plaintiff for injunction under its own name. Although this was a case involving a design patent ('Hair Brush Case' Osaka District Court, 20 December 1984,

Hanrei-Jiho No. 1138 p. 137), it can also be used in relation to trademark cases. On the other hand, another precedent provided that a licensee of a non-registered exclusive licence may seek an injunction on behalf of a trademark owner by utilizing the 'Obligee's Subrogation Right' under the Civil Code (Article 423 (1) of the Civil Code, Tokyo District Court, 31 August 1965, Hanrei-Times No. 185 p. 209).

2.3.7. Claim for Compensatory Damages by a Licensee of a Non-registered Exclusive Licence

With respect to a claim for compensatory damages, according to the precedents[1], it is likely that a non-registered exclusive licensee will be entitled to bring a claim for damages, although the Trademark Act does not explicitly grant such right.

3. RIGHTS AND OBLIGATIONS UNDER LICENSING AGREEMENT

3.1. Basic Approach to Licensing Agreement

As mentioned above, the Trademark Act provides only the basic rules for licences; thus, the Civil Code governs contractual provisions for a licence agreement. As the principle of 'freedom of contract' applies, parties can set forth any provisions unless they are against public policy or other mandatory provisions. The following are some key legal issues to note and practical tips to consider when entering into a licensing agreement.

3.2. Confirmation of the Status of Trademark Rights

The first step for a licence agreement is to confirm the subject of the licence. The JPO publishes its trademark application gazette, trademark registration gazette and trademark register and makes them available to anyone who wishes to confirm the status of a trademark. This makes it quite easy to confirm such status.

For example, you should confirm whether the trademark is properly registered, whether the licensed trademark rights cover the goods/services on which the licensee wants to use the mark, whether the trademark right is owned solely or jointly, and whether a trial for invalidation is pending, etc.

In addition to the above-described trademark search, the licensee should request the licensor to make representations and warranties under the licensing agreement to the effect that the licensor is legally entitled to the licensed trademark and that it is not infringing upon any third-party rights.

---

1. For example, the 'Hair Brush Case' Osaka *Chiho Saibansho* [Osaka District Court] 20 December 1984, HANJI No. 1138 p. 137, etc.

3.3. Contract Term

3.3.1. Perpetual Licence

In Japan, there is no rule for contractual durations; therefore, the parties to a licence agreement can freely determine the term. Accordingly, perpetual term licences are allowed in Japan.

However, one needs to be aware that the trademark right must be renewed every ten years in Japan and, if the trademark registration is expired, the value of the licence will decrease, especially in the case of an exclusive licence. The mark may possibly be protected under the Unfair Competition Prevention Act as a famous mark after the expiration of the trademark registration; however, expiration of the registration of a trademark will lead to uncertainty regarding the protection of the mark, and moreover, any third party may apply for and register the respective trademark and then request the licensee to cease using the mark. Therefore, in order to secure the rights of the licensee granted under the licence agreement, in concluding a perpetual licence agreement, the licensee should make sure that the licensing agreement has a provision to oblige the licensor to renew the trademark registration in perpetuity.

3.3.2. Doctrine of Continuous Contracts

Once the parties agree to the contract term, either party may terminate the contract at the end of the term, in principle; however, even if the parties agree on the specific term of the licensing agreement, Japanese courts have prohibited them from terminating the agreement as an abuse of rights in order to protect the expectation of a long-term contractual relationship under certain circumstances. Such restriction to termination is known as the 'doctrine of continuous contracts'.

It is generally considered that the 'doctrine of continuous contracts' is applicable in cases where a certain long-term contractual relationship exists, and the termination thereof is considered unreasonable taking into account various elements of the cases, including the purpose of the contract, the period of the term, the history of previous renewals, and the reason for termination of the contract, and the applicability of the doctrine is determined by the court upon a case-by-case basis. Thus, if a licence agreement has continued for a long term, the parties should be aware of the possible application of 'the doctrine of continuous contracts' in the case of termination of the contract.

3.4. Use of the ® Mark

3.4.1. Necessity of Use of the ® Mark

Article 73 of the Japanese Trademark Act provides that the trademark owner or a licensee of a registered exclusive or non-exclusive licence shall 'make efforts' to affix an indication stating that the trademark is registered (the 'indication of trademark registration') pursuant to the provisions of the Ordinance of the Ministry of Economy, Trade and Industry (the 'Ordinance'). In other words, it is not mandatory for the trademark owner or the licensee to affix the indication of trademark registration under Japanese law.

The provisions of the Ordinance provide that the indication shall consist of the words 'registered trademark and the registration number or number of the international registration' (e.g., 'Registered Trademark No. XXX').[2] In Japanese practice, however, the ® mark is commonly used as it enables consumers to acknowledge that the trademark is protected as a registered trademark and thus to prevent unintentional infringement. It also contributes to avoiding the trademark from becoming a generic term.

Therefore, in a licence agreement in Japan, it is common to set forth a provision requiring the licensee to use the licensed trademark together with the ® mark.

It should be noted that the ® mark should not be affixed to a trademark if the mark is not actually registered as a trademark in Japan as this may be considered as a misrepresentation which is restricted under Article 74 of the Trademark Act. Therefore, for unregistered marks, the 'TM' mark or an indication stating 'trademark pending', which does not indicate that the trademark is registered as a trademark, should be used.

3.5. Importance of Monitoring

Article 53 (1) of the Trademark Act stipulates that where a registered trademark or a trademark similar thereto is used by a licensee and is misleading as to the quality of the goods or services or causes confusion in connection with the goods or services of another person, a trial for cancellation of the trademark registration may be filed, unless the holder of the trademark right was unaware of such fact and exercised reasonable care. This provision requires the trademark owner to monitor how the licensee uses the trademark.

Based on this provision, the trademark registration may be cancelled when, for example, the licensee provides inferior goods bearing the licensed trademark that undermine the expectations of consumers. To avoid such consequence, the licensor should set forth various provisions such as specifications of the use or processes to confirm the actual use or conduct an audit to make sure the trademark right is being used in the correct manner.

3.6. Provisions in a Licence Agreement Possibly Conflicting with the Competition Law

3.6.1. Whether the Competition Law Applies to a Licence Agreement for Trademark Rights

Article 21 of the Act on Prohibition of Private Monopolization and Maintenance of Fair Trade (the 'Competition Law') stipulates that the Competition Law shall not apply to acts recognizable as an exercise of rights under the Trademark Act. Under this

2. Article 17 of the Enforcement Regulations of the Trademark Act.

provision, the interpretation of 'exercise of rights' is crucial. This term excludes not only acts which are not the exercise of rights but also acts which are not substantially an 'exercise of rights' even if it seems to be an 'exercise of rights'. In other words, the Competition Law will apply to cases where the act in question impedes free or fair competition beyond the purpose of maintaining the credibility of the trademark. The following are typical provisions that may potentially cause a conflict with the Competition Law.

3.6.2. Inhibition of Parallel Imports

A provision inhibiting parallel imports is one which prohibits a licensee from exporting the licensed goods or selling the same for exportation. The act of importing authentic goods legally sold overseas ('parallel import') is not considered to be substantially illegal in Japan because it does not harm the source-indicating function and quality assurance function of trademarks.[3] Since parallel importation generally has an effect of promoting price competition, it may be against the Competition Law if the parties to a licence agreement attempt to impede parallel imports for the purpose of maintaining the prices of goods or services.

For example, the following cases may be illegal under the Competition Law because they hinder price competition between the goods of the licensee and the parallel imported goods by impeding the distribution of the parallel imported goods:[4]

- obligating the licensor not to sell the goods to a parallel importer or the supplier for the parallel importer even if the licensor receives an offer from them to purchase the goods;
- causing a licensee to promise not to handle parallel imported goods; or
- obligating the licensee to notify the licensor when the licensee finds parallel imported goods and buys them up so that such parallel imported goods do not reach the customers.

In addition to the above examples, one needs to consider what will occur if a licensor requires a licensee to reject a customer's request to repair a parallel imported good or sets different conditions for repair. In this case, it is unlikely to be against the Competition Law so long as there are objectively justifiable reasons that the licensor should give priority to its own products in terms of repair of the products it supplies. However, if it is extremely difficult for a third party to repair parallel imported goods and the licensee refuses to repair solely because the product is a parallel imported good, such refusal may be illegal under the Competition Law as an obstruction to parallel imports for the purpose of price maintenance.[5] Therefore, it is necessary to examine whether there are grounds to justify the difference between the products handled by the licensee and the parallel imports under specific circumstances.

3. Judgment by the Supreme Court (27 March 2003 Minshu 57-2-125).
4. Article 19 of the Antitrust Law; Articles 12 and 14 of the Designation of Unfair Trade Practices.
5. Article 19 of the Antitrust Law; Article 14 of the Designation of Unfair Trade Practices.

3.6.3. *Resale Price Maintenance*

A resale price maintenance clause sets a minimum resale price or a pricing range for the goods or services bearing a licensed trademark. As it is important for a trademark owner to maintain its brand image and retail price is an important factor in the value of a brand, the licensor has an incentive to set a minimum resale price in the licence agreement.

However, the licensee's free determination of the resale price for the goods depending on market conditions is of the utmost importance in order to maintain competition in the market, and this type of clause is therefore highly likely to fall under a violation of the Competition Law.[6]

The issue in practice is whether a licensor can lawfully indicate a specific price or price range as a 'reference price' or 'recommended price'. Such indication is not illegal per se; however, it may constitute a violation of the Competition Law if a licensor imposes any substantial sanctions on a licensee when the licensee does not follow such indication.

3.6.4. *Restrictions on Raw Materials*

In some licensing agreements, there is a clause which restricts the supplier and/or quality of raw materials, parts, etc., used for products bearing the licensed trademarks. While this type of clause is not intrinsically against the Competition Law to the extent it is necessary for any reasonable reason, such as the need to maintain the credibility of the licensed trademarks or the safety of the goods or for protection of confidential information, if such restriction is not found to be reasonable or is imposed beyond the level necessary, it may be illegal under the Competition Law due to preventing the licensee from trade opportunities with other suppliers of alternative raw materials.[7]

3.6.5. *Market Allocation*

In some licence agreements, a licensor may limit the sales territory of each licensee. Even in this case, such limitation is likely to be legitimate if price competition within the territory is substantially ensured, such as if there are two or more distributors of the licensed goods in the territory or consumers can easily move between the territories.

In addition to the restriction on the territory, the quantity of sales, customers, etc., may be subject to restriction under a licence agreement; however, if there are no reasonable grounds to justify such restrictions causing an unreasonable limitation on the business activities of the licensee, this may also constitute an unfair trade practice.

6. Article 19 of the Antitrust Law; Article 12 of the Designation of Unfair Trade Practices.
7. Article 19 of the Competition Law; Articles 10, 11 and 12 of the Designation of Unfair Trade Practices.

3.7. Licensor's Product Liability

Under the Japanese Product Liability Act (the 'PL Act'), the following types of entities and persons are liable for damage to life, limb or property of others which is caused by defects in the delivered products:[8]

(a) any person or entity who has manufactured, processed or imported the product in the course of trade;
(b) any person or entity who: (i) provides its name, trade name, trademark, or any other indication (collectively, 'representation of the name') on the product as the manufacturer of the product, or (ii) provides the representation of the name on the product which misleads others into believing that it is the manufacturer of the product; and
(c) in addition to the persons or entities listed in the preceding items, any person who provides the representation of the name on a product that can be regarded as the substantial manufacturer thereof, considering all relevant facts such as the way of manufacturing, processing, importing or selling the product.

The issue here is whether a licensor in a trademark licence agreement is liable for the damage which is caused by products bearing the licensed trademark. Since the licensor is not categorized in (a) above, it is important to consider whether the licensor falls under category (b) or (c).

As to category (b) (i), since the licensee of the trademark is usually indicated as the manufacturer, it is rare for the licensor to fall under this category. On the other hand, as for (b) (ii), the licensor may fall under this category, taking into consideration various circumstances such as the characteristics of the product and how it is distributed in the market. For example, in the case where a very small item does not state 'Licensor XXX' but merely bears the licensor's trademark, there can be an appearance as if the licensor was a manufacturer of the product.

With regard to category (c) above, the licensor can fall under such category not only when it authorizes the use of its trademark on the product but also when it plans the product and provides instructions on how to manufacture the product. For example, when a parent company grants a licence to its subsidiary for a trademark that the parent company controls in a unified manner, the parent company may be liable under the PL Act as a substantial manufacturer of such products due to its influence in the planning or design thereof.

As described above, a licensor may be liable under the PL Act in certain conditions and should therefore take the following measures to mitigate against unexpected liability:

8. Articles 2(3) and 3 of the PL Act.

- include a provision describing how to use the licensed trademark and how to monitor such use in the licence agreement, and then actually monitor whether the licensee complies with such provision;
- set out a provision that requires the licensee to indemnify the licensor against any loss, damage, cost or expense caused by any third party's claims against the licensor in connection with the products in the licence agreement;
- add a quality assurance clause which enables the licensor to control the quality of products; and
- oblige the licensee to buy product liability insurance.

4. RIGHTS AND OBLIGATIONS AFTER TERMINATION OF LICENCE AGREEMENT

4.1. General Rules

As a matter of contract, the rights and obligations incurred under a licence agreement generally extinguish at the time such agreement terminates. Therefore, it is common to stipulate a grace period allowing the licensee to use the trademark for the purpose of inventory clearance sales.

If the licensee has granted a sublicence, the termination of the licence agreement will not only affect the licensee but also cause the sub-licensee to lose its rights and may result in the licensee becoming liable for default in connection with the sub-licence agreement. Therefore, it is important to set forth provisions as fully as possible to cover the treatment of the trademark after termination of the licence agreement.

4.2. Ownership of Trademark after Termination of Licence Agreement under Which Licensee Obtains Registration of Licensor's Trademark in Japan

In some cases, a licensor grants a licence for a trademark that is unregistered in Japan and allows the licensee to file an application for and obtain its trademark registration in Japan under the licensee's name. In such cases, the ownership of the licensed trademark may become an issue after termination of the licensing agreement. The issue, in other words, is whether the licensee is obligated to transfer the trademark registration to the licensor after the end of the licence agreement.

As the Japanese Trademark Act has no provision regulating the licensing of unregistered trademarks, the decision on which party should own the trademarks basically depends on the agreement between the licensor and licensee. Therefore, an issue may arise where the licence agreement does not clearly specify which party owns the rights to the trademarks after the termination. The licensor will probably seek the transfer of the registered trademarks, alleging that the licensee is only the nominal and temporary owner of the trademark registrations under the licensing agreement (i.e., the substantial owner of the trademarks is the licensor). On the other hand, the licensee may claim that it is the owner of the registered trademark and that it has no duty to transfer it to the licensor since the registered trademark is not covered by the licence agreement.

The *'TROY'* case is the leading case regarding this issue.[9] In this case, an American corporation (the licensor) which had been selling sportswear with the trademarks including 'TROY' granted a licence to a Japanese corporation (the licensee) to use the trademarks. The licensor allowed the licensee to become the registered holder of the licensed trademarks, and thus the licensee registered four trademarks; however, the licence agreement did not clearly specify the trademarks (a related clause only stated that the licensor granted a licence to use the licensor's trademarks, including marks identical therewith and altered) and did not indicate which party would be the owner of the trademarks after termination of the licence agreement. Upon termination of the licence agreement, the licensor requested the licensee to transfer the four registrations of the trademarks to the licensor and to stop using the trademarks.

The court held that one of the four trademarks belonged to the licensee, but the remaining three trademarks belonged to the licensor and ordered the transfer of the registrations of such three trademarks and an injunction against the licensee's use thereof.

To reach this conclusion, the court took into account all of the relevant facts such as the purpose of the licence agreement, the process of reaching the agreement and the words and behaviour of both parties. The reasoning was that, based upon the interpretation of the agreement, the subject of the licence agreement would be *the trademarks designed by the licensor to be used by its own and used now and in the future including the same or similar marks therewith ideologically*, and the licensee was therefore obliged to transfer the trademarks which were the subject of the licence agreement. On the other hand, the licensee could keep the trademark which was not the subject of the licence agreement because *a trademark which the licensee designed and increased its value as a result of its marketing efforts should belong to the licensee.*

According to this case, the following points should be noted in allowing the licensee to apply for registration of the licensed trademark:

- clearly specify the scope of the specification, design, and variation of the licensed trademark;
- confirm that the substantial owner of the trademark which is applied for registration in Japan is the licensor and that the licensee is only the nominal and temporary owner of the trademark; and
- oblige the licensee to transfer the licensed trademarks to the licensor upon termination of the licence agreement.

9. 'TROY Case' Osaka *Koto Saibansho* [Osaka High Court] 10 December 1985, MUTAISHU 17-3-614.

Mexico

Zarina Beltrán[*]

1. INTRODUCTION TO TRADEMARK LICENSING IN MEXICO

1.1. Legislation on Trademark Licensing in Mexico

The Mexican legal system is based on civil law. The license agreement will be governed by and subject to the terms agreed by the parties, as well as by the provisions set out in the new Federal Law of Protection of Industrial Property Law (FLPIP) and its implementing Regulation and, for aspects not regulated in the FLPIP, the general rules of the Federal Civil Code and the Commercial Code. The government agency in charge of applying the FLPIP is the Mexican Institute of Industrial Property (IMPI).

The FLPIP entered into full force on November 5, 2020.

1.2. Trademarks Subject to the License Agreement

The FLPIP provides that not only trademark registrations but also trademark applications can be subject to a license.

Traditional trademarks could only be protected in Mexico, until the amendments to the legislation that entered into force on 10 August 2018. Derived from the amendments, now it is viable to obtain registration for: (1) nontraditional trademarks - sound, olfactory and holographic trademarks - can be registered; and (2) the amendment introduces the possibility of registering as a trademark a plurality of operative and image elements that combine to distinguish products or services in the market, which in the international market is known as trade dress.

* The author would like to thank the following colleagues for their valued contributions to this chapter: Teresa Espinosa, Jesus Colunga, Jose Massas, Francisco Matus, Mónica Roldan and Rodolfo Barreda.

1.2.1. Brand Search

Clearance word searches may be conducted online through the Mexican Institute of Industrial Property (IMPI) database. The word search will provide trademarks that are identical, similar or have a word in common. The results are mostly reliable, but, given that the IMPI takes certain time to update the database, the provided information may not include a trademark that could constitute a legal impediment or data corresponding to possible designations to which Mexico could be subject, pursuant to the Protocol Relating to the Madrid Agreement Concerning the International Registration of Marks.

The information contained in the search result does not constitute an official communication in terms of the FLPIP.

1.2.2. Brand Protection

In Mexico, it is not possible to file multi-class applications; rather, individual applications, per mark and per class, should be filed. If a trademark application has been previously submitted in another jurisdiction, priority may be claimed within six months of the filing date of the foreign application.

The approximate time frame for obtaining the registration of a trademark is three to six months. However, if an opposition is filed by a third party or if the trademark examiner issues an office action to clarify the listed goods or services, or citing an identical or confusingly similar trademark or otherwise objecting to the registrability of the proposed mark, the registration process will be extended up to a year or in some cases even more than a year.

Once the application is filed, it is published for opposition and will be studied by the examiner.

The trademark should be used by the owner or by a licensee to distinguish the products or services for which it was registered. If the owner and licensee do not use the trademark during three consecutive years, a third party could request a nonuse cancelation action based on lack of use.

2. LICENSE AGREEMENT

The FLPIP does not provide a definition of a license per se; however, Article 239 establishes that the owner of a registered or pending trademark may grant, by agreement, a license to use to one or more persons, in relation to all or some of the products or services to which said trademark is applied.

This said, when providing a license, certain aspects must be defined, such as:

(a) the trademarks that will be licensed;
(b) if the license will be exclusive or nonexclusive;
(c) if it will be onerous or royalty-free;
(d) for all or certain goods or services protected under the trademarks;
(e) the territory;
(f) time frame;

(g) if the licensee shall have the power to exercise the legal actions for the protection of the rights over the trademark;
(h) the know-how that may be provided.

It is important to differentiate between a license and a franchise; these concepts should not be confused since a franchise involves different legal requirements that must be fulfilled.

A franchise is defined in Article 245 of the FLPIP, which establishes that a franchise exists when, with a license to use a trademark granted in writing, technical knowledge is transmitted or technical assistance is provided, for the licensee to produce or sell goods or render services in a uniform manner and with the operating, commercial and administrative methods established by the owner of the trademark, to maintain the quality, reputation and image of the products or services distinguished by the trademark.

Additionally, the franchise agreement must comply with minimum legal provisions, and franchisor must fulfill certain legal obligations, such as providing a Franchise Disclosure Document (FDD) to the prospective franchisee, at least thirty business days before executing the franchise agreement. The FDD includes the relevant company information, such as technical, economic and financial information that will allow the prospective franchisee to be able to make an informed decision before entering into the agreement.

After timely delivery of the FDD, no additional requirements must be met before executing the agreement. There is no obligation to register the FDD with the IMPI.

A lack of veracity in the information disclosed in the FDD will entitle the franchisee, in addition to demanding the nullity of the agreement, to claim for losses and payment of damages. This right to claim payment of damages may be exercised by the franchisee within the first year of the execution of the agreement, and the franchisee must be able to prove that the damages arose as a consequence of the lack of veracity in the information contained in the FDD.

Failure to provide the FDD upon request by the prospective franchisee is considered an administrative infraction of the FLPIP. The IMPI may sanction this conduct with an economic fine, temporary or permanent closure of the premises or administrative arrest.

2.1. License Legal Requirement

The FLPIP and its Regulation establish certain legal requirements when granting a license of a trademark. The agreement must be in writing, indicate the name or denomination or business name of the licensor and the licensee, as well as the nationality and domicile of the latter.

Furthermore, the goods sold or the services provided by the licensee must be of the same quality as those manufactured or provided by the owner of the trademark.

In addition, those products or the establishment where the services are provided must indicate the following information:

(a) Name and address of the owner of the registered trademark.
(b) Name and address of the licensee.
(c) The use under license of the registered trademark.

This obligation is in order for the final consumer to be able to identify that the offered goods or services are being provided by a person different than the owner.

As previously mentioned, a license and a franchise are different, and should be treated accordingly. Unlike a license, a franchise agreement must comply with stricter obligations.

According to Article 246 of the FLPIP, franchise agreements must be in writing and contain at least the following minimum provisions:

(a) The geographical territory.
(b) The location, minimum size and investment characteristics of the infrastructure, relating to the premises in which the franchisee shall carry out the activities deriving from the agreement.
(c) If applicable, the inventory, marketing and advertising polices, and the provisions relating to the merchandise supply and to contracting with suppliers.
(d) The policies, procedures and terms for any reimbursement, financing and other considerations that fall within the parties' charge in the terms agreed in the agreement.
(e) The criteria and methods applicable to determining the franchisee's commission and profit margins.
(f) The characteristics of the technical and operational training of the franchisee's personnel and the manner in which the franchisor shall provide technical assistance.
(g) The criteria, methods and procedures of supervision, information, evaluation and valuation of the performance and quality of the services under the responsibility of the franchisor and the franchisee.
(h) The terms and conditions governing sub-franchising, in the event that it is agreed by the parties.
(i) The reasons for termination of the franchise agreement.
(j) The assumptions under which the terms or conditions relating to the franchise agreement may be reviewed and, if applicable, modified by mutual agreement.
(k) Unless otherwise agreed, the absence of an obligation for the franchisee to sell its assets to the franchisor or whoever the franchisor designates at the end of the agreement.
(l) Any provisions regarding the franchisee's obligation to sell or transfer the shares of its company to the franchisor or to make the franchisor a partner in the company.

2.2. Requirement of Recordal of a License

The new FLPIP eliminates the obligation to register the license with the IMPI in order to be binding to third parties.

In Mexico, trademark owners must prove use to prevent a cancelation action by any third party, and the recordal of the license agreement with the IMPI would serve for use of the licensee to be considered as of the owner. However, although recommended, there is no legal obligation to record the license agreement.

In order to be able to record the agreement with the IMPI, an original or a certified copy of the agreement containing the license or authorization of use must be accompanied with the application of recordal. The document must contain the signatures of the parties to the aforementioned agreement, and to maintain certain aspects confidential, a short version of the license agreement may be recorded with the IMPI.

The FLPIP establishes that the agreement may omit the provisions that refer to royalties and other considerations that must be paid by the licensee; those that refer to confidential information, referring to the forms or means of distribution and commercialization of the goods and services. The application for recordal may be submitted by any of the parties involved in the license agreement.

Additionally, if the agreement is in a language other than Spanish, the translation of the document must be accompanied by the application of recordal. If the document is a certified copy, then it must be legalized by means of apostille.

The recordal of the license for two or more pending applications or two or more registered trademarks may be requested through a single promotion, when the licensor and the licensee are the same parties.

Finally, even when the agreement is recorded with the IMPI, it is important to bear in mind that the IMPI is not the authority in charge that will resolve in case of dispute arising from the agreement.

2.3. Enforcement and Cancelation of the Recordal of the License

According to Article 241 of the FLPIP, the cancelation of the registration of a license will proceed in the following cases:

(a) When jointly requested by the trademark owner and the user to whom the license has been granted.
(b) Due to nullity, expiration or cancelation of the trademark registration, or in the case of pending trademarks if their registration is not obtained.
(c) By expiration of its term.
(d) By court order.

Licensee must be aware that certain actions or conducts may result in an Administrative Infringement. The FLPIP establishes several types of conduct that constitute administrative infringements, such as the unauthorized use of a registered mark. For example, if the agreement has expired or has been terminated due to lack of compliance of the obligations under the agreement, to continue with the unauthorized use of the trademarks will result in an Administrative Infringement.

Administrative infringements can be sanctioned with: (1) a fine; (2) temporary closure; and (3) permanent closure. The infringement action is filed with the IMPI, which conducts an investigation. Additionally, a breach of obligations stipulated in the agreement, such as payment of royalties, will incur civil liabilities.

3. CONSUMER PROTECTION

According to the provisions established by the FLPIP, the goods sold or the services provided by the licensee must be of the same quality as those manufactured or provided by the owner of the trademark. In addition, those products or the establishment where the services are provided must indicate the name and address of the licensee, name and address of the owner and the use under the license of a registered trademark.

This obligation is foreseen in order to protect the reputation of the owner and maintain the quality of its products or services. The goods sold or the services provided by the licensee must be of the same quality as of those manufactured or provided by the owner of the trademark. In order to avoid confusion and be specific regarding the quality control, it is common for the licensor to provide a Brand Standard Manual, with the specifications of the goods or services.

Furthermore, the parties must not overlook the legal requirements established by the Consumer Protection Law; this will vary depending on the licensed goods. The currently valid Mexican standards are not aimed to establish quality standards other than those required for the safety of the user. Generally, the standards are primarily addressed to the manufacturer of the product, and therefore, Authorities have the power to impose sanctions on the manufacturer of the goods if they find breaches to the standards. However, even when there is no risk for the owner of the brand to have a sanction imposed, there is a reputational risk that must be taken care of. Therefore, when licensing, it is advisable to establish in the license agreement provisions regarding the quality control and evaluation of goods and services.

Therefore, it should contain a description of the quality standard expected to protect the brand from any reputational harm. Thus, if the Mexican licensee does not comply with the quality requirements and causes a reputational harm, it would have to pay a compensation to the owner.

In Mexico, consumer protection is regulated by the Federal Consumer Protection Law (FCPL) and its Regulations. The FCPL applies to both domestic and foreign companies rendering services or providing goods in Mexico.

According to the FCPL, the consumer is the individual or company that acquires or enjoys goods or services as end user, while the supplier is someone who offers, distributes, or sells a product or renders a service to consumers.

Licensees or franchisees could be deemed as consumers to the extent that they acquire or use goods or services as part of a production process or to provide services to third parties; however, their entitlement for presenting claims is capped to a certain amount, which is yearly updated and for 2020, e.g., it is MXP $561,970.57.

4. FOREIGN EXCHANGE AND TAX

4.1. Foreign Exchange

Mexico does not have foreign currency exchange restrictions. The considerations agreed under a license or franchise agreement could be in either Mexican pesos or a foreign currency. There are certain rules applicable to the actual payment of the consideration. If it is agreed to carry out payment within Mexican territory, the payer could elect to pay with the elected foreign currency or with Mexican pesos using the exchange rate published by the Central Bank of Mexico on the day of payment. Mexico follows the Organization for Economic Co-operation and Development (OECD) international tax standards. Thus, all transactions carried out with foreign residents (related parties or not) should fulfill the requirements of the arm's-length principle. Income earned by foreign residents from a Mexican source is, in general, subject to withholding tax at various rates, which will depend on various factors, such as type of income (royalties, technical assistance), the tax residence of the receiving party, among other circumstances, but, in general, the withholding rate is 25 per cent over gross income. In the case of royalties, the withholding tax rates are between 25 per cent and 35 per cent, depending on the type of royalty paid to the foreign resident. Foreign residents are subject to tax in Mexico for income earned from a source of wealth located in Mexico. Mexico currently has over seventy-five tax treaties in force with other countries, including the United States, the United Kingdom, Canada, Japan, Germany, Spain, France and Switzerland. Mexico is constantly negotiating tax treaties with other countries. In addition, on 7 June 2017, Mexico signed the Multilateral Instrument, which allows it to swiftly amend existing bilateral tax treaties to implement tax avoidance measures developed by the OECD. Tax treaties can reduce taxation or even completely remove the withholdings described above.

4.2. Tax

4.2.1. Licensor Tax Liabilities

A licensor or franchisor resident for tax purposes in Mexico is required to pay income tax on its worldwide income. A legal entity is deemed to be a Mexican resident for tax purposes if its main administration or seat of effective management is located in Mexico. Mexican residents are subject to income tax on their profits at a general rate of 30 per cent. Regarding income from foreign sources, Mexico allows legal entities to credit direct and indirect foreign income taxes capped at the Mexican corporate tax rate, provided the income is subject to tax in Mexico. Licensors or franchisors may deduct only expenses that are strictly necessary to fulfill their corporate purpose, and these include business expenses, certain local taxes and social security contributions, among others. Mexico has controlled foreign corporation rules, whereby income derived from foreign investments must be taxed in Mexico when accrued in the foreign jurisdiction, even if it has not been distributed to the investor. The foregoing applies where income subject to foreign taxation is taxable at a rate of less than 75 per cent of the applicable income tax rate in Mexico or not taxed at all. Mexican transfer pricing rules apply to business transactions entered into by and between related parties. These provisions are based on the arm's-length standard, as Mexico has adopted most of the OECD Transfer Pricing Guidelines for Multinational Enterprises and Tax Administrations.

Additionally, domestic law provides that foreign residents obtaining income arising from a source of wealth located in Mexico are required to pay income tax in Mexico. In the case of income arising from royalties or technical assistance (if the technical assistance qualifies as a royalty (know-how)), the source of wealth shall be considered to be in Mexican territory when the goods or rights for which the royalties or the technical assistance is paid are used in Mexico, or when the royalties or the technical assistance is paid by a Mexican resident or by a foreign resident with a permanent establishment in Mexico. The income tax must be withheld by the person making the payments if this is a Mexican resident (Mexican licensees or franchisees). The income tax withheld or paid by the foreign licensor or franchisor may be creditable in its country of tax residency. If the income for royalties is earned by a foreign licensor/franchisor whose income is subject to a preferential tax regime, the income for royalties shall be subject to a 40 per cent withholding tax rate, without any deductions, rather than at the tax rates indicated above.

4.2.2. Licensee Tax Liabilities

Pursuant to domestic law, the income tax associated with royalties paid to foreign residents must be withheld by the person making the payments if this is a Mexican resident (Mexican licensees or franchisees) or even a foreign resident. If the payment is made by a licensee or franchisee Mexican resident, the licensee or franchisee should withhold the income tax and pay it directly to the Mexican tax authority. In practice, it could be complicated for the foreign withholding party to pay the relevant tax in Mexico since there is no easy mechanism for foreign residents to pay the relevant tax directly. Mexican licensees or franchisees should determine whether the payments for royalties fulfill the Mexican requirements to be deducted as expenses for tax purposes, including in relation to transfer pricing rules.

5. COMPETITION LAW

The economic competition framework in force in Mexico is grounded in Article 28 of the Federal Constitution, and further regulated by the Federal Economic Competition Law (FECL). The agency in charge of enforcing the FECL is the Federal Economic Competition Commission (FECC), although it is enforced by the Federal Telecommunications Institute in the broadcasting and telecommunications sectors.

The FECL applies to economic agents, construed as individuals, legal entities, economic groups and in general any private or public agent involved in economic activity.

The FECL regulates four main types of anticompetitive behavior, namely: (1) absolute monopolistic practices, including hardcore cartel behavior; (2) relative monopolistic practices, which refer to abuses of a dominant position in the market; (3) anticompetitive concentrations or mergers; and (4) barriers to competition.

There are no specific provisions or exceptions applying specifically to licenses or franchises (or e-commerce) in terms of competition enforcement, and as such, these will be governed by general provisions. Because of their nature, however, it is common for license or franchise agreements to include provisions that will be relevant in terms of antitrust assessment and enforcement.

Regarding restrictive covenants, as a general rule, the will of the parties is the governing law of the agreement. That is to say, the parties are free to agree on the terms and conditions to be included in an agreement, provided they are not contrary to law.

Accordingly, any contractual covenants will be governed and subject to the terms agreed by the parties, as well as, in specific cases, provisions set out in the FLPIP and civil and commercial principles.

Notably, Article 5 of the Mexican Constitution grants all persons the right to develop the activity, industry, commerce or job they choose as long as it is legal. However, according to the criteria sustained by the Supreme Court of Justice, restrictive agreements or clauses (e.g., noncompete clauses) may be enforceable as long as they are subject to a determined term and territory, and a consideration is paid in exchange. Nevertheless, enforceability may be subject to a court proceeding, which may be time sensitive, and, as in any proceeding of this nature, results cannot be anticipated.

6. DATA PROTECTION

Following constitutional amendments that included the right to data protection as a basic right of individuals, in 2010 the Federal Law on Protection of Personal Data held by Private Parties was enacted, followed, in 2011, by its Regulations (together with the Data Protection Law). These pieces of legislation – which are complemented by guides issued by Mexico's data protection authority, the National Institute for Transparency, Information Access and Personal Data Protection – apply at a federal level and make up the Mexican data protection legal framework. The Data Protection Law applies to all processing of personal data by private entities or individuals, except when it is processed for personal or domestic use or by credit bureaus.

The parties will be data controllers with respect to certain personal data they process; for example, licensees will be controllers of their employees' personal data, and, in some cases, a franchisor or licensor is a data controller of customer data. In this regard, when processing personal data or any information concerning identified or identifiable individuals, both franchisors and franchisees need to be aware of their obligations and responsibilities, which are more onerous for data controllers. Some of the obligations of data controllers are to: (1) maintain appropriate physical, technical and organizational security measures; (2) provide a privacy notice to all data subjects; (3) collect consent from data subjects, where necessary; and (4) allow data subjects the exercise of their rights (access, rectification, cancelation, objection, etc.). Personal data can be transferred to third countries regardless of the level of protection a country provides if transfers are covered by an agreement that is in compliance with the Data Protection Law and with the privacy notice that was made available to data subjects. Consent from data subjects for the transfer of their personal data is sometimes required. Failure to comply with the provisions of the Data Protection Law may result in hefty fines and, if personal data is processed deceitfully or for profit, penalties of imprisonment may be imposed.

7. SOCIAL MEDIA AND E-COMMERCE

There are no specific regulations or provisions applying to licenses, franchises and social media, nor codes of conducts in this regard; however, social media activity is mainly governed by the Data Protection Law and consumer protection legislation. In addition, certain products which may cause a risk to health such as foods, beverages, tobacco products, alcoholic beverages, medical devices, pharmaceutical products, fertilizers, pesticides, cleaning supplies and cosmetic products are further governed by the General Health Law and its Regulations and could either require a notice or obtain a permit from the Federal Commission for the Protection Against Sanitary Risks to advertise on social media.

E-commerce is a growing activity and the governing legal provisions in our country are contained in Mexican Code of Commerce, Federal Civil Code and Federal Consumer Protection Law, which are complemented with a Mexican Standard of voluntary compliance. These provisions are applicable throughout Mexico for goods and services commercialized in the country regardless of the suppliers' location.

8. TERMINATION

Mexican law differentiates between termination and rescission of an agreement. Termination is the consequence of the expiration of the term, or achievement of its subject matter, while rescission is the consequence of a breach, which might be declared by the nonbreaching party without judicial intervention if this possibility is expressly agreed in the contract. In the case of both termination and rescission, under Mexican law and based on the freedom to contract, the parties can validly agree on restrictive covenants that would survive the termination or rescission of the contract and can be enforced at the request of the interested party.

For franchise agreements, pursuant to the provision of the FLPIP, the franchisor and the franchisee cannot terminate the agreement unilaterally, unless it has been executed for an indefinite time, or there is a just cause for termination. Should the franchisee (or franchisor) wish to terminate the agreement in advance, whether this happens by mutual agreement or rescission, the franchisee (or franchisor) must comply with the requirements and procedures established in the agreement. In the case of a violation of the provisions, the early termination of the agreement made by the franchisor or franchisee will result in payment of the conventional penalties established in the agreement, if any, or compensation for the damage and lost profits caused.

Post-termination of the agreement, certain specific provisions will continue in full force and effect, for example, confidentiality provisions.

9. DISPUTE RESOLUTION

In Mexico, when a dispute exists, the parties can choose to resolve their disputes through the courts (litigation) or by alternative dispute resolution mechanisms, such as arbitration.

If the parties have agreed to submit any resulting disputes to the jurisdiction of any of the local courts of the states of Mexico to be decided under Mexican law, the judicial proceeding will be heard by a local court, generally referred to as a first level or first instance court, which will be responsible for resolving the dispute through a final judgment. This judgment may be challenged through an appeal, which will be decided by a higher-level court, generally referred to as a second instance court. The parties can file a writ of amparo against a final judgment from a second instance court whenever they consider fundamental or constitutional rights to have been violated by an unlawful act or omission by the local courts. The writ of amparo will be heard and resolved by a federal court, which will issue a final judgment.

In the event that the parties have agreed to arbitrate, either through an arbitration clause in the agreement or after the controversy has arisen, the parties will be forced to honor the terms of the arbitration agreement and have their dispute decided by an arbitral tribunal. There are two types of arbitration: ad hoc arbitration and institutional arbitration. It is fairly common for parties to agree to institutional arbitration for commercial and business matters. By submitting to arbitration, the parties agree that their dispute will be decided by an impartial adjudicator, identified as the arbitrator, whose decision will be final and binding to the parties (the award).

Foreign judgments and arbitral awards that do not contravene Mexican law (public order) are enforceable through a procedure of recognition and enforcement that is carried out before a first instance court. As one of the 163 states contracting to the New York Convention, Mexico is obliged to enforce arbitral awards.

Mediation is a nonbinding alternative dispute resolution mechanism available to any of the parties in a franchise dispute, either through any of the mediation centers of the Superior Court of Justice or through other institutions that have certified mediators. Mediation will not proceed if the counterparty does not agree to mediate and resolve the dispute through a settlement agreement between the parties.

In Mexico, as the administrative authority in matters of industrial property, the IMPI is in charge of resolving any claim of Administrative Infringement initiated by a franchisor against any person who violates the provisions of the FLPIP. In this regard, the FLPIP provides for an administrative conciliation process, in which a neutral intermediary (the IMPI), at the request of one or both parties and at any time during the dispute, will strive to provide an alternative solution. However, this conciliatory process is not common in practice.

Russia

Natalia Gulyaeva & Elizaveta Semenova

1. LEGAL OR FORMAL REQUIREMENTS FOR TRADEMARK LICENSING IN RUSSIA

1.1. Licence Recordal and Written Form

Issues of intellectual property are regulated by legal provisions of Part IV of the Civil Code of the Russian Federation (CCR). A definition of a licence agreement is provided in Article 1235 of the CCR: under a licence agreement, one party, the holder of an exclusive right to a result of intellectual activity or to means of individualization (the licensor), shall grant or shall undertake the commitment to grant to the other party (the licensee) the right to use such result or such means within the limits provided for by the agreement. The licensee shall use the result of intellectual activity or means of individualization only within the limits of those rights and by those means as provided for by the licence agreement. The right to use a result of intellectual activity or means of individualization not expressly indicated in a licence agreement shall not be considered as granted to the licensee.

Under paragraph 2 of Article 1235 of the CCR, the licence agreement to an intellectual property asset shall be concluded *in written form*, unless otherwise provided for by the CCR. The licence shall be subject to official registration in cases provided for by paragraph 2 of Article 1232 of the CCR. Failure to conclude the licence agreement in a written form or to meet the requirement on official registration shall entail the invalidity of the licence agreement.

Pursuant to paragraph 2 of Article 1232 of the CCR in cases where the result of intellectual activity or a means of individualization are subject to state registration in accordance with the CCR, assignment of the exclusive right to such a result or to such a means under an agreement, a pledge of this right and the granting of the right to use such a result or such a means under an agreement (licence), as well as the transfer of the exclusive right to such a result or to such a means without a contract are also subject to state registration, the procedure and conditions of which are established by the Government of the Russian Federation.

Paragraph 1 of Article 1490 of the CCR, which specifically addresses trademarks, explicitly provides that 'a license agreement...must be concluded in *written form* and ... [is]...subject *to state registration* with the Federal executive body for intellectual property [emphasis added]'. Thus, Part IV creates the mandatory recordal requirement and the rule according to which a failure to record the licence leads to invalidity of the licence agreement.

Paragraph 37 of the Resolution of the Plenum of the Supreme Court of the Russian Federation dated 23 April 2019 No. 10 'On application of Part IV of the Civil Code of the Russian Federation' (Resolution of Plenum No. 10) also explicitly states that granting of the right under a licence agreement is considered valid from the moment of state registration of granting the right. At the same time, the obligatory relations arising from the agreements, the transfer or grant of rights under which are subject to state registration, arise regardless of state registration (paragraphs 1 and 2 of Article 433 of the CCR).

Moreover, it is not possible to record a licence against a pending application, as the rule on mandatory state registrations assumes that there is a registered intellectual property asset, the transfer or grant of rights to which shall be publicly registered. Thus, licence agreements with respect to the registered intellectual property assets are subject to mandatory registration, which is considered to be a condition for completeness, validity and enforceability of the licence agreements against third parties. In other words, a non-registered licence agreement in relation to the registered intellectual property asset will be incomplete and generally unenforceable against third parties. However, the law does not provide any obligatory deadline within which the licence agreement must be registered in order to be completed.

The mandatory licence recordal, thus, continues to impose substantial burden on companies wishing to expand their business to the Russian Federation, as opposed to the countries where registration is not mandatory.

1.2. Substantial Terms of the Licence Agreement

Based on paragraph 6 of Article 1232 of the CCR, the licence agreement shall provide for:

1) the subject of the agreement by indicating the result of intellectual activity or means of individualization, the right of the use of which to be granted under the agreement, with an indication, in appropriate cases, of the reference number and date of the granting a document confirming the exclusive right to such result or to such means (patent, certificate);
2) ways of use of the result of intellectual activity or means of individualization.

The agreement shall also contain the provisions governing consideration for the trademark use. Specifically, pursuant to paragraph 5 of Article 1232 of the CCR under a licence agreement, the licensee shall be committed to pay the licensor the remuneration provided for by the agreement unless the agreement provides otherwise. In case of absence in a remunerated licence agreement of provisions on the amount of remuneration or on the procedure for determining it, the *agreement shall be considered as not concluded*. In this case the provisions for determination of the price provided for by paragraph 3 of Article 424 of the CCR (where the price for analogous contracts is taken into account) shall not apply.

These terms reveal substance of the licence agreement, and may be taken into account when individuals are trying to circumvent the law by concluding assignment agreement instead of the licence agreement. In this respect, paragraph 37 of the Resolution of Plenum No. 10 states that an agreement providing for the assignment of the exclusive right to the result of intellectual activity or means of individualization, but at the same time introducing restrictions (e.g., by the timing, territory, methods of use of the corresponding result or means) or setting the duration of this agreement, may be qualified by the court as a licence agreement. In the absence of such a possibility, the agreement shall be declared invalid in full or in the corresponding part (Articles 168, 180 of the CCR).

There are also other terms usually included in the licence agreement, which are not essential under Russian law (i.e., their absence does not result in qualification of the respective agreement as not concluded). According to paragraph 3 of Article 1232 of the CCR, the licence agreement shall contain the indication of the territory within which the use of the result of intellectual activity or means of individualization is permitted. If the territory within which use of such result or such means is permitted is not indicated in the agreement, the licensee shall have the right to exercise its use throughout the territory of the Russian Federation.

Based on paragraph 4 of Article 1232 of the CCR, the duration of the licence agreement shall not exceed the term of validity of the exclusive right to the result of intellectual activity or to means of individualization. In case the duration of the licence agreement is not defined in the licence agreement, the agreement shall be considered to be concluded for five years, unless otherwise provided for by the CCR. In case of termination of the exclusive right, the licence agreement shall be terminated.

The transfer of the exclusive right to a result of intellectual activity or to means of individualization to a new rightholder shall not be the ground for change or dissolution of a licence agreement concluded by the previous rightholder.

2. PERMISSIBILITY OF NON-COMPETE AND NON-CHALLENGE CLAUSES

2.1. Non-compete Clauses

Generally, non-compete clauses are not permitted in Russia, and, thus, are considered unenforceable.

However, regulation of the franchise (commercial concession) agreements that are usually based on trademark licensing provides for non-compete clauses. Specifically, according to Article 1033 of the RCC, the contract of the commercial concession may provide for the restrictions on the rights of the parties to this contract, in particular may provide for the obligation of the franchisee not to compete with the rightholder in the territory to which the franchise contract extends in terms of business activity carried out by the user with the use of the exclusive rights belonging to the rightholder.

Additionally, the current trend in antitrust regulation also shows that non-compete clauses, if included in joint venture agreements between entrepreneurs, might be acceptable subject to several conditions. However, the norms that govern competition-restraining agreements (within the scope of which non-competes also fall) explicitly exclude agreements on IP assignment and licensing. Thus, potentially non-compete clauses might form a part of a complex agreement that encompasses provisions on trademark licensing, as well as other matters, but should not be included in the licensing or assignment agreement per se.

As stated in Clarifications of the Federal Antitrust Authority on the procedure and methodology for the analysis of agreements on joint activities dated 7 August 2018 (FAS Clarification) non-compete provisions may be deemed admissible if they: (1) are consistent with the objectives of the joint venture agreement; (2) do not apply to product markets, other than those where the parties to the agreement operate as part of the joint activity; (3) are limited by a reasonable time frame; and (4) do not provide for the exchange of unnecessary information. Furthermore, such non-compete clauses are usually subject to the Federal Antitrust Authorities' approval, if the total value of assets or revenue exceeds the thresholds set in clause 8, paragraph 1 of Article 27 of the Federal law of 26 July 2006 No. 135-FZ 'On Protection of Competition' (Law on Protection of Competition) (e.g., see Decision of the Federal Antitrust Service of Russia dated 07 November 2017 No. AK / 76988/17). The threshold is exceeded if the total value of the assets of the entities establishing the joint venture (assets of their groups of persons) according to the latest balances exceeds RUB 7 billion (approximately EUR 77 million), or the total revenue of such economic entities (their groups of persons) from the sale of goods for the calendar year preceding the year of the conclusion of the agreement exceeds RUB 10 billion (approximately EUR 110 million).

Non-compete obligations should apply exclusively to activities that constitute a subject of the transaction at issue. This means that the parties to the agreement are not limited in the right to carry out any other types of activities and compete with each other in other areas of business, except for activities, for example, carried out as part of a joint venture.

It is worth noting that under part 1 of Article 13 of the Law on Protection of Competition when substantiating the admissibility of non-compete clauses, it needs to be proven that such obligations do not create opportunities for the parties to the transaction to eliminate competition in the relevant market.

Non-competition obligations must be strictly limited in time. Specifically, the term of non-compete clause shall be tied to the time frame necessary for return of the investments and gain of the profit. In accordance with clause 5.3 of the FAS Clarifications, the reasonable duration of non-competition restrictions in the framework of a joint venture agreement is seven years.

It is worth noting that under part 1 of Article 13 of the Law on Protection of Competition when substantiating the admissibility of non-compete clauses, it needs to be proven that such obligations do not create opportunities for the parties to the transaction to eliminate competition in the relevant market. Based on the foregoing, in order to ensure that there is an enforceable non-compete clause, it is preferable to frame the relations between the parties in the form of a joint venture agreement (potentially with the inclusion of provisions on licensing or an undertaking to conclude the licence agreement in the future), bearing in mind the above-mentioned guidelines and the need for authorization from the relevant state authorities.

2.2. Non-challenge Clauses

Under part 3 of Article 4 of the Arbitrazh Procedure Code of the Russian Federation, waiver of the right of appeal to a court is invalid. Thus, generally, undertakings not to pursue judicial remedies are invalid under Russian law. Nonetheless, challenge of the trademark protection concerns administrative procedure, and, thus, there is a dispute in legal doctrine and lack of uniform approach in the judicial practice on the question of whether the right to initiate administrative proceedings, e.g., file a trademark cancellation action, can be waived.

In the past, provisions regarding the obligation not to challenge protection of the trademark were considered invalid in court practice (e.g., in the Ruling of the IP Court of 10 February 2014 in Case No. SIP-192/2013) and the courts, for instance, refused to approve settlement agreements that contained such an obligation.

However, recent developments show that the courts are adopting the opposite approach, where the obligation to abstain from challenging the rightholder's trademark's protection is recognized and upheld (see, e.g., the Ruling of the IP Court of 11 December 2018 in Case No. SIP-584/2018; the Ruling of the IP Court of 29 May 2018 in Case No. SIP-54/2018). At the same time, available judicial practice concerns settlement agreements and does not provide guidelines with respect to the potential enforceability of such clauses incorporated into other types of contracts.

To sum up, the non-challenge clauses with respect to administrative proceedings are not explicitly prohibited by Russian law and, therefore, may be used in the Russian licensing or assignment practice. The licensee's action to the contrary might be considered as a breach of contract containing such a non-challenge clause, or even as an abuse of rights, that may be eventually remedied by the licensor.

3. RULES ON THE LICENSEE'S STANDING TO SUE THIRD PARTIES FOR TRADEMARK INFRINGEMENT

The licensee's legal opportunity to sue third parties for trademark infringement stems from the type of licence agreements they are parties to. Exclusive and non-exclusive licensees have different scope of rights with respect to protection of the licensed intellectual property assets.

The CCR does not provide a non-exclusive licensee with the right to sue third parties for trademark infringement. This is a mandatory rule, which cannot be altered by licence agreements. In other words, a non-exclusive licensee cannot directly deal with the trademark infringement and has to resolve such issues through the rightholder.

On the contrary, according to Article 1254 of the CCR, exclusive licensees can take advantage of almost all claims available to the rightholder, including claims for withdrawal of infringing goods from circulation and claims for destruction of counterfeit tangible media, as well as claims for compensation.

Interestingly, initially, Article 1253 of the CCR granted an exclusive licensee a right to claim liquidation of a legal entity or the cessation of the activities of an individual entrepreneur in case one of these entities violated the rights of the licensee. Subsequently, such an opportunity was recognized as excessive and not in accordance with the nature of the rights of the licensor. Currently, remedies provided by Article 1253 of the CCR can be requested only by the prosecutor.

Despite having access to a wide arsenal of legal instruments regarding IP enforcement, exclusive licensees are entitled to sue third parties when their alleged trademark infringement affects use of the rights granted by the licence agreement. This means that the exclusive licensees' rights to enforce the IP at issue are, in fact, limited by the rights provided by the agreement.

This rule is further elaborated by paragraph 79 of the Resolution of Plenum No. 10, which states that the basis for the licensee's submission of a claim for the recovery of compensation for the intellectual property rights infringement is a violation of the rights the licensee obtained on the basis of the licence agreement, and not the trademark owner's rights.

With this in mind, licensees can protect the rights in the ways provided for in Articles 1250 and 1252 of the CCR (which establishes general rules on different means of protection of the IP rights) only if the infringement at issue affects the granted right to use the trademark (for instance, in a particular way, e.g., via the Internet).

Exclusive licensees are entitled to protect their rights independently from the rightholder to the extent they are entitled to use the licensed intellectual property asset. According to the mentioned paragraph 79 of the Resolution of Plenum No. 10, the exclusive licensee independently challenges the provision of legal protection to other results of intellectual activity and means of individualization if such is in violation of a granted right. The rightholder may be involved in the case (e.g., as a third party to the dispute).

Meanwhile, rightholders who issue an exclusive licence still retain an opportunity to protect their exclusive right, since they remain an owner of the exclusive right, albeit limited by the licence.

There is an unresolved question whether a rightholder and a licensee have a right to sue an infringer simultaneously. If an infringement is still ongoing, prohibitory preliminary or permanent injunctions might be sought by both since both – the trademark owner and the licensee – have an obvious legitimate interest to stop the unlawful actions and to reduce potential harm.

Answering the question becomes much more problematic when both plaintiffs seek damages or statutory compensation: the principle prohibiting double compensation and the principle which entitles the trademark owner to protect their rights seem to contradict each other.

On the one hand, courts leave room for such claims, trying to separate the owner's and the licensee's interests, while, on the other hand, they tend to limit the trademark owner's interest to claim damages given a concurrent interest of the exclusive licensee.

According to paragraph 79 of Resolution of Plenum No. 10, it is not the IP right itself which might be protected by exclusive licensees, but a special interest. Thus, as the Supreme Court concludes, an exclusive licensee has to prove not only a violation of the right to the relevant intellectual property asset but also a violation of its own rights obtained on the basis of the licence agreement to the respective intellectual property asset.

In other words, the holder of an exclusive licence has an opportunity to protect its violated rights, but is not entitled to sue with respect to the infringement of the exclusive right of the trademark owner not granted to the licensee, and even more so not with respect to the entire range of their intellectual property rights. Having issued an exclusive licence, trademark owners retain the opportunity to protect their exclusive rights from violations by all methods provided by the law since they retain the right itself.

Thus, when the violation of an exclusive right affects the rights of the licensee obtained on the basis of a licence agreement, the licensee can protect these rights on its own, to the extent that there is a legal interest for the licensee in such protection. This reasoning presumes the existence of a separate interest of the trademark owner, which might be protected independently from the licensee's interest.

Courts sometimes support the described position, according to which both the interests are qualified for simultaneous protection, but nevertheless take into account the nature of compensation and reduce the amount of damages when satisfying claims of the trademark owner along with those of the licensee. For instance, in Case No. A40-251571/2018 the courts decided that full amount of compensation should be distributed between the exclusive licensee and the trademark owner in parts based on the need to maintain a balance of rights and legitimate interests of the parties, fairness in determining the amount of compensation for violation of exclusive rights, and proportionality of compensation for the consequences of the violation. However, the courts decreased the amount of compensation sought, taking into account, *inter alia*, that the trademark owner did not incur any losses in connection with the infringement, since the licence agreement concluded between them provided for use of the trademark free of charge.

This supports the position that in any case, the court will take into account danger of double redress in lieu of concurrent claims of the trademark owner and the licensee and will reduce the amount of compensation on this basis. Legal ground for such reduction is formed by paragraph 62 of the Resolution of Plenum No. 10, which stipulates that in cases relating to recovery of compensation, the court, as a general rule, determines the amount of compensation: (1) within the limits established by the CCR (subparagraph 2 of paragraph 3 of Article 1252), (2) based on the evidence presented by the parties, (3) in the amount not higher than requested by the plaintiff, given that the latter is expected to submit evidence clarifying on the amount of their actual loss (paragraph 5 of Article 132, part 1 of Article 149 of the CCR). The defendant has the right to challenge both the fact of violation and the amount of compensation claimed by the plaintiff (paragraphs 2 and 3 of part 2 of Article 149 of the CCR). In other words, although the law specifically states that upon claiming statutory compensation, the plaintiff does not have to prove that they have sustained any damages, they yet have to justify the amount of compensation they are seeking.

Thus, when determining the amount of compensation, the court takes into account, in particular, the circumstances associated with the type of violated rights, nature of the infringement, period of unlawful use of the disputed intellectual property asset, guilt of the defendant, probable losses of the trademark owner (or a licensee, dependent on who is acting as a plaintiff) as well as whether the use of the disputed intellectual property asset constituted an essential part of the defendant's business, and makes the decision based on principles of rationality and justice, as well as proportionality of compensation to the consequences of the infringement. All of these factors are assessed by the court.

4. INVALIDATION OF THE LICENSED TRADEMARK

Licensing agreements concluded prior to the decision to invalidate the legal protection of a trademark remain in force to the extent that they were executed at the time of the decision under paragraph 6 of Article 1513 of the CCR. In other words, despite the trademark being cancelled, the licensee is still considered to be using the trademarks lawfully prior to such cancellation with respect to their obligations owed to the licensor. Particularly, all licence fees due at the moment of the trademarks cancellation are to be paid by the licensee.

The basis for this was clarified by the Constitutional Court of Russian Federation in its Ruling No. 966-O-P dated 4 December 2007. The Constitutional Court pronounced that a licensee benefits from use of the invention (in particular, in the form of saving time, material resources, advantages over competitors), and that such benefit justifies the need to pay the licensor the licence payments and, thus, excludes the possibility of applying the rules on unjust enrichment. If the licensee believed that IP protection was granted unreasonably, thus claiming its right to use the licensed IP freely and without the licensor's permission, they could file an objection to the grant of protection instead of entering into licence agreement.

Thus, according to the Constitutional Court, Russian patent law in its constitutional and legal meaning does not imply any possibility of invalidation of existing licence agreements in case of a patent being declared invalid to the extent in which such agreements were executed by the time of declaration of the invalidity. This reasoning also applies to trademark law. For instance, in the Ruling of the IP Court of 17 July 2017 in Case No. SIP-716/2016, the court stated that cancellation of trademarks does not automatically render void all relevant licence agreements entered into before such cancellation, citing the mentioned decision of the Constitutional Court.

In that case, the plaintiff, TERMOPHORE LLC (Main State Registration Number 1035401509010), challenged Rospatent's rejection to grant cancellation actions filed against a series of trademarks containing the 'TERMOPHORE' word element.

The claim was granted since the challenged trademarks were identical to the company name of the TERMOPHORE LLC (Main State Registration Number 1035401509010), exclusive right to which was acquired earlier than the priority dates of the trademarks, as well as due to the fact that the trademarks were registered in relation to similar goods, with respect to which the plaintiff carried out business activities.

This decision was appealed by another company with the same business name, Thermophore LLC (Main State Registration Number 1105405008444), a licensee of the holder of the cancelled trademarks. The company claimed that the court's ruling violated their rights as a licensee. Thermophore LLC (Main State Registration Number 1105405008444) asserted that the plaintiff in this case committed an act of unfair competition, destroying the scheme of use of the annulled trademark.

However, the IP Court did not support Thermophore LLC (Main State Registration Number 1105405008444). It ruled that the court did not make a decision or draw any conclusions about any rights and obligations of Thermophore LLC (Main State Registration Number 1105405008444), which, according to the procedural law, constitutes a ground to overturn a respective court act. Particularly, the court in the appealed decision did not conclude that the licence agreement between the trademark owner and Thermophore LLC (licensee) was invalid or otherwise flawed, and that the agreement was contrary to the law or violated the rights of any person. The IP Court further explicitly stated that a revocation or invalidation of the trademarks does not mean that licence agreements concluded before such revocation or invalidation are null and void, and dismissed the appeal of Thermophore LLC (Main State Registration Number 1105405008444).

5. CONSEQUENCES OF TERMINATION OR EXPIRATION OF THE LICENCE AGREEMENT

Under paragraph 3 of Article 1238 of the CCR, licence termination *automatically triggers termination of all sublicences*. This consequence is usually considered to follow from the general principle, according to which terms of a sublicence agreement should not exceed terms of the licence agreement, neither in relation to time period nor in relation to scope of uses granted by the rightholder.

Thus, signing additional document in order to terminate the sublicence agreement in case of termination of licence is not required.

However, an automatic termination of sublicence agreements might be seen problematic by many sublicensees, who have complied with the terms of the sublicence and invested much in the relevant IP asset. Thus, the question arises on whether the rights of such sublicensees may and should survive termination of the licence agreement.

Russian law does not recognize such pre-emptive right of a sublicensee to substitute for a licensee in relevant legal relations. This approach is based on an assumption that the personality of a licensee bears a certain degree of personal significance to the licensor, and, thus, protects the rightholder from 'imposition' of the sublicensee's figure by default.

Licensors often agree to negotiate in good faith with former sublicensees of terminated licences and permit the sublicence to survive if the sublicensee assumes financial terms of the licence itself. Moreover, in practice, some licensors might allow automatic survival of sublicences under the condition of the prior explicit approval of such sublicence. In such cases, an implicit consent of the licensor to survival of the sublicence on substantially same terms as the licence might be derived from the very consent to the sublicence itself.

Thus, from the sublicensee's perspective, it is advisable to ensure obtaining the licensor's prior explicit consent to sublicense.

Sublicensing issues highlight fundamental tensions between licensors and licensees; careful consideration of these issues early in the negotiation process is very important to successfully negotiate a licence that will satisfy the business needs of the parties.

Another noteworthy aspect of the problem is whether the sublicensor (licensee under the master agreement) might be held liable for termination of the sublicence agreement in case of termination of the licence agreement.

In its Ruling of 11 August 2016 No. C01-660/2016 in Case No. A56-59702/2015, the IP Court seemed to be pointing to the affirmative answer to the posed question.

This case related to the agreement between the two publishing houses, one of which granted another a right to use the IP asset. According to the terms of the agreement, the party, who granted rights to the IP at issue, guaranteed the licensee that there will be no adverse claims from third parties, as well as guaranteed the right to use the IP freely for a certain period of time. The wording of the agreement explicitly stated that the licensor is the owner of the respective IP asset, and nothing in the text implied that the rights are provided under a sublicence.

However, after the agreement's execution, the grantor notified the grantee on revocation of the IP rights to the asset at issue with reference to termination of the grantor's rights under the master licence agreement. The grantee brought a lawsuit, seeking restoration of a non-exclusive (sub)licence and access to the IP asset from the grantor.

The IP Court ruled that the grantor (defendant) guaranteed the grantee (plaintiff) that they are the owner of all rights transferred under the contract and that there are no obligations of the defendant that prevent the plaintiff from using the IP. The court also noted that the defendant failed to prove that the agreement at issue can be qualified as a sublicence, as well as did not provide evidence of the defendant's lack of the exclusive rights to the works at issue. Due to this, according to the IP Court, the situation should be governed by the norms regulating licence agreements, under which the licence should survive transfer of the licensed IP rights from one rightsholder to another. While the conclusion of the court is mostly driven by the failure of the defendant to actually prove that their title to the copyrighted work at issue now lapsed, the ruling highlights the need for the licensees to be ready to prove the sublicence nature of the agreements between them and their sublicensees. Otherwise, the termination of the respective contracts (which would be in line with the law if the sublicence nature thereof is explicit) will be held unlawful.

Sweden

Stojan Arnerstål

1. INTRODUCTION TO TRADEMARK LICENSING IN SWEDEN

The Swedish Trademark Act (SFS 2010:1877) was adopted in 2010 and entered into force on 1 July 2011. The Act has later been updated in connection with the transposition of the EU Directive (2015/2436) approximating the laws of the Member States relating to trademarks. Article 25 of the Directive is the main provision dealing with licensing of trademarks, which has been transposed in Chapter 6, section 4 of the Swedish Trademark Act.

The first paragraph of that provision stipulates that the holder of a trademark may grant another party a right to use the trademark (licence) for a part of, or all, the goods and services for which it is protected and for the whole or a part of the country. It is further stated that the licence may be exclusive or non-exclusive and that the licensee may not sub-license the rights without consent from the trademark holder. The provision further sets out under what circumstances the trademark holder is entitled to invoke the trademark rights against a licensee, which is further discussed below in section 3.

Chapter 6, section 5 of the Trademark Act sets out the requirements for recordal of the licence. Such recordal does, however, not have any material effect under Swedish law. As such, the validity of the licence agreement does not depend on a recordal. Further, a recordal is not necessary for the licensee to rely on the rights conferred by the licence agreement vis-á-vis third parties, for example against a party infringing the trademark (see further below in section 6). Last of all, section 2 of Chapter 10 stipulates under which circumstances a licensee is entitled to bring an action for trademark infringement against a third party (see further below in section 6).

For franchise licensing in particular, there exists a particular Franchise Disclosure Act that contains provisions on the franchisor's obligations to provide the franchisee with certain information before the franchise agreement is concluded. Section 3 of the Disclosure Act holds that the franchisor, in due time before the agreement is concluded, shall give the franchisee written information about the agreement and any other necessary conditions that, depending on the circumstances, need to be disclosed. The information, which shall be clear and understandable, shall at least contain:

1. a description of the franchise;
2. information on other franchisees and the extent of their business;
3. information on the compensation that the franchisee shall pay and other economic conditions for the franchise activity;
4. information concerning intellectual property rights that will be granted to the franchisee;
5. information on the goods or services that the franchisee is obligated to buy or rent;
6. information on covenants not to compete that will apply during and after the term of the agreement;
7. information concerning the term of the agreement, conditions for modification, prolongation and termination of the agreement; and
8. information on dispute resolution.

However, the Disclosure Act does not provide any substantive rules or govern the contractual aspects of franchising or the permitted use of the intellectual property rights, once the contract is in place. Other than the few provisions of the Disclosure Act, there is no comprehensive body of legislation covering trademark licences, or any other additional provisions dealing specifically with licences or the legal effects of such agreements. Consequently, the interpretation or analysis of contractual issues and problems in trademark licensing must be assessed from the general perspective of Swedish contract law.

2. CONTRACT LAW AS A BASIS FOR DETERMINING THE LEGAL EFFECTS OF A TRADEMARK LICENCE AGREEMENT

Contract law in Sweden, similarly as the other Nordic countries, is distinguished from most continental European countries due to the lack of a comprehensive civil code. Rather than having a uniform legislative system covering all aspects of contract law, the Swedish model is founded on a set of separate, yet central, acts. These sets of acts constitute the core of contract law, providing guidance on how to navigate systematically through the judicial system. However, the legislation is incomplete. For instance, distribution agreements are not subject to any specific legislation in Sweden, aside from that the sale and purchase of goods are governed by the Sale of Goods Act (SFS 1990:931).

In situations where a contract is silent in relation to a particular obligation, the contract needs to be supplemented by filling the gaps left by the parties. When there is no applicable legislation that provides explicit guidance, the commonly used method under Swedish law is to review regulations and principles applicable to similar types of contracts and apply such principles by way of analogy or to apply general principles of contract law. This is the basic method that would apply also when analysing contractual issues relating to a trademark licence agreement, e.g., when filling gaps. Such method will, nonetheless, also take into consideration additional factors such as contractual interpretation, custom or trade usage, case law and other circumstances relevant in each individual case, taking into consideration the specific risks and characteristics of the contractual object at hand. Thus, analogies constitute one of the multiple steps which arise in each case of resolving a dispute.

The main source for analogies in Swedish contract law is the Sale of Goods Act. This is the closest Swedish law comes to a civil code, as the Act is considered to set out the broader principles of contract law. However, the Sale of Goods Act is not directly applicable for licence agreements since a licence only grants a limited right. In the legal literature, it has been debated whether the principles and systematics set out in the Sale of Goods Act are at all relevant for analysing licence agreements.[1] There is a fundamental distinction between a momentary exchange of obligations in an assignment and a long-term licensing contract where the lasting performance normally causes uncertainty due to the risk of changed circumstances in the future - circumstances which cannot be foreseen at the time the contract was concluded. Even though the Sale of Goods Act can be useful as a starting point when discussing the general principles of contract law and licence agreements, it is generally considered that an assessment by way of analogy must be carried out with caution.

As a complement to the Sale of Goods Act, the Commercial Agency Act (SFS 1991:351)[2] and the Commission Agents Act (SFS 2009:865) are important sources for analogies and for determining general principles of contract law. The Commercial Agency Act applies to commercial agents who, in business activities on behalf of the principal, act independently while promoting the sale and purchase of goods, by forwarding tenders for the principal or concluding agreements in the principal's name. The Commission Agents Act applies in situations in which a commission agent undertakes to sell or buy movable property, on behalf of another person (the commissioner) - but in his own name.

The Acts have traditionally been considered as prominent sources for general law principles as well as constituting a foundation for analogies such as distribution agreements.[3] Based on the lasting exchange of obligations for contractual relationships under these Acts, they are suitable and significant when determining the legal effect of a trademark licence agreement.

In addition to national legal sources, Swedish contract law is subject to an increased influence of international development and harmonization. For example, the Swedish Sale of Goods Act is clearly influenced by the United Nations Convention on Contracts for the International Sale of Goods (CISG). Further, the academic project

1. Bengt Domeij, Patentavtalsrätt. Licenser, överlåtelser och samägande av patent (2010) p. 18 f.; Christina Hultmark, Köplagens tillämplighet på fel i patent (JT 1993/94) p. 690 and Jon Kihlman, Fel. Särskilt vid köp av lös och fast egendom (1999) p. 273.
2. The Act transposes EU Directive 86/653/EEC on the coordination of the laws of the Member States relating to self-employed commercial agents.
3. The Swedish Supreme Court has in NJA 2007 p. 909 (Jehander) and in NJA 2009 p. 672 (Allbröd) pointed out that the Commercial Agency Act gives rise to similar circumstances as for exclusive distribution agreements and can therefore justify an analogous application to such types of contracts.

Draft Common Frame of Reference (DCFR) as well as the Principles of European Contract Law (PECL) are increasingly influencing the development of Swedish contract law and therefore also relevant for discussing and assessing the legal effects of licence agreements.

3. THE DELIMITATION BETWEEN PROPRIETARY TRADEMARK RULES AND CONTRACT LAW

Trademark licences, as all intellectual property licences, are characterized by that the licensed object is intangible, which may result in difficulties when determining the scope as to what usage that is permitted under the agreement. A breach of the licence agreement will result in contractual liability for the licensee. However, a breach of a trademark licence agreement may have both contractual and proprietary implications. If the breach relates to the licensed trademark, trademark law may provide alternative remedies. Consequently, a breach of the agreement can, to a certain extent, result in a proprietary liability for trademark infringement.[4]

The motive for a licensor to invoke proprietary liability is that trademark law may provide alternative sanctions and procedural safety measures, in comparison with a breach of contract. Obtaining a preliminary injunction for trademark infringement can be an effective way of exerting pressure on the licensee. An injunction effectively prohibits the licensee from using the trademark. It would be difficult for the licensee to continue the business activities under the licence if consent to use the trademark is withheld by the licensor. The alternative that enables the licensor to invoke proprietary sanctions clearly represents an advantage in relation to the licensee if compared to other contractual relationships.

The delimitation between proprietary trademark rules and contract law is expressed in Chapter 6, section 4 of the Trademark Act, which transposes Article 25 of the EU Trademark Directive. The provision stipulates:

> The proprietor of a trade mark may invoke the rights conferred by that trade mark against a licensee who contravenes any provision in his licensing contract with regard to:
> 1. the duration of the license;
> 2. the form covered by the registration in which the trademark may be used;
> 3. the scope of the goods or services for which the license is granted;
> 4. the territory in which the trademark may be used; or
> 5. the quality of the goods manufactured or of the services provided by the licensee.

A breach of any of the aforementioned provisions will have the effect that the trademark owner is entitled to choose between invoking contractual liability for breach of the agreement or invoking proprietary liability for trademark infringement. As set out by the CJEU in *Copad* (case C-59/08), the listed provisions are exhaustive. This

4. The differences between invoking contractual and proprietary liability due to a breach of trademark licence agreement under Swedish law are discussed in Stojan Arnerstål, Varumärket som kontraktsföremål (2014) pp. 196 ff.

means that a breach of a contractual obligation not listed in the provision will not trigger proprietary liability, i.e., trademark infringement. For example, if the licensee does not pay the agreed royalties under the licence agreement, the licensor can only invoke rules on contractual breach. The licensor cannot 'withhold' the consent to use the trademark due to non-payment as long as the agreement is in force. However, if the agreement is terminated due to non-payment, any continued use of the trademark after termination may constitute an infringement under p. 1 (the duration of the licence).

It follows from p. 5 above that if a licensee breaches a provision concerning the quality of the goods manufactured or services provided, the licensor may invoke the rights conferred by the trademark. The rationale of the rule is based on the quality function of the trademark. The rule safeguards the trademark owner's interests as it provides additional control over the goods or services bearing the trademark.[5]

One important aspect of trademark law is that the trademark must offer a guarantee that all goods bearing it have been produced under the control of a single undertaking which is accountable for their quality.[6] Thus, trademark law is based on the notion that there is one undertaking that ultimately bears responsibility and exercises control over the goods and services placed on the market under the trademark.[7] For licensing, the licensor can control the quality of the licensee's production by including obligations in the trademark licence agreement requiring the licensee to comply with certain instructions or specifications, and by providing the licensor the possibility to verify such compliance.[8]

A further rationale is that it protects consumer interests because it constitutes a mechanism for the trademark owner to ensure the quality level of the goods or services in relation to consumers and end-users who enjoy the goods or services. It is therefore considered reasonable that the trademark proprietor is entitled to invoke sanctions provided by trademark law if the licensee manufacturers or provides defective or substandard goods or services.[9]

Given that the provision expressly refers to 'the quality of the goods manufactured', it would be easy to conclude that its application is limited to tangible properties of the goods, that is to say which involve the features obtained in the production process. Such an interpretation would be in line with how the quality function of the trademark has traditionally been perceived.[10] However, the provision is not construed that strictly. The reference to quality includes regard to abstract properties of the trademark, a question that was discussed in *Copad*.[11] The case pertained to an

5. Cf. Stojan Arnerstål, Varumärket som kontraktsföremål (2014) pp. 219 ff.
6. Cf. CJEU Case C-9/93 (Ideal Standard) p. 37.
7. Cf. Stojan Arnerstål, Varumärkesanvändning (2018) p. 219.
8. See also section 5 below, regarding the notion of quality control for trademark licences under Swedish law.
9. The breach of Article 22(2) EUTMR also has implications for when the trademark rights vested in the goods are exhausted in accordance with Article 13 EUTMR. Cf. CJEU case C-59/08 (Copad) paragraph 50.
10. Cf. Stojan Arnerstål, Marknadsidentitet, irrationella konsumenter och varumärket som en kvalitetsgaranti (Nordic Intellectual Property Review 2015/4) pp. 401 ff.
11. CJEU case C-59/08 (Copad).

interpretation of Article 25(2) (previously Article 8) of the Trademark Directive. The principles set forth in the case have important implications for trademark licences.

The facts of the case concerned the company Christian Dior, which had entered into a trademark licence agreement with the company SIL in respect of the manufacture and distribution of luxury corsetry goods bearing the Christian Dior trademark. The agreement stated that SIL was only entitled to distribute the goods within a selective distribution network. In the agreement, the licensee agreed not to sell the licensed products to wholesalers and discount stores, etc., without prior written consent from the licensor. The objective of the restriction was to protect the repute and prestige of the trademark. However, due to economic difficulties - and in spite of the restriction and the lack of consent - SIL sold licensed goods to Copad, a company operating a discount store business.

Christian Dior argued that the prohibition on sales outside the selective distribution network aimed to protect the quality of goods. Since SIL sold goods outside the selective distribution network this, according to Christian Dior, constituted an infringement of their trademark rights. It was also argued that the infringement by SIL meant that Copad had a responsibility for infringement for the subsequent sales that occurred.

The CJEU held that the quality of luxury goods, such as the ones at issue in the main proceedings, is the result not only of their material characteristics but also of the allure and prestigious image which bestows on them an aura of luxury.[12] According to the court, the provision of the licence agreement aimed at ensuring that the goods would be displayed in sales outlets in a manner that enhanced their value. That would contribute to the reputation of the goods at issue and therefore to sustain the aura of luxury surrounding them. Consequently, it was conceivable that the sale of luxury goods outside the scope of the selective distribution network might affect the *quality* of those goods. A contractual provision prohibiting such sale must therefore be considered as falling within the scope of Article 25(2) of the Trademark Directive.

With reference to the origin and quality functions of the trademark, the court stressed that the aura of luxury emanating from this type of prestigious goods is essential in that it enables consumers to distinguish them from similar goods.[13] The aura of luxury is held to encompass a capacity to distinguish goods. Therefore, impairment to that aura of luxury is likely to affect the quality of the goods.[14] The approach adopted by the CJEU emphasizes that the form of distribution may have significance for how the goods, in a trademark law relevant sense, are perceived by the consumers or end-users. The trademark's attractiveness is held to be determined by not only the product or service that bears the trademark but also *how* this product or service is marketed.

The reasoning of the court makes a clear connection between the trademark's capacity to attract consumers into buying the goods or services and the trademark's origin and quality function. The judgment explicitly refers to the prestigious image that is essential in enabling the goods to be distinguished from other similar goods (origin

12. CJEU case C-59/08 (Copad) paragraph 24.
13. CJEU case C-59/08 (Copad) paragraphs 22 and 25.
14. CJEU case C-59/08 (Copad) paragraph 26.

function) and that an action which impairs this image therefore can affect the actual quality of the goods (quality function).[15] In this sense, the quality function does not only encompass that the consumer or end-user is able to distinguish the goods from each other and that this choice can be made with the perception that there is a single company that has exercised its control over the goods. According to *Copad*, the notion has a broader scope.

A breach of a provision relating to the duration of the trademark licence may also trigger proprietary sanctions. The requirement in p. 1 of Chapter 6, section 4 of the Trademark Act, is however not limited to use after the expiration of the ordinary term of the agreement. The provision will also have effect if the agreement is terminated in advance, as follows from the decision by the Swedish Supreme Court in NJA 1997 p. 109 (Partyman).

The case concerned a claim for interim injunction for trademark infringement. The plaintiff was the registered proprietor of the trademarks and had licensed the rights to the defendant. After a dispute between the parties regarding alleged delays in deliveries and payments as well as other disloyal behaviour, the licensor terminated the licence agreement and brought an infringement action against the licensee. The parties were in agreement that the trademark licence had terminated, but they had different views on whether the licensor was entitled to terminate and which of the parties were entitled to the trademarks after termination.

The Supreme Court held that the interim action concerned an infringement based on trademark law since the licensee had continued the use after the termination of the licence. Therefore, the interim injunction should be assessed as a trademark infringement, regardless of the fact that the licensee had asserted that the trademarks should be transferred to the licensee. According to the Supreme Court, the question of which of the parties was the rightful proprietor of the marks post-termination should not be considered in the interim case, but later when the full case was heard.

A similar question was dealt with by the Supreme Court in NJA 1982 p. 738 (Esselte). A design rights holder had brought action for design infringement against a licensee. The licensee objected and asserted that the licence agreement contained an arbitration clause, according to which any dispute concerning the application or interpretation of the agreement should be settled by arbitration. The licensor claimed that the licensing agreement had been terminated due to the licensee's breach of contract. The Supreme Court decided that the question of validity of the licensing agreement was a preliminary question that should be assessed prior to considering the infringement case. Therefore, the Supreme Court decided that the District Court should have requested the licensor to initiate arbitration, after which the infringement proceedings should have been stayed pending the outcome in the arbitration.

A fundamental prerequisite for the licensor to initiate an infringement claim against the licensee is that the breach as such constitutes an infringement. For example, if the trademark is used for goods and services other than what follows from the licence, an infringement claim will only be successful if the licensor has protection for

15. CJEU case C-59/08 (Copad) paragraphs 25–26.

those goods or services that are disputed. Otherwise, the licensee's violation of the licence will only amount to a contract breach. This was discussed by the Svea Court of Appeal in RH 2008:29 (Golden Gate).

The case concerned two parties that had entered into a supply agreement, with an oral addendum that the purchaser was allowed to use the seller's trademark, free of charge, on the goods in addition to the purchaser's own trademark. The plaintiff's (the seller's) trademark was not protected in Sweden and had not been used in the country prior to that agreement. In breach of the parties' agreement, the defendant (the purchaser) registered the trademark in its own name and used the trademark for goods not included in the agreement. The unauthorized use resulted in that the plaintiff brought an action for trademark infringement and breach of contract. The Court of Appeal ruled that the defendant's trademark registration in its own name and use of the trademark for goods not covered by the agreement constituted a breach of contract. Irrespective of the abovementioned, the plaintiff's action was dismissed in so far as it concerned infringement of the trademark since the company did not hold any exclusive rights to the trademark in Sweden (the only rights that existed were held by the defendant and were subsequently invalidated due to the bad faith registration).

4. TRADEMARK LICENSING AND COMPETITION LAW

In the negotiation and execution of a licence agreement, it is imperative to consider the effects that may follow from competition law and antitrust principles. Competition law sets out the outer limits for what two parties may agree upon. Intellectual property law and competition law share the common purpose of promoting innovation and welfare – intellectual property law by providing incentives for creation and investments and competition law by prohibiting certain measures that could potentially harm competition on the existing market or in new ways of meeting consumer demands. In the interface between intellectual property law and competition law, tension may arise, for example, with regards to which limitations the licensor may impose on the licensee.

In Chapter 2, section 1 of the Swedish Competition Act, it is set out that companies are prohibited from entering into agreements or cooperating in a way that prevents, restricts or distorts competition in the market. A similar prohibition is provided for in Article 101 of the Treaty on the Functioning of the European Union, which applies if the cooperation may affect trade between EU Member States. The purpose of these provisions is to protect competition in the market in order to promote consumer welfare and an efficient allocation of resources.

However, there are some exceptions to this prohibition for agreements and collaborations that ultimately benefit competition in the market. This may be the case, for example, if the collaboration promotes technical or economic progress, e.g., by streamlining production or distribution in a way that also benefits consumers in terms of lower prices or higher quality.[16] It is up to the parties to assess for themselves

16. Cf. Chapter 2, section 2 of the Swedish Competition Act and Article 101 (3) of the Treaty on the Functioning of the European Union.

whether the agreement in question meets the conditions for this exemption. No prior notification from the Swedish Competition Authority is necessary.

Further guidance on what limits competition law imposes on licence agreements is set out in the so-called block exemptions. The block exemptions prescribe certain special conditions that must be met for an agreement to be exempted from the prohibition against anticompetitive agreements in accordance with Chapter 2, section 1 of the Competition Act. The Swedish Competition Act in essence refers to the corresponding EU regulations on block exemptions, which means that the principles laid down in the EU regulations also apply to purely national conditions.

Two important block exemptions for assessing licensing agreements are:

(1) Regulation (EU) no 316/2014 on the application of Article 101 (3) of the Treaty on the Functioning of the European Union to groups of technology transfer agreements; and
(2) Regulation (EU) no 330/2010 on the application of Article 101 (3) of the Treaty on the Functioning of the European Union to groups of vertical agreements and concerted practices.

The block exemptions set out certain important principles, all of which must be taken into account by the parties to a licensing agreement. However, these block exemptions are not directly applicable for trademark licence agreements, although they do appear to have a strong normative effect on companies' market conduct also in terms of trademark licensing.

For example, the block exemption on vertical agreements is not directly applicable to licensing. The field of application of the Regulation is limited to the purchase and sale of goods and services. Article 2 of the Regulation states that, although the block exemption may be applied to agreements which contain provisions on the buyer's use of intellectual property rights, this applies provided that the licence does not constitute the primary purpose of the agreement.

According to the guidelines presented by the Commission on vertical restraints, intellectual property rights must be provided in the context of an agreement to purchase or distribute/supply goods or services, and the provisions on intellectual property must serve the implementation of the vertical agreement. In the guidelines provided by the Commission, a franchise agreement is used as an example, in which the franchisor sells goods to the franchisee for resale and, additionally, grants the franchisee a licence to use a trademark and know-how to market the goods. An additional situation covered by the exemption is the one where a supplier gives the buyer a licence to mix and pour extracts into bottles and then sell them as drinks.

Even if the block exemption is not directly applicable on trademark licences, it provides important guidance on how the parties should relate to restrictions that may follow from competition law. Otherwise, there is a risk that the licensing agreement, in an individual assessment according to Chapter 2, sections 1-2 of the Competition Act (alternatively Article 101 (1) and 101 (3) TFEU), is considered to be in breach of competition law. Consequently, it is advisable to, e.g., carefully assess what territorial restrictions that the licensor can impose on the licensee, which influence the licensor may have on the determination of the licensee's sales prices or the duration of any direct or indirect non-compete obligations on the licensee.[17]

5. PROTECTION OF THE REPUTATION AND GOODWILL OF THE TRADEMARK IN A CONTRACTUAL RELATIONSHIP

Trademark law affords protection by ensuring that the goods or services bearing the trademark are put on the market under the control of the trademark owner, which is responsible for the quality of the goods or services. The protection is, however, restricted in such a way that it merely enables the trademark owner to ascertain control of the quality – and thereby protect the reputation of the trademark. It does not require that any actual quality control is carried out by the licensor.[18]

The trademark owner will bear sole responsibility if he tolerates the marketing of substandard products or services despite having the contractual means of preventing it. In this respect, trademark law merely protects the trademark owner's ability of preventing use of the trademark for goods or services provided outside his control. It does not protect against the risk that consumers may be deceived due to the proprietor's failure to act against inferior products or services. Consequently, there is no legal basis within Swedish trademark law for requiring the licensor to maintain the reputation or image of the licensed products or services.

Moreover, there is no such obligation to maintain this reputation under contract law. There is no explicit rule in Swedish contract law stipulating an obligation to maintain the reputation or goodwill of a licensed intellectual property.

However, a non-mandatory rule setting out such obligations for franchising particularly is included in the Draft Common Frame of Reference (DCFR). The DCFR was a joint pan-European academic project, setting out non-binding common principles with the objective to achieve a uniform European contract law. Although it has not lead to any compulsory legislation, the DCFR is referenced in a few decisions by the Swedish Supreme Court giving it semi-relevance when discussing contract law from a strict national perspective.

Article IV. E. – 4:207 of the DCFR sets out the franchisor's obligations concerning the reputation of the franchise network and advertising. It requires the franchisor to make reasonable efforts to promote and maintain the reputation of the franchise network. In particular, the franchisor is obligated to design and co-ordinate the appropriate advertising campaigns aiming at the promotion of the franchise network. The activities of promotion and maintaining reputation are to be carried out without additional charges to the franchisee.[19]

---

17. Cf. Articles 4 and 5 of Regulation (EU) no 330/2010 on the application of Article 101 (3) of the Treaty on the Functioning of the European Union to groups of vertical agreements and concerted practices.
18. CJEU Case C-9/93 (Ideal Standard) paragraph 38.
19. The provision concerning which of the parties should pay for the advertising appears somewhat peculiar. It is not obvious that only the franchisor should be responsible for the costs associated with marketing, especially in situations with transborder franchising. If the franchisor undertakes to promote the franchise network internationally, it is not uncommon to establish an

Nonetheless, the provision does not have any equivalent under Swedish contract law. One alternative would be to argue that there exists an obligation similar to that set out in the DCFR as an implied term in the trademark licence agreement. As an example, it is sometimes held that a similar implied obligation exists for lease of goods under Swedish law, whereby the lessor is held to have an obligation to preserve the object of the contractual arrangement (*Sw: bevarandeplikt*).[20] Such an obligation is explicitly provided for in the DCFR in relation to the lease of goods. The provision stipulates that the lessor must ensure that throughout the lease period, and subject to normal wear and tear, the goods: (a) remain of the quantity, quality and description required by the contract; and (b) remain fit for the purposes of the lease, even where this requires modifications to the goods.[21] The application of a similar obligation, however, is not settled under Swedish law. It cannot be assumed that a lessor of movable property has a general obligation, as an implied term, to preserve the object of the contract.[22]

It has been discussed in the legal literature whether the principle of *bevarandeplikt* is applicable to licensing agreements in such way that the licensor has an implied obligation to maintain the licensed object.[23] However, those discussions are related to the mere existence of the exclusive right. To say that the principle should also include maintaining a reputation or image would be to stretch its application even further. It therefore appears too excessive to argue that under Swedish law an implied contractual obligation exists for the licensor or the licensee to maintain the reputation of the licensed trademark, in similar way as set forth for franchising in the DCFR.

Consequently, any obligations on the licensee or the licensor to maintain a particular quality of the products or to uphold the reputation or goodwill of the trademark must be laid out in the licence agreement. It cannot be invoked as an implied term. However, given the central importance of the reputation and brand image for attracting consumers and retaining their loyalty, the inclusion of a provision of this nature seems very reasonable.

It is therefore reasonable to expect a trademark licence agreement to commonly contain obligations, for either the licensor or the licensee, to protect the quality and the reputation and goodwill of the licensed trademark. The contract will function as the primary instrument for safeguarding the interests of both the licensor and the licensee.

advertising fund to which all the sub-franchisors or franchisee's will contribute advertising fees, cf. UNIDROIT Guide to International Master Franchise Arrangements (2007) p. 57. There are more options that are conceivable, e.g., that the franchisee bears a substantial part of the responsibility for advertising in its territory or that the franchisee contributes to the marketing with a small percentage of its gross revenues for the franchisor's advertising in the territory.

20. Jacob W. F. Sundberg, Om ansvaret för fel i lejt gods (1966) pp. 223 ff.
21. DCFR Article IV. B. - 3:104.
22. Cf. Eric M. Runesson, Licens till patent och företagshemligheter i avtals- och kontraktsrätten (2014) p. 140.
23. Stojan Arnerstål, Varumärket som kontraktsföremål (2014) p. 105 f. and Eric M. Runesson, Licens till patent och företagshemligheter i avtals- och kontraktsrätten (2014) p. 101 and 128.

6. LICENSING AND TRADEMARK INFRINGEMENT

A trademark licence agreement will normally include provisions on how to deal with third parties infringing the licensed rights. If the licence is exclusive and for a territory where the licensor normally does not conduct business, it is also common to include an obligation for the licensee to monitor the market to detect any unauthorized use of the trademark.

If the licence agreement does not provide for any provisions in this respect, the agreement will be supplemented with the principles set out in the Trademark Act. Chapter 10, section 2 of the Trademark Act stipulates the following:

> A licensee may bring proceeding for infringement of the trademark only if the proprietor consents thereto. However, the holder of an exclusive license may bring such proceedings if the proprietor of the trademark, after formal notice, does not himself bring infringement proceedings within a reasonable period. This paragraph shall apply also for actions for declaratory judgements.

A similar provision applies for EU trademarks according to Article 25(3) of the Regulation. The rights for the licensee to invoke infringement proceedings against a third party are not dependent on the licence being recorded in the trademark registry.[24]

The court shall ex officio examine that the conditions for bringing an action by a licensee are met. If the requirements are not fulfilled, the court will request that the licensee supplements the claim. If the licensee does not rectify the deficiency, the court will dismiss the claim as inadmissible. As mentioned, the parties can agree on a different solution than set out in the Trademark Act, for example, by prohibiting the licensee from bringing any infringement actions.

In the second paragraph of Chapter 10, section 2, the following is set out:

> If a trademark holder brings proceedings for trademark infringement, the licensee is entitled to intervene for the purpose of obtaining compensation according to Chapter 8, Section 4.

Chapter 8, section 4 of the Trademark Act is the general provision on the right to compensation and damages suffered due to an infringement of the trademark. Consequently, the licensee is entitled to intervene obtaining compensation for the damage suffered by the licensee. This right for the licensee to claim compensation cannot be waived in the agreement. However, it appears as if such compensation claim presupposes that the licence is exclusive.

In a case tried by the Göta Court of Appeal, a holder of a non-exclusive trademark licence brought an action for compensation due to a trademark infringement.[25] In a previous proceeding, the court had declared that the defendant was guilty of trademark infringement. However, the licensee's claim for compensation was rejected on the ground that the non-exclusive licence did not encompass any rights to prevent others from using the trademark.

24. CJEU case C-163/15 (Youssef Hassan) paragraph 26.
25. Göta Court of Appeal, judgment 2012-09-25 in case T 3050-11.

7. TERMINATION OR EXPIRATION OF THE TRADEMARK LICENCE AGREEMENT

7.1. All Trademark Use Must Cease upon Termination or Expiration of the Agreement

The termination or expiration of a trademark licence agreement generally has the effect that the licensee must cease all use of the trademark.[26] Once the licence agreement has expired, the licensee no longer has any rights to use the trademark.

The obligation to cease all trademark use corresponds to the general contractual obligation to return leased movable property after the expiration of the lease period. For example, in Article III. - 3:510.1 of the DCFR the following is stipulated:

> On termination under this Section a party (the recipient) who has received any benefit by the other's performance of obligations under the terminated contractual relationship or terminated part of the contractual relationship is obliged to return it.

A similar provision is set out in the Principles of European Contract Law (PECL), Article 9:308:

> On termination of the contract a party who has supplied property which can be returned and for which it has not received payment or other counter-performance may recover the property.

It follows from the nature of a licence agreement that the use must cease in connection with the termination of the licence relationship, unless the parties have agreed that otherwise shall apply. Continued use of the trademark may constitute an infringement, in addition to constituting a breach of contract.[27]

The cessation of all trademark use encompasses all activities over which the licensee has direct or indirect control. This entails a relatively far-reaching obligation for the licensee to ensure that all uses of the trademark end, similarly as an infringer's obligation to comply with an injunction. According to case law, this includes an obligation to investigate the extent of ongoing use and to make far-reaching attempts to end all such use.[28] It may also include an obligation to request from third parties, from which the licensee have ordered advertisements, to remove the advertisements or the reference to the trademark contained therein.[29]

7.2. Licensee May Not Sell Off Remaining Inventory Without Permission

The principles discussed in the previous section only apply if the licence agreement does not stipulate otherwise. For trademark licence agreements, it is common to include a provision providing the licensee the right to sell off any remaining inventory

26. Cf. Stojan Arnerstål, Varumärket som kontraktsföremål (2014) pp. 311 ff. and Bengt Domeij, Patentavtalsrätt. Licenser, överlåtelser och samägande av patent (2010) pp. 373 ff.
27. Cf. section 3 above.
28. Cf. Svea Court of Appeals in RH 2006:42 (BMW).
29. CJEU case C-179/15 (Mercedes-Benz) paragraph 39.

during a transition period after the expiration of the licence. The purpose of such provision is typically to give the licensee a chance to sell products already manufactured, to avoid wasting resources by the goods having to be discarded.

Without a sell-off provision, the licensee would be prohibited from selling any remaining inventory after the expiration of the licence agreement, unless the trademark rights in the inventory are exhausted. Trademark exhaustion occurs when the goods are placed on the market within the European Economic Area, by the trademark holder or with his consent.[30] After exhaustion, the trademark holder cannot prevent the resale of the products.

The licence agreement generally entails a consent for the licensee to place products on the market. As set out above, the consent ceases when the agreement expires, unless the agreement stipulates otherwise. In the absence of permission to sell off remaining inventory, the licensee is prohibited from marketing the products after the agreement has terminated. The licensee cannot rely on the exhaustion principle since exhaustion occurs when the products have been put on the market. Products in the licensee's inventory are normally not subject to exhaustion. Even the offering for sale of the products does not trigger exhaustion if the goods are not actually sold.[31]

A sale of inventory after the licence agreement has been terminated or expired will therefore constitute an infringement. The same will apply if the licence agreement is terminated due to the insolvency of the licensee. The bankruptcy trustee is not permitted to sell off any inventory without the consent from the trademark holder.[32]

A consequence of the abovementioned is that there is a strong incentive for the licensee to include provisions on post-termination winding down of the trademark use. This can be achieved either as an explicit right for the licensee to sell off the products or as an obligation for the licensor to purchase any remaining inventory. The other option for the licensee would be to plan the manufacturing and stock in view of the duration of the licence agreement, to avoid being left with a substantive inventory that needs to be destroyed after the expiration of the agreement.

30. Chapter 1, section 12 of the Trademark Act. A corresponding provision for EU trademarks is set out in Article 15 in EU Regulation 2017/1001 on the European Union trade mark.
31. CJEU case C-16/03 (Peak Holding) paragraph 44.
32. A similar situation was addressed by the Supreme Court in NJA 2005 p. 510, in which a copyright licensee was declared bankrupt, after which the bankruptcy trustee sold off the inventory. It follows from the decision by the Supreme Court that the sale of the inventory, after the licensor had terminated the licence due to the bankruptcy, constituted an infringement of the licensors' copyright.

Switzerland

Gregor Wild & Fabio Versolatto

1. INTRODUCTION TO TRADEMARK LICENSING IN SWITZERLAND

1.1. Legislation on Trademark Licensing in Switzerland

The licence agreement is a contract whereby the licensor undertakes to grant the licensee the use of an intellectual property right. The *Swiss Federal Act on the Protection of Trademarks and Indications of Source* (Trademark Protection Act, TmPA) contains only a few provisions which specifically deal with trademark licensing.[1]

The main legal provision and definition are found in *Article 18 paragraph 1 TmPA* which reads under the title 'Licence' as follows: 'The proprietor of a trademark may permit others to use the trademark for the goods or services for which it is claimed, in whole or in part, and for the whole territory or a part of Switzerland only.'

1.2. Trademarks as Objects of Contractual Arrangements

Licence agreements, in general, deal with rights to use intangible goods granted to the licensee. These intangible goods can be absolute rights, such as artistic works protected by copyright, patent-protected inventions or *trademarks*,[2] or relatively protected rights, such as know-how, trade secrets or unregistered signs.[3]

Under Swiss law, licence agreements are so-called *innominate contracts*, which mean that they are not explicitly regulated by Swiss (contract) law.[4] In particular, there are no specific provisions in the Swiss Code of Obligations (SCO), the law governing general contract law (general part of the SCO) and special contract law (specific

1. For example, Articles 18, 27, 27e, 53 paragraph 3, 55 paragraph 4, 71 or 78a TmPA.
2. Apart from trademarks, absolute rights are, e.g., rights to patents, designs, copyrights or plant variety protection.
3. Cf. Federal Supreme Court ruling (BGE) 115 II 255 no. 2a.
4. BGE 133 III 360 no. 8.1; BGE 96 II 154 no. 2; BGE 92 II 299 no. 3a; BezGer Höfe, sic! 2007, 140.

classification of contracts, specific part of the SCO) in Switzerland. The specific part of the SCO regulates certain types of contractual arrangements such as sale, exchange, gifts, tenancy, lease, loan, employment contract, agency contract or simple (unregistered) partnership. However, there is no section in the SCO dealing with licence agreements (such as trademark licensing).

With that said, there are no exhaustive regulations on the rights and obligations of the licensor and the licensee, when faced with contractual problems relating to a trademark licence, such as assignability, sublicences, royalties, record-keeping, warranty, maintaining and defending the licensed trademark, third-party infringement, liability, confidentiality, duration or termination of contract and associated consequences.

In order to create legal certainty, the local *doctrine and jurisdiction* apply – depending on the specific structuring of the contractual relationship at hand – certain rules of the specific part of the SCO (contracts falling under a specific classification) to licence agreements *analogously*, where appropriate due to their nature.[5] Furthermore, the provisions of the general part of the SCO apply without reservation. Accordingly, contractual issues are answered in Switzerland by way of analogy to other similar legislation, through application of general contractual principles or, as the case may be (case comparable), by making reference to other similar case law (which however is sparse in Switzerland).

Depending on its specific nature and content, a licence agreement can have primarily elements of tenancy, lease or sales contracts (or, as the case may be, a simple partnership):

- Generally, licence agreements are *continuing obligations*.[6] Nevertheless, licence agreements can include one-time obligations (e.g., if the parties agreed on a one-off payment as royalty) and therefore show the characteristics of a purchase agreement (sale) in this respect. One example might be the purchase of standard software off the shelf.
- However, in contrast to purchase agreements, where the seller transfers ownership of goods to the buyer, the licensor will remain the holder of the trademark rights. The licensor grants the licensee a *(contractual) right to use* an intangible good, such as a trademark, in a contractually agreed manner and for certain purposes.[7] In this respect, a trademark licence agreement rather bears resemblance to a tenancy or lease agreement.[8]

5. Cf. BGE 115 II 255 no. 2b; BezGer Höfe, sic! 2007, 140; i.e., no direct applicability.
6. BGE 92 II 299 no. 3b.
7. BezGer Höfe, sic! 2007, 140; BGE 92 II 279 and BGE 101 II 293 no. 2c; or rather: The licensee gains a contractual (personal) claim against the licensor whereby the latter has to tolerate the use of the licensed trademark by the licensee (licensor grants licensee the use of the trademark).
8. Cf. BGE 124 III 456 no. 4b/bb; BGE 92 II 299 no. 3a; Heinrich Honsell, Schweizerisches Obligationenrecht, Besonderer Teil, 10th ed., Zurich 2017, no. 3801.

- Licence agreements can sometimes even show some elements of a simple (unregistered) partnership (contractual relationship) since they are characterized by an *increased obligation of the parties to cooperate* on various issues to achieve (at least partially) a common goal.[9]

One significant difference between those contracts falling under a specific classification, and licence agreements, however, is the *contractual object*: Whereas tenancy, lease and purchase contracts regulate the rights to (tangible) objects, properties or land, the contractual object of licence agreements can only be *intangible goods*. In the case of trademark licence agreements, those intangible goods are trademarks. Furthermore, licence agreements between commercial customers (B2B) also lack the idea of social protection (legislative concept), which is still very much prevalent under Swiss tenancy or lease law (protection of the weaker party).

Therefore, caution and, under certain circumstances, restraint are always advisable when it comes to the question of analogous application of other similar legislation.

In any event, this demonstrates how important it is under Swiss law that the parties explicitly regulate the individual points which they regard as essential in a contract. The parties ought to make use of this (contractual) freedom in Switzerland. This legal position is both an advantage (extensive freedom in drafting) and a challenge (not to forget anything essential) for the parties at the same time.

1.3. Delimitation Between Proprietary Trademark Rules and Contract Law

As outlined above, by concluding a trademark licence agreement, the licensee gains a contractual (personal) claim against the licensor to tolerate the use made by the licensee of the licensed trademark.

The trademark, an absolute right (*erga omnes*), and the licence agreement, a legal relationship by its relative nature between the contracting parties (contract), exist in parallel as a legal basis.

If the licensee breaches the contract, e.g., by actively marketing the branded goods outside the contract territory or beyond the extent permitted (e.g., other goods and/or services), the licensor may claim a breach of contract. Moreover, the licensor may invoke trademark infringement remedies since the licensor is contractually only obliged to tolerate the use made by the licensee if and to the extent executed in the contractually agreed manner. Beyond this scope (contractual toleration), the licensee, like any third party, must respect the exclusive rights of the licensor and trademark owner.

It should be noted, however, that not every breach of the licence agreement in each case also constitutes a trademark infringement. Regarding the breach, there is a need for reference to the trademark right or the permission of use. For example, the

9. Articles 530 et seq. SCO; Claire HUGUENIN, Obligationenrecht – Allgemeiner und Besonderer Teil, 3rd ed., Zurich 2017, no. 3803; BGE 92 II 299 no. 3b.

mere breach of contractual accounting and reporting obligations (towards the licensor) by the licensee would probably not constitute a trademark infringement.

2. NATURE AND CONTENT OF TRADEMARK LICENCE AGREEMENTS

2.1. Characteristics of a Trademark Licence Agreement

Under a trademark licence agreement, the licensor undertakes to grant the licensee the use of a trademark. The licensee, in return, generally owes a licence fee.[10] The latter is, however, not absolutely necessary. A licence can theoretically also be granted free of charge, against benefits in kind or in exchange for a cross-licence.

As already mentioned, the licensor will remain the holder of the trademark rights within the scope of this contractual relationship. Hence, there is no actual assignment (transfer) of title or any absolute rights. The licensee 'just' gains a contractual (personal) claim against the licensor to tolerate the use of the licensed trademark.

Hence, trademark licence agreements have an *inter partes* effect (relative nature), which means the licensee may assert his right of use only against the licensor, but not against any other third parties.[11] This differentiation is relevant for the question as to:

- whether and to what extent the licence has an effect if the licensed trademark is assigned to a third party and
- whether the licensee has a standing to sue (a right to sue for trademark infringement).

If the licence is entered in the Swiss trademark register at the request of one of the contracting parties, the licence then becomes binding on any rights to the trademark subsequently acquired.[12]

And any person who holds an exclusive licence is entitled to bring a separate action – irrespective of the registration of the licence in the trademark register – unless this is expressly excluded in the licence agreement.[13] This right to bring an action (as exclusive licensee) is therefore independent of the entry of the licence in the trademark register. However, the licence agreement may exclude this entitlement.

10. BSK OR I-Amstutz/Morin/Schluep, see also Articles 184 et seq. N 238.
11. SHK MSchG-Bühler, Article 18 no. 8; BGE 92 II 279, 280; cf. BGE 105 II 49 no. 2a; BGer 4A_317/2016 no. 2.5; BezGer Höfe, sic! 2007, 140, 142.
12. Article 18 paragraph 2 TmPA.
13. Article 55 paragraph 4 TmPA.

2.2. Contracting Parties

2.2.1. Trademark Licensor

The licensor is generally the holder of the trademark as registered in the relevant trademark register.[14] Alternatively, an usufructuary can act as a licensor. Likewise, even a licensee can license the trademark to other parties and act as licensor if the licensee is permitted to grant trademark sublicences.

A licensor can have a multitude of reasons for licensing his trademarks. For one thing, a trademark licence agreement allows the licensor to profit from his trademark, even if the licensor is unable or not willing to market it himself. Where the trademark is used by the licensee in connection with new products and services, the trademark's value may even be increased.[15]

2.2.2. Trademark Licensee

The licensee can be any natural or legal person.

In the case of a so-called sublicence, the licensee himself becomes the licensor, however, without establishing a contractual relationship between (main) the licensor and the sub-licensee.

According to the prevailing doctrine, the licensee must be authorized by the licensor to grant sublicences, at least in the case of a non-exclusive (simple) licensee.[16] The question of the permissibility of granting sublicences should in any case be regulated in the contract so as not to create legal uncertainty.

2.3. Types of Trademark Licence Agreements

2.3.1. Exclusive Trademark Licence Agreement

A trademark licence agreement is considered exclusive if the licensor is contractually prohibited from granting any further (non-exclusive or exclusive) licences in addition to the exclusive licence. The licensor is *also prohibited* from using the trademark himself. This grants the licensee a relatively strong position.[17]

However, the licensor may grant several exclusive licences if these licences have different geographic or material scopes and therefore do not coincide.

14. The Swiss trademark register can be accessed through https://www.swissreg.ch/srclient/faces/jsp/start.jsp. The Swiss designations of international trademark registrations are available under: https://www3.wipo.int/madrid/monitor/en/.
15. SHK MSchG-Bühler, Article 18 no. 1.
16. SHK MSchG-Bühler, Article 18 no. 23; cf. Federal Patent Court decision O2014_002 no. 6.6.3; Reto M. Hilty, Lizenzvertragsrecht, 759 et seq., according to which the exclusive licensee may grant sublicences even without the licensor's consent, as long as no estimable interests of the licensor are affected.
17. Cf. also Article 55 paragraph 4 TmPA (standing to sue).

2.3.2. *Non-exclusive (Simple) Trademark Licence Agreement*

If the licence agreement is non-exclusive (also called simple licence), the licensor is free to grant other non-exclusive licences and to use the trademark himself. Therefore, a single licensee has a relatively weak position under a non-exclusive licence. This position can be strengthened by agreeing on a most-favoured licensee clause, which may guarantee the licensee that later licensees will not get better conditions.

2.3.3. *Sole Trademark Licence Agreement*

Like an exclusive trademark licence agreement, the licensor must not grant any further licences. This means that only one sole licensee has the right to use the trademark. However, the licensor is *still allowed* to use the trademark and all rights in and to the trademark himself.

2.3.4. *Qualified Trademark Licence Agreement*

Under a qualified trademark licence agreement, the licensor may grant several licences, but to a limited number of additional licensees only.

2.4. Scope of Trademark Licence Agreements

The parties are free to agree on the contractual content within the limits of the law (principle of freedom of contract). This means, *inter alia*, that the licensor can freely decide on the scope of the licence agreement. This is also shown by Article 18 paragraph 1 TmPA, saying that the proprietor of a trademark may permit others to use the trademark for the goods or services for which it is claimed, in whole or in part, and for the whole territory or a part of Switzerland only.

As stated in Article 18 paragraph 1 TmPA, a trademark licence can be geographically restricted. The entitlement of the licensee to market the product under the licensed trademark might, e.g., be restricted to certain cantons or regions. If the licence agreement is not about a Swiss trademark, but rather, e.g., an international trademark, the licence can be restricted to one or several designations or even certain regions within one designation.

Other restrictions may concern certain Nice classes for which the trademark is claimed,[18] or the field of use. For example, the licensee might be entitled to use the trademark only for the manufacturing or distribution and the corresponding marketing of a product.[19] Or the licensee might, e.g., be entitled to use the trademark to commercialize only a certain face cream or a whole series of skincare products or all cosmetics, but not his textile products.

Similarly, the setting of a fixed contractual period can be considered a restriction. The licensee might be entitled to exploit a trademark during a certain period of time

18. SHK MSchG-Bühler, Article 18 no. 29.
19. SHK MSchG-Bühler, Article 18 no. 31.

only. If there is no explicit temporal limitation, this regularly means that the licence agreement is valid during the term of validity of the trademark rights.

2.5. Formation (Conclusion) of Trademark Licence Agreements in Switzerland

2.5.1. Formal Requirements

A trademark licence agreement can be concluded *without* any formal requirements under Swiss law (principle of freedom of form). Implied consent is sufficient.[20] In practice, however, the written form is recommended in view of a possible registration of the licence or possible questions of evidence.

There are no particular legal requirements to be complied with prior to entering into a trademark licence agreement in Switzerland, apart from the usual general requirements such as legal capacity to act, mutual expression of intent or circumstances with no impossible, unlawful or immoral terms and the like.

Further, there are no national pre-contractual disclosure requirements (e.g., pre-contractual disclosure by the licensor for franchising agreements) in Switzerland.

2.5.2. Register Entry

There is no necessity to record a licence with the national trademark office where a trademark licensing agreement is concerned (matters like conclusion of contract, validity, enforcement, etc., are independent of the register entry).

However, the trademark licence can be entered in the Swiss trademark register *at the request of one of the contracting parties*. The licence then becomes binding on any rights to the trademark subsequently acquired by third parties (protection by succession planning).[21] This means that when the trademark is sold by the licensor or otherwise transferred to a third party in the course of bankruptcy proceedings, the licensee may hold the licence out towards the acquirer.

Any person who holds an exclusive licence is entitled to bring a separate action irrespective of the registration of the licence in the register, unless this is expressly excluded in the licence agreement.[22] Hence, the possible standing to sue third parties for trademark infringement is independent of such recordal of a licence (but limited to exclusive licensees).

2.6. Pledgeability

A licence, just as debts or other rights in general, may be pledged provided the licence is assignable (Article 899 Swiss Civil Code).

20. BGE 101 II 293, no. 2c.
21. Article 18 paragraph 2 TmPA; BGer 4A_317/2016 no. 2.
22. Article 55 paragraph 4 TmPA.

3. CONTRACTUAL OBLIGATIONS

3.1. Typical Obligations of the Trademark Licensor

3.1.1. Granting the Right to Use

The licensor has the obligation to grant the licensee the right of use and economic exploitation of the licensed trademark. The licensor must therefore *tolerate* the use of the licensed trademark by the licensee (licensor's main obligation).

3.1.2. Maintaining the Trademark and Defence

In this context, the licensor generally has to take measures necessary to *maintain* the trademark, such as renewals and paying all necessary fees.[23]

Within the scope of the obligation to maintain the trademark, the licensor is further obliged to *defend* the trademark against actions by third parties for invalidity of the licensed trademark,[24] such as nullity suits, opposition or cancellation proceedings.

3.1.3. Enforcing the Trademark (as the Case May Be)

Within the scope of defending the trademark, the licensor has to take action against infringements by third parties if these infringing actions affect the licensee's right of use granted under the trademark licence agreement.[25]

Such an obligation to take legal action therefore exists in the case of exclusive licences, as otherwise the exclusivity promised in the contract is lost.

In case of a most-favoured licensee clause, the licensor is in practice obliged to take action against infringements as well because the licensor must also grant the existing licensee the same favourable conditions as any third parties are granted.[26]

However, there is no need for the licensor to take action against any and all trademark infringements by third parties, but only against the significant ones, i.e., only in cases where the infringements have reached such an extent that the sales of licensed products are threatened to be impaired. Thus, the licensor has no general duty to monitor the market for possible infringements.[27]

3.1.4. Warranty

The licensor shall warrant to be the owner of the trademark and that the trademark is registered in the contract territory. The licensor shall further warrant not to be aware of any defects of title in the trademark at the time the agreement is concluded. However, the licensor shall not guarantee the legal validity of the trademark. According to the licensor, he is not aware of any rights of third parties that conflict with

23. BGE 61 II 142 et seq.; BezGer Höfe, sic! 2007, 140 et seq.
24. SHK MSchG-Bühler, Article 18 no. 32.
25. SHK MSchG-Bühler, Article 18 no. 34.
26. SHK MSchG-Bühler, Article 18 no. 34, this means that the licensor would have to grant the licensee a free licence if the licensor tolerated an infringement of trademark rights.
27. SHK MSchG-Bühler, Article 18 no. 35.

registration and/or use of the trademark for the contractual products in the contract territory. However, the licensor shall not guarantee that the rights of third parties are not infringed by making use of the trademark.

3.2. Typical Obligations of the Trademark Licensee

3.2.1. Licence Fees

In return for being allowed to use a certain trademark, most trademark licence agreements oblige the licensee to pay a licence fee to the licensor (licensee's main obligation). There are several models of how those fees can be paid.

First of all, the licensee may owe a one-time fee which can be due at once or payable by instalments. By agreeing on a one-time fee, the trademark licence agreement obtains the characteristics of a purchase agreement. For the licensor it is thus important to explicitly clarify in the agreement that the licensor remains the holder of all trademark rights (no assignment), and that the licensee loses his right to use the trademark after termination of the licence agreement.

In practice, the contracting parties might also encounter periodic flat-rate fees. These can be dependent on the expected number of sold goods or the expected revenue. Whereas this allows the licensor to reduce his administrative efforts, the licensee might be freed from having to render a detailed account.

However, use-dependent or performance-dependent fees are most common in trademark licence agreements in practice. The licensee is obligated to pay a fixed amount for each sold product or a certain percentage of the achieved turnover. Profit could also be a calculation parameter, but is not optimally suited due to its 'controllability' on the part of the licensee. It is important to clarify the method of calculation so as to prevent legal uncertainty among the contracting parties. The licensor can minimize the risk of an unsuccessful commercialization by obligating the licensee to periodically pay a minimum amount (minimum royalties). Such a clause can act as an additional incentive for the licensee to use the trademark actively.

3.2.2. Accounting and Inspection of Records

In case of use-dependent or performance-dependent fees, the licensor must be able to track the licensee's exploitation of the trademark. Therefore, the licensee is often contractually obligated to keep records and to render account to the licensor periodically. The licensor, on the other hand, is generally entitled to access and inspect those records. Alternatively, should the licensee have concerns about his trade secrets, the licensee may grant the licensor the right to appoint a neutral auditor to audit the records.

3.2.3. Obligation to Use

The licensor generally has an interest in the trademark being used. It is only through usage in relation to goods and/or services that the trademark can gain high profile and that its value can be increased.

Furthermore, Article 12 paragraph 1 TmPA stipulates that where the proprietor has not used the trademark in relation to the claimed goods and/or services for an uninterrupted period of five years following the expiry of the opposition period (grace period), the proprietor may no longer assert his right to the trademark (challenge due to non-use). Non-use of the licensed trademark by the licensee can therefore lead to a loss of rights for the licensor, which increases his interest in contractually binding the licensee to actively use the trademark or to ensure that the trademark is being used by the sub-licensee.

According to Article 11 paragraph 3 TmPA, the use of the trademark with the consent of the proprietor is regarded as use by the proprietor himself (representative use). In the case of an exclusive licence, the licensee is assumed to be obliged to use (the trademark), even if this duty is not expressly stipulated in the licence agreement.[28] A further indication for the existence of an obligation to use is the arrangement of a profit- or revenue-based licence fee.[29]

3.2.4. Quality Management

The licensor has an imminent interest in ensuring that the integrity and reputation of the trademark are not diminished by the licensee, e.g., by marketing low-quality products under the licensed trademark.

The licensor will therefore often include his quality standards in the trademark licensing agreement. Depending on the circumstances, the licensor will use existing quality standards or the parties may negotiate such standards. Quality standards usually contain provisions on market presentation, advertising and the individual representation of the sign on the products, packaging, promotion material, etc.

By insisting on a licence notice ('made by [licensee] under licence from [licensor]'), the licensor ensures that his name will be associated with the trademark.

In order to ensure that the licensee upholds such quality standards, the licensor will often insist on stipulating corresponding control rights or a subject-to-approval clause.

4. TRADEMARK LICENSING AND COMPETITION LAW

A trademark licensing agreement can in principle be freely formulated within the limits of the legal system. The Swiss Cartel Act (CartA) is one of these legal limitations (antitrust law).

The CartA applies to trademark licensing agreements which have an effect in Switzerland (i.e., in the Swiss market), even if they originate in another country (Article 2 paragraph 2 CartA). The CartA does basically not apply to effects on competition that result exclusively from the legislation governing intellectual property. However, import restrictions based on intellectual property rights shall be assessed under the CartA (Article 3 paragraph 2 CartA).

28. BGE 96 II 154 no. 3; BGE 85 II 38 no. 6c.
29. Cf. BGE 85 II 38 no. 6c (regarding a quota licence).

Trademark licensing agreements may be qualified as agreements affecting competition, in the sense of Article 4 paragraph 1 CartA, which have a restraint of competition as their object or effect. As such, they must comply in particular with the antitrust restrictions of Article 5 CartA (unlawful agreements affecting competition between undertakings operating at the same or at different levels of production) and Article 7 CartA (unlawful practices by dominant undertakings).

4.1. Obligation Not to Attack (Non-challenge Clause)

Just like any other party, the licensee might potentially have an interest in attacking the trademark with a nullity suit. If the arrangement between the licensor and the licensee is based on a loyalty relationship (special fidelity), such a suit might be considered as bad faith. According to the Swiss Federal Supreme Court, such a fiduciary duty can be assumed if the parties have formed a simple (unregistered) partnership or a similar legal relationship (e.g., exclusive licence) for the purpose of joint exploitation with special fidelity.[30] Legal certainty can be obtained by inclusion of an explicit contractual obligation not to attack, or (at least) a right of termination in favour of the licensor in case of an attack.

However, non-attack or non-challenge clauses must be in compliance with the applicable antitrust law. The effects of non-attack clauses do not result exclusively from trademark rights (exclusivity) (cf. Article 3 paragraph 2 CartA). If such agreements extend an unjustly existing exclusivity by preventing an attack on the trademark (as licensed object), the respective clause may have restrictive effects on competition.[31]

4.2. Other Restrictions

Agreements merely intended to limit the licence to a certain territory or to a particular Nice class (or classes), to grant an exclusive licence or to restrict the licence according to the individual acts of use in the sense of Article 13 paragraph 2 TmPA, are basically admissible as such and not contrary to Swiss antitrust law. For instance, a licence may be granted for manufacture only, for distribution only or comprehensively for manufacture, distribution and related marketing. As a rule, such restrictions result from the legislation governing intellectual property (trademark law).

The following examples of (additional) contractual restrictions do not result exclusively from the legislation governing intellectual property and have thus to be examined, on a case-by-case basis, regarding their antitrust compatibility (risk assessment): general, unlimited or otherwise excessive non-compete obligations to the disadvantage of the licensee, e.g., not to distribute goods or services of competitors of the licensor, non-challenge clauses, vertical resale price maintenance (direct or indirect fixing of resell prices), prohibition of passive sales or artificial partitioning of the

30. BGE 95 II 271 no. 2, in relation to a patent licence agreement. It can be assumed that the requirements for fiduciary duties are the same between parties to a trademark licence agreement.
31. SHK MSchG-Bühler, Article 18 no. 42.

market (e.g., regional foreclosure of the Swiss market, prevention or restriction of parallel imports, etc.).

In contrast, the following clauses should in general be less risky (of course subject to individual assessment): prohibition of sub-licensing and transfer (for brand quality reasons), fixing the licensee to a specific production plant (for brand quality reasons), requirements in connection with quality assurance (including rights of control), obligation to use, guidelines in terms of advertisement and packaging, prohibition of selling branded products at loss, or post-contractual confidentiality in terms of manufacturing and business secrets or secret know-how.

Certain contractual restrictions are more likely to be acceptable in the case of an exclusive licensee than in the case of a simple licence. This has to be examined on an individual case-by-case basis.

5. BREACH OF TRADEMARK LICENCE AGREEMENT

5.1. Protecting the Reputation and Goodwill of the Trademark in a Contractual Relationship

The Swiss TmPA (and contract law) is based on the principle of free trademark licensing. This means that a licensor may grant a trademark licence to a licensee without having specific economic ties in place with the licensee or providing for any instruction or control rights in the trademark licence agreement. However, in view of the possible damage to the brand value or a possible degeneration of the trademark into a free sign, an uncontrolled granting of licences is unlikely to be in the long-term interest of the licensor and trademark owner.[32]

Thus, in order to ascertain quality control of the licensee's trademark use, it may be advisable for the licensor to integrate the necessary standards of use into the trademark licence agreement which the licensee has to comply with when utilizing the trademark. Such standards can, for example, be marketing and advertising guidelines which may be attached to the licence agreement as an annex and integrated part of the agreement.

There are no statutory provisions providing for obligations of the trademark holder to maintain the reputation or goodwill of the trademark. If the licensor shall be obligated to design, co-ordinate, approve and/or finance the appropriate marketing or advertising campaigns aiming at the promotion of the brand network, such clauses must be expressly included in the contract.

5.2. Licensing and Trademark Infringement

There are no default rules or principles that apply in case the licensee infringes a third-party-owned trademark when using the licensed trademark. In principle, each party/legal subject is responsible (and liable) for its own use of a certain sign (trademark). Trademark law primarily implies a right of prohibition, i.e., an exclusive

32. SHK MSchG-Bühler, Article 18 no. 20.

right according to which the owner may prohibit others from using an identical or confusingly similar sign for the same or similar goods and services, and not a (positive) permission to use a certain sign. Earlier (better) rights of third parties must always be observed, under certain circumstances also by the trademark owner and licensor. Thus, the licensee is a potential infringement defendant if a third party takes legal action against the use of the licensed trademark on the basis of earlier trademark rights.

Pursuant to Article 55 paragraph 4 TmPA, the licensee himself, who holds an exclusive licence, is entitled to bring a separate action (standing to sue third parties for trademark infringement) irrespective of the registration of the licence in the trademark register, unless this is expressly excluded in the licence agreement. This right of the exclusive licensee, however, applies only to licence agreements that have been concluded or confirmed after 22 June 2007 (Article 78a TmPA). Furthermore, any licensees may join an infringement action in order to assert claims for their own damage.

6. TERMINATION OF TRADEMARK LICENCES

6.1. Post-termination Rights

When the licence agreement does not deal with the issue concerned, the licensee has basically no post-termination rights to claim entitlement to goodwill in the trademark, or a right to compensation for investments made in the trademark, e.g., if the licensee has successfully adapted the trademark and brand image in the licensee's territory. Thus, in order to ascertain 'return on investment', it may be advisable for the licensee to integrate the necessary clauses into the trademark licence agreement (if the bargaining power of the licensee allows to do so).

However, there is an exception according to case law if the trademark licensing is part of an exclusive distribution agreement: Under certain conditions, the exclusive distributor can be awarded a compensation for clientele by analogous application of Article 418u SCO (mandatory provision under commercial agency contract law).[33] This is the case if the licensee is economically dependent on the licensor (like an agent), i.e., if the licensee is integrated into the licensor's sales organization (extensive powers to direct and control in favour of the licensor) and if the licensee invests in customer expansion, but loses these customers to the licensor at the end of the contract.[34]

6.2. Consequences of Termination of Sublicences Granted

The fate of a sublicence in case of termination of the main licence is not regulated by statutory law and has not been decided by case law (so far). In view of the relative nature of the licence, the Swiss doctrine operates based on the principle that the sub-licensee loses his right to use the trademark in case of termination or cancellation of the main licence agreement.[35]

33. BGE 134 III 497.
34. BGE 134 III 497 no. 4.
35. Maria Iskic / Eva-Maria Strobel, sic! 2013, 686 et seqq.

This can lead to unfair results. Therefore, the licensor and the licensee should include explicit provisions in the trademark licence agreement on what happens to the sublicence if the main licence ceases to exist. For instance, will the sublicence automatically be terminated or does the sub-licensee have a right to step into the licensee's place in the event that the original agreement with the licensee is terminated.

6.3. Invalidation or Expiry of the Licensed Trademark

The existence of trademark protection regularly forms the basis of a licence agreement. If the trademark granted to the licensee for use turns out to be invalid, the prevailing opinion is that the licence agreement will also lapse (termination).[36]

A trademark licence agreement always bears the risk of the trademark being annulled, e.g., by way of opposition proceedings (Article 31 TmPA), cancellation (expiry) or cancellation proceedings (Articles 35 et seqq. TmPA) or a nullity suit (civil action). The nullity of the trademark generally leads to the lapse (nullity) of the licence agreement since it is subsequently impossible to fulfil the contractual obligations (Article 20 SCO). In any case, the licensee is no longer obligated to pay royalties when the trademark has ceased to exist or has been formally declared null and void.

According to the long-standing jurisprudence of the Swiss Federal Supreme Court, the licensee has been able to profit from a registered trademark during the apparent validity of the licence agreement (at least to some degree). A complete reverse transaction of the contract will therefore often not be justified since there were actual effects of the 'phantom trademark', at least until its invalidation or expiry. In such a constellation, a refund of already paid licence fees would be considered bad faith in accordance with Article 2 Swiss Civil Code (if the licensee could actually benefit so far).[37]

6.4. Consequences of Bankruptcy

In view of the relative nature of the licence and based on the characterization as a continuing obligation, the Swiss Federal Supreme Court held that licence agreements are not automatically terminated in the case of bankruptcy if the licence is entered in the trademark register.[38] The licence then becomes binding on any rights to the trademark subsequently acquired (Article 18 paragraph 2 TmPA).

Hence, if the other party becomes bankrupt (conceivable scenario), it is advisable for the licensee or the licensor to enter the trademark licence in the trademark register in order to protect their interests or investments.

36. BGE 116 II 191 no. 3.
37. BGE 116 II 191 no. 3; BGE 85 II 38 no. 6; BGE 75 II 169 no. 3a; Eugen Marbach/Patrik Ducrey/Gregor Wild, Immaterialgüter- und Wettbewerbsrecht, 4th ed., Bern 2017, no. 938 et seq.
38. BGer 4A_317/2016 no. 2.

7. STATUTORY (OR COMPULSORY) TRADEMARK LICENCES

There is one case in which the TmPA provides for a statutory licence: Following Article 53 paragraph 1 TmPA, the plaintiff may bring an action for the assignment of the trademark instead of a declaration of nullity of the trademark registration if the defendant has usurped the trademark. If the court orders the assignment under this provision, then licences or other rights granted to third parties in the intervening period lapse; however, if the said third parties have used the trademark commercially in Switzerland in good faith or have made special preparations for this purpose, these third parties are entitled to be granted a non-exclusive licence (by law).

Other than that, Swiss trademark law, in contrast to patent or copyright law, for example, does not provide for statutory or compulsory licences.[39]

39. The limitation concerning previously used signs ('right of continued use' or limitation to trademark rights) according to Article 14 TmPA, a Swiss law speciality, is still sometimes referred to as a statutory licence (although this is controversial).

United Kingdom

Arthur Artinian, Sunny Kumar & Keisha Phippen

1. OUTLINE OF THE LAW IN UNITED KINGDOM

1.1. Legislation on Trademark Licensing

1.1.1. The Trademarks Act 1994

The main provisions governing trademark licensing are set out in the Trademarks Act 1994 (the '**TMA**')[1] in sections 28 to 31. These provisions also apply to the licensing of trademark applications.

The aim of the TMA is to ensure that trademark owners are given adequate trademark protection against the use of their trademarks by third parties.

1.1.2. The Trademarks Regulations 2018

On 14 January 2019, there were a number of changes made to the TMA, implemented by the Trademarks Regulations 2018. The changes affected the rights and remedies of licensors and licensees of registered trademarks in the UK and included changes related to the right to bring proceedings.

The specifics of these changes are set out below:

- Under the amended TMA, non-exclusive licensees are unable to commence proceedings for infringement without the trademark owner's permission (which may be given in the licence agreement itself or separately).

Previously non-exclusive licensees were entitled to ask the owner of the licensed registered trademark(s) to commence proceedings against a third-party infringer and, if the owner refused or failed to do so within two months, the non-exclusive licensee could commence proceedings.

1. Trademarks Act 1994. Available at: https://www.legislation.gov.uk/ukpga/1994/26/section/25.

- Under the amended TMA, it is not possible for exclusive licensees to contract out of the right to be excluded by contractual provision in the licence.

Previously exclusive licensees could request the owner of the licensed registered trademark(s) to commence infringement proceedings and, if the owner refused or failed to do so within two months, the exclusive licensee could commence proceedings itself.

However, Section 31 of the TMA (relating to an exclusive licensee having the same rights and remedies of an assignee) was not amended and still allows exclusive licensees to bring actions in their own name, if given the right to do so in the licence agreement.

Where the owner of a registered trademark brings infringement proceedings, the court will take into account any loss suffered by any licensee and, if successful, the court may order that the owner holds some or all of the damages on behalf of the relevant licensee. Under a new section 30(A) of the TMA, a licensee has a direct right to intervene in infringement proceedings in order to seek compensation/damages.

The licensing provisions in the TMA (including the amendments to the licensing provisions as outlined above) also apply to applications for trademarks made on or after 14 January 2019. For example, a licensor could bring proceedings against a licensee that is in breach of a licence of a trademark application. However, caution should be exercised since an application may not be granted or the goods or services covered by the trademark may be revised before grant, which could impact the rights and obligations under the licence agreement.

Under the TMA, it has always been possible to transfer a registered trademark or an application for a trademark in connection with the goodwill of a business or independently. As of 14 January 2019, the TMA now includes a provision that a contractual obligation to transfer a business is to be taken to include an obligation to transfer any registered trademark or application of that business, except where there is agreement to the contrary or it is clear in all the circumstances that this presumption should not apply.

1.2. Types of Trademark Licence

The provisions in the TMA concerning licences are congruent with Article 25 of Directive (EU) 2015/2436 of the European Parliament and of the Council of 16 December 2015.[2]

Article 25 of the Directive provides specifically that licences may: (i) be exclusive or non-exclusive; (ii) relate to some or all of the goods or services for which the mark concerned is registered; and (iii) be for all or part of the Member State to which the registration relates.

2. Directive (EU) 2015/2436 of the European Parliament and of the Council of 16 December 2015 to approximate the laws of the Member States relating to trademarks (Recast) (text with EEA relevance). Available at: https://www.legislation.gov.uk/eudr/2015/2436/article/25#.

These provisions are echoed in sections 28 to 30 of the TMA, which also permit licences to be partial as to the manner of use of the trademark.

1.2.1. Exclusive Licence

An exclusive licence is the grant of a licence in which only the licensee can use the licensed rights. The licensor cannot use the licensed rights or grant any further licences within the scope of the original grant.

As outlined in section 1.1.2 above, an exclusive licensee can be granted the same rights as the trademark proprietor, for example, to bring infringement proceedings in their own name (section 31 of the TMA). If the licence does not expressly grant any such rights, exclusive licensees can call on the proprietor to take action, or take action themselves if the proprietor refuses or fails to do so within two months of being called upon (sections 30(2) and 30(3) of the TMA).

1.2.2. Non-exclusive Licence

A non-exclusive licence is a licence in which the licensor can use the licensed rights and can grant any number of non-exclusive licences.

Non-exclusive licensees may only bring infringement proceedings with the consent of the trademark proprietor (section 30(1A) of the TMA).

A non-exclusive licensee will occasionally seek to prevent the licensor from granting a licence on more favourable terms to another licensee (in relation to the same territory (or possibly a foreign territory) and the same licensed IP right) or to require the licensor to extend the more favourable terms to the licensee. The licensor is likely to resist or seek to limit such a clause.

1.2.3. Sole Licence

A sole licence is a licence in which only the licensor and sole licensee can use the licensed rights. The licensor cannot grant any further licences within the scope of the original grant.

1.3. The Law Relating to Sub-licensing

There is no statutory right to sublicense in the UK, and section 28(4) of the TMA refers to sublicences being grantable only insofar as is provided for in the relevant licence agreement.

1.4. The Law Relating to Successors

Under section 28(3) of the TMA, licences are binding on a successor to the grantor's interest (and references to the consent of the proprietor elsewhere in the TMA must be construed accordingly, i.e., to refer to the consent of the proprietor or, in the case of a licence, the predecessor who granted the licence).

Indeed, section 28(3) of the TMA might be thought inconsistent with section 25 of the TMA, which provides that licences do not bind unknowing parties to later inconsistent dealings unless an application for registration has been made. There is, however, no inconsistency. Section 28 of the TMA states the general rule that successors are bound. It is necessary that there should be such a provision because there is usually no privity of contract between the grantee of the licence and the grantor's successor. However, section 25 of the TMA has the effect that section 28 will only bite when an application for registration of the licence has been made (or when the successor has knowledge of the licence). Purchasers of the grantor's interest without knowledge of the licence will not be bound in the absence of an application for registration.[3]

1.5. Competition Law

Trademark licensing is essential for innovation purposes and ensuring that innovators' rights are adequately protected. Although generally, licensing agreements can have anticompetitive effects, intellectual property licensing, such as trademark licensing, has the potential for pro-competitive effects (increased efficiencies, strengthened incentives to innovate and increased engagement in research and development initiatives (while reducing duplication in such activities)).

However, arrangements involving the transfer of intellectual property rights (particularly where competitors are involved) can have negative implications for competition, particularly where such arrangements result (directly or indirectly) in price-fixing, output limitations or the sharing, partitioning and/or foreclosure of markets.[4]

1.5.1. The Competition Act 1998

The Competition Act 1998 introduced a new regulatory regime within the UK. The Competition Act 1998 is interpreted consistently with European Union competition law and, as such, licence conditions will generally be treated in the same way under both.

The Competition Act 1998 prohibits all agreements between undertakings which may affect trade within the UK and which have as their object or effect the prevention, restriction or distortion of competition within the UK or a part of the UK.

Generally, an agreement (such as a trademark licence) will have no tangible effect on competition if the parties' combined share of the relevant market does not exceed 25%. Exceptions to this are agreements which directly or indirectly fix prices, impose minimum resale prices, or share markets, and such agreements will be judged as having an appreciable effect on competition (even where the parties' combined market share is less than 25%).

---

3. David Keeling et al., *Kerly's Law of Trademarks and Trade Names* § 15-086-15-087 (16th ed. Sweet & Maxwell 2020).
4. *Competition, IP Rights and Technology Transfer Block Exemption – Overview*, Lexis Nexis PSL, https://www.lexisnexis.com/uk/lexispsl/competition/document/391329/57RD-97D1-F187-5490-00000-00/Competition__IP_rights_and_Technology_Transfer_Block_Exemption_overview.

Depending on the circumstances, it may be that a trademark licence can be brought within an exemption or an exception. As a general rule, terms which are necessary to maintain the reputation of a trademark will not normally fall foul of the competition rules provided that they do not go beyond what is necessary. Accordingly, it is unlikely that terms regulating the quality of marked goods will infringe competition laws. It will also generally be acceptable to tie the use of the trademark to the purchase of ancillary goods or services from the licensor if this is necessary to maintain the quality of the branded goods.[5]

Certain provisions in trademark licences should be avoided, for example, price-fixing terms and absolute bans on the export of marked goods outside of a territory. With reference to the latter example and depending on the circumstances, it may be acceptable for a licensor to seek to prevent a licensee from actively marketing goods outside a territory.

2. FORMALITIES

2.1. Formation of Trademark Licence Agreements in the UK

Although licences are registrable transactions under the TMA, there is no statutory requirement that they must be recorded at the UK Intellectual Property Office. However, there are shortcomings to not doing so, and recordal gives a licensee certain statutory rights under section 30 and section 31 of the TMA relating to where there has been an infringement of a registered trademark and various rights and remedies as if the licence had been an assignment.

A trademark licence can be limited to use of the mark in a particular manner or a particular locality (Section 28 of the TMA).

A UK-registered trademark can be licensed in relation to all, or some, of the goods or services for which it is registered (section 24 of the TMA), and section 28(2) of the TMA provides that 'a licence is not effective unless it is in writing signed by or on behalf of the grantor'.

If the formalities set out in section 28(2) of the TMA are not complied with, then:

- an informal licensee cannot benefit from any of the other provisions of the TMA conferring rights on a licensee (sections 28, 29, 30 and 31 of the TMA);
- the licensee is in danger of their informal licence being overridden by either a subsequent conflicting licence which does comply with section 28(2) of the TMA or a subsequent effective assignment of the registered trademark; and
- provided privity of contract remains with the grantor of the informal licence, the informal licensee has rights vis-à-vis the grantor, but no security against the position of third parties who may acquire rights or interests in or under the registered trademark.[6]

5. *Fox Williams Brand Licensing*, https://www.fashionlaw.co.uk/cms/document/Brand_licensing.pdf.
6. David Keeling et al., *Kerly's Law of Trademarks and Trade Names* § 15-081 (16th ed. Sweet & Maxwell 2020).

2.2. Pre-contractual Disclosure

There are no formal requirements for pre-contractual disclosure in the UK. Subject to the transaction and resources at hand, parties may wish to agree upon a due-diligence process similar to that for a corporate acquisition; however, for many small-scale licences, this is neither feasible nor necessary. Licensors should be aware of the impact of inducing a licensee to enter into an agreement by misrepresentation, which can lead to rescission of the contract, or a payment in damages to the licensee. Silence may constitute misrepresentation in some circumstances, and, accordingly, a licensor may wish to make some limited disclosure, or include some level of warranty in any licence.[7]

2.3. Payment

Royalty payments (either fixed or a percentage linked to sales of the licensed product), with or without an upfront fee, are the most common payment mechanism for trademark licences.

There are no standard royalty rates in trademark licensing, as the value of the licence in each case will depend very much upon the reputation of the trademark in question and market rates, such as rates for fast-moving consumer goods, apparel, and technology products. The licensee will need to decide how much value the use of the trademark will add to its business, over and above the profit which it could make without using the trademark.

The value of the trademark may lie in it increasing the market value of goods and services upon which it is used, or in increasing the licensee's share of the market, or in enabling the licensee to break into a new market.

In considering the value of the trademark, a licensee will need to take many factors into account, including:

- the level of market recognition of the trademark;
- how long the trademark has been established;
- whether it is time or fashion sensitive;
- whether its use might be extended to other goods or to other countries; and
- whether the licensee will need to spend substantial sums on marketing.

2.4. Taxation

Trademarks are assets and, in some instances, highly valuable ones. Dealings with trademarks may involve the valuation of the rights concerned plus the payment of substantial sums of money for the transfer or granting of rights.

As is the case with tangible assets, the ownership, disposal and licensing of intellectual property rights all have potential tax implications. When transferring or

7. Alice Esuloa, Claire Smith, Helena Connors, Sophie Lawrance, *Licensing* (27 January 2021), https://www.lexology.com/gtdt/tool/workareas/report/licensing/chapter/united-kingdom.

licensing trademarks, the tax consequences of the proposed transaction should be carefully considered.

3. PROTECTION OF THE REPUTATION AND GOODWILL OF A TRADEMARK IN A CONTRACTUAL RELATIONSHIP

3.1. Brand Protection

A strong brand protection strategy may help to protect both the reputation and goodwill of a trademark that is subject to a trademark licensing arrangement. Such a strategy may include the following steps:

- Ensuring trademarks subject to licensing agreement are being used correctly and properly as per the terms of the licensing agreement;
- Implementing appropriate monitoring policies and procedures to help with the monitoring of the licensed trademarks; and
- Taking appropriate action against parties that infringe or misuse the trademarks licensed to them.

Breach of contractual provisions regarding use of trademarks will generally give the licensor the right to terminate a licence agreement. Similarly, infringement of the trademark licence by a licensee would also entitle the licensor to seek redress through the courts - for example, by seeking an injunction to restrain the infringing use or by claiming damages in respect of it. The licensor may also be entitled to delivery up and destruction of any such trademarked goods or an account of profit for its sale.

A licensor could also request an undertaking from the licensee not to infringe its intellectual property in future.

3.2. Trademark Infringement

The rights of licensees in case of infringement are dealt with in sections 30 and 31 of the TMA and both provisions are mutually exclusive.

3.2.1. Non-exclusive Licensees

The right afforded under Section 30 of the TMA is a more limited right of action than section 31 of the TMA. It confers a right on non-exclusive licensees and on exclusive licensees whose agreement with the proprietor falls outside of the remit of section 31 of the TMA.

Unless the right is excluded by the agreement(s) from which they derive their licence, a licensee may, under section 30(2) of the TMA, call upon the proprietor to take infringement proceedings in respect of any matter 'which affects his interests'.

If the proprietor refuses to bring proceedings, or fails to do so within two months after being called upon, then the licensee may bring proceedings in its own name as if it was the proprietor.

Both sections 31(4) and (5) and sections 30(4) and (5) of the TMA set out that the proprietor must be joined as a party unless the court permits otherwise. However, this requirement does not impact the granting of interim relief. In addition, the proprietor is not liable for costs if it does not take part in the proceedings.

Section 30 of the TMA is unclear as to the remedies which a licensee may obtain if successful in an action brought under section 30, and in particular its right to recover damages.

While the section provides for the licensee to sue 'as if he were the proprietor', it lacks the provision set out in section 31 of the TMA giving an exclusive licensee "the same rights and remedies" as if the mark had been assigned to them.

Section 30(6) of the TMA provides that where infringement proceedings are brought by the proprietor, loss suffered by a licensee is to be taken into account, without stipulating what is to be done if the licensee is the claimant, although it is widely assumed that there is no intention to exclude such persons from recovering financial relief altogether and that non-exclusive licensee can recover damages under section 30.

Although it is not expressly stated, it seems that, whatever the position in relation to damages, a non-exclusive licensee must at the very minimum have the right to obtain an injunction to restrain further infringements through proceedings under section 30; without it, the ability to bring an action at all would be worthless.[8]

3.2.2. Exclusive Licensees

Unless an exclusive licensee's licence provides otherwise, licensees under a registered trademark may bring proceedings to restrain infringements which affect them, should the proprietor fail to do so.

Because exclusive licensees have a right to sue in their own name, this impacts not only the manner in which they may bring proceedings but also, in certain circumstances, the manner in which the proprietor may do so.[9]

The rights of action which an exclusive licensee obtains under section 31 of the TMA are concurrent with those of the proprietor, and the defendant may avail themselves of any defence which would have been available to them had the proprietor brought the action.

Section 31(4) of the TMA sets out that 'where proceedings for infringement of a registered trademark brought by the proprietor or an exclusive licensee relate wholly or partly to an infringement in respect of which they have concurrent rights of action, the proprietor, or, as the case may be, the exclusive licensee may not, without the leave of the court, proceed with the action unless the other is joined as a plaintiff or added as a defendant'.

8. David Keeling et al., *Kerly's Law of Trademarks and Trade Names* § 22-026 (16th ed. Sweet & Maxwell 2020).
9. David Keeling et al., *Kerly's Law of Trademarks and Trade Names* § 22-011 (16th ed. Sweet & Maxwell 2020).

This means that if an exclusive licence relates to some, but not all, of the types of goods the subject of a registration, and gives the licensee a right to sue in its own name, and an infringer uses the mark on those types of goods, or on those types of goods and other goods covered by the registration but not by the licence, then the proprietor and the licensee can both sue, but both must be made parties.[10]

Section 31(5) of the TMA provides that where a proprietor or licensee is joined to proceedings under section 31(4) but takes no part, then they shall not be made liable for any costs. Unusually, section 31(8) of the TMA appears to allow the proprietor and exclusive licensee to contract out of the provisions of section 31(4) and (5) of the TMA, and it is surprising that the parties should be able to vary the requirement of section 31(4) that both should be joined if their rights are concurrent, since such provisions are usually made in order to protect a defendant from being sued twice for the same infringement.[11]

The relationship between proprietor and licensee may also affect the relief which each can obtain in an action for infringement where their rights are concurrent in sections 31(6) and (7) of the TMA.

Section 31(6) provides that, where there are concurrent rights of action, the court is to take the terms of the licence into account in assessing damages, as well as any award of damages already made.

Section 31(7) provides that the proprietor must notify an exclusive licensee with a concurrent right of action of any application for an order under section 16 of the TMA and empowers the court to make an order under section 16 upon the application of an exclusive licensee, having regard to the terms of the licence.

3.3. Termination of Trademark Licences

Typical trademark licence termination triggers include:

- a material breach that has not been remedied after notice;
- insolvency and related events;
- challenging the other parties' intellectual property rights; and
- a change of control of the licensee.

Upon termination, there is a risk that a trademark will be diluted as a result of the terminated licensee. For example, the former licensee may have strong commercial reasons to continue exploiting the trademark, even without a licence. This may particularly be the case if the termination was hostile.

Even if the termination occurs by agreement of the parties, there should be a transitional period where a licensee may make limited use of the licensed mark, such

10. David Keeling et al., *Kerly's Law of Trademarks and Trade Names* § 22-013 (16th ed. Sweet & Maxwell 2020).
11. David Keeling et al., *Kerly's Law of Trademarks and Trade* Names § 22-015 (16th ed. Sweet & Maxwell 2020).

as through sale of its inventory, which would be deemed as reasonable behaviour between the parties. A 'winding-down' clause could, for example, specify the channels by which any remaining inventory can be sold and limit the period of time over which these sales may take place.

United States of America

Pam Kohli Jacobson, Mary Atkinson, Ryan Edmondson & Michael Meredith

1. INTRODUCTION TO TRADEMARK LICENSING IN THE UNITED STATES

Trademark licensing is one of the most effective means of leveraging the value and geographic scope of a licensor's brand. Yet, a successful licensing strategy remains elusive to many brand owners, largely because it is complex and fraught with pitfalls for the unwary. A successful licensing strategy not only requires a level of business savvy that accommodates diverse market realities but also requires knowledge of how laws interact across global jurisdictional borders. This chapter seeks to address these issues through a discussion of trademark licensing in the United States and global licensing strategies from a U.S. perspective.

Trademark licensing in the United States is largely governed by two sources of law: the federal Lanham Act and the state common law of contract. The Lanham Act is the primary federal trademark statute in the United States. It is important to remember, however, that a trademark license is first, and foremost, a contract between parties whereby a trademark owner, a "licensor," allows another party, a "licensee," to use its trademark in association with making, selling and/or distributing goods/services in a particular way. As such, the Lanham Act and state common law operate together to form the legal foundation for trademark license agreements in the United States.

2. LEGISLATION ON TRADEMARK LICENSING IN THE UNITED STATES

The central piece of federal legislation that governs trademark licensing in the United States is the Lanham Act, which was passed by the United States federal government in 1946. Prior to that date, the Act's predecessor statute, the 1905 Trademark Act, did allow trademark owners to register their marks with a federal trademark registry, but did not include any provision expressly permitting the licensing of those marks, federally registered or otherwise. As a result, for decades, licensing in the United States was regulated almost exclusively by common law courts.

The common law rule that developed was succinctly stated by the United States Court of Appeals for the Eighth Circuit in *Macmahan Pharmacal Co. v. Denver Chemical Manufacturing Co.*, which held that: "[a] trademark cannot be assigned or its use licensed, except as incidental to a transfer of the business or property in connection with which it has been used."[1] The rule laid out in *Macmahan* was used by United States courts to invalidate a number of licensing agreements that did not include a contemporaneous transfer of the licensor's business.[2] Nevertheless, and despite the *Macmahan* rule, early courts did find licensing agreements to be enforceable if the licensor exercised meaningful control over the quality of their licensee's goods and services, or if the licensor owned a majority interest in their licensee's business.[3] Similar exceptions were also made for American businesses that were granted an exclusive trademark license to serve as a domestic representative for a foreign entity.[4]

These piecemeal rulings, however, generated some counterintuitive results. Most notably, a decision by the United States Commissioner of Patents in *United States Steel Corp.*, 23 U.S.P.Q. 145 (Comm'r 1934) found that a trademark owner was permitted to license the use of its mark to its subsidiary businesses, but was not permitted to register its ownership of that same mark under the 1905 Trademark Act because only its subsidiaries had made use of the mark. The *United States Steel Corp.* decision, among others, highlighted the long-standing deficiencies of the 1905 Trademark Act and gave rise to calls for revised federal law.

2.1. The Lanham Act of 1946

In response to the *United States Steel Corp.* decision, Congress sought to supplant the 1905 Trademark Act with the passage of the federal Lanham Act of 1946, which formally approved trademark licensing arrangements in the United States. Specifically, in Section 5 the Act provides that:

> Where a registered mark or a mark sought to be registered is or may be used legitimately by related companies, such use shall inure to the benefit of the registrant or applicant for registration, and such use shall not affect the validity of such mark or of its registration, provided such mark is not used in such manner as to deceive the public.[5]

1. 113 F. 468, 474-75 (8th Cir. 1901).
2. *See, e.g.*, *Everett O. Fisk & Co. v. Fisk Teachers' Agency, Inc.*, 3 F.2d 7 (8th Cir. 1924); *Independent Baking Powder Co. v. Boorman*, 175 F. 448 (C.C.D.N.J. 1910).
3. *See, e.g.*, *Ralston Purina Co. v. Saniwax Paper Co.*, 26 F.2d 941 (W.D. Mich. 1928); *Coca-Cola Co. v. Bennett*, 238 F. 513 (8th Cir. 1916), rev'g 225 F. 429 (D. Kan. 1915).
4. *See, e.g.*, *Scandinavia Belting Co. v. Asbestos & Rubber Works of America, Inc.*, 257 F. 937, 955-56 (2d Cir.), cert. denied, 250 U.S. 644 (1919).
5. 15 U.S.C. § 1055 (1964).

The Act then goes on to define "related company" as:

> [A]ny person who legitimately controls or is controlled by the registrant or applicant for registration in respect to the nature and quality of the goods or services in connection with which the mark is used.[6]

The effect of these provisions is to allow trademark owners in the United States to enter into valid and enforceable licensing arrangements, and register their marks based upon the use of their licensees.[7] They also codify the common law rule that only a licensor who exercises meaningful control over the quality of its licensee's goods and services is entitled to enforce a licensing agreement and failure to do so may result in a finding that the licensed mark has been abandoned.[8] The 1946 Act did not, however, detail how much control a licensor must exercise or the manner in which they must exercise it, again leaving that question for the courts to interpret.

Hoping to provide some clarity on the matter, the United States Court of Appeals for the Second Circuit explained: the "critical question" regarding quality control in a licensing arrangement is "whether the [licensor] sufficiently policed and inspected its licensees' operations to guarantee the quality of the products they sold under its trademarks to the public."[9] Agreements containing various levels of control have been found to be enforceable by United States courts applying the Second Circuit's standard, depending on the situation. But, as a general matter, courts have advised that trademark owners not only include a provision in any licensing agreement permitting the licensor to exercise quality control over their licensee's goods and services but also actually exercise that control, in order to fall within the scope of the Act.

3. TYPES OF TRADEMARK LICENSE AGREEMENTS

A trademark license agreement grants a licensee the right to use a mark or brand on specified goods and services, in a specified geographic territory, for a specified period of time. Three types of licenses are typical in the United States: (i) exclusive license; (ii) sole license; and (iii) nonexclusive license.

3.1. Exclusive License Agreement

In an exclusive license agreement, the owner of a mark grants to a licensee exclusive rights to use a licensed mark or brand, even to the exclusion of its owner. An exclusive license, however, can be limited to specified goods and services, and to a specified geographic territory. In such circumstances, the owner is free to license the mark to other parties and to use the mark itself outside of the scope of the agreement. Because of the nature of an exclusive license, care should be taken in drafting the license to

6. *Id.* at § 1127.
7. *See, e.g.*, *C. B. Donald Co.*, 117 U.S.P.Q. 485 (Comm'r 1958).
8. 15 U.S.C. § 1064(c) (1964); *see, e.g.*, *Sterling Drug, Inc. v. Lincoln Laboratories, Inc.*, 322 F.2d 968 (7th Cir. 1963).
9. *Dawn Donut Co. v. Hart's Food Stores, Inc.*, 267 F.2d 358, 367 (2d Cir. 1959).

preclude the licensee, due to ambiguous language, from using the mark outside the scope of the licensor's intended grant.

3.2. Sole License

In a sole license agreement, the owner of a mark or brand grants to a licensee exclusive rights to use a mark or brand to the exclusion of other parties, but the owner of the mark retains the right to use the mark. It is prudent when drafting a sole license to make clear that the license is subject to the licensor's right to continue to use the mark.

3.3. Nonexclusive License Agreement

In a nonexclusive license agreement, the owner of a mark or brand is free to grant rights to use a licensed mark to other parties and the licensor also is free to use the mark itself. A nonexclusive license places the least restrictions on the owner of the mark. Nonexclusive licensees are often attractive to licensors as they permit the licensor to grant a number of overlapping licenses, and introduce competition between licensees, while at the same time allowing the licensor to continue to exploit its own intellectual property.

4. FORMATION OF TRADEMARK LICENSE AGREEMENTS

At the outset, the parties to a license agreement should take the time to perform an audit and undertake due diligence on the particular trademark rights at issue to ensure that the targeted licensed products and territories are adequately protected by the licensed portfolio and to address any gaps.

4.1. Formal Requirements

U.S. trademark law requires the following six licensing elements: (1) clear identification of licensed marks; (2) identification of licensed goods/services; (3) quality control; (4) territory; (5) termination; and (6) consideration.

The United States treats consideration as a legal requirement for an enforceable contract. This is broader than just a monetary exchange. Generally, U.S. courts define consideration as a bargained-for exchange. This not only can include money but also may be satisfied by a promise or a licensee's ability to use the mark. It is important for trademark license agreements to clearly identify the consideration exchanged by all parties to the agreement to ensure its validity.

4.2. Oral and Implied Licenses

Although both oral and implied trademark licenses are not recommended, United States courts recognize both types of licenses.[10] An implied trademark license is found where parties, by their course of conduct, are found to have intended to license the use of a trademark. As further discussed below, implied and oral license agreements must still provide for the requisite quality control over the use of the mark. Courts have found that the lack of express quality control provisions in a trademark license supports a finding of naked licensing, which may result in the abandonment of the trademark.[11] Because of these risks, it is highly recommended that the parties to a licensing agreement enter into a written trademark license and set forth express quality control provisions in the agreement.

4.3. Recordal of License

Under U.S. law, parties are permitted, but not required, to record license agreements with the United States Patent and Trademark Office.[12] Recordal of a license will provide constructive notice of the licensee's rights to use the trademark.[13] Because recorded documents are publically available, the parties to a license may not wish to record the license agreement itself if its provisions contain confidential or sensitive business information, and may instead elect to record a redacted or skeletal version of the agreement with the USPTO. If the license agreement is to be recorded, it should provide for the cooperation of the parties to also record the termination of the agreement.

5. RIGHTS AND OBLIGATIONS

5.1. Quality Control

The cornerstone of any U.S. trademark license in the U.S. is its quality control provisions. These provisions serve two functions: they safeguard the licensed brand by ensuring that it continues to serve as a source identifier for the associated goods and they also provide a means to control the quality of those goods.

Entering into a trademark license agreement without quality control provisions and without any exercise of quality control may result in the abandonment of the licensed trademark. In the U.S., this uncontrolled licensing is also known as "naked"

---

10. *Transgo, Inc. v. Ajac Transmission Parts Corp.*, 768 F.2d 1001, 1017 (9th Cir. 1985) (acknowledging oral trademark license between plaintiff and third party); *Dep't of Parks & Recreation for California v. Bazaar Del Mundo Inc.*, 448 F.3d 1118, 1129-30 (9th Cir. 2006) (implied license).
11. *FreecycleSunnyvale v. Freecycle Network*, 626 F.3d 509, 516 (9th Cir. 2010).
12. TMEP § 503.02 ("Some instruments that relate to registered marks or to marks in pending applications may be recorded, even though they do not constitute a transfer or change of title to the mark or do not convey the entire title or interest in the business in which the mark is used. Typically, these instruments are license agreements, security agreements, and agreements between parties limiting future extension of use of a mark with regard to the goods/services or other circumstances of use. These instruments are recorded to give third parties notification of equitable interests or other matters relevant to the ownership of a mark.").
13. *Id.*

licensing, and courts have invalidated trademark registrations under these circumstances because the marks ceased to serve their source-identifying function and led to consumer deception.

To prevent naked licensing, a licensing agreement should provide for the licensor's supervision and control over the use of the mark, and the licensor should exercise that control. Reliance on the licensee's own quality control is not sufficient; there must be an indication of control by the licensor.[14]

The level of quality control will vary in each case based on the relationship between the parties and particular concerns over the related goods and services. But typical terms may include inspection of facilities or prototypes, approval of marketing material, periodic reporting requirements, regulation of materials used in products, review of customer comments or complaints, and use of appropriate trademark notices.

It is also recommended that quality control provisions provide for consistent and proper use of the licensed marks. Such provisions are important to prevent dilution of the licensed trademarks and to protect against genericide. Sophisticated licensors will often include trademark use guidelines as an exhibit to a license agreement. This document can provide further guidance on the size, color and placement of trademarks; ensure that textual marks are only used as adjectives modifying a noun; prohibit modification of the licensed marks; and bar use of the licensed mark in association with the licensee's own marks.

Where the parties to a licensing agreement allow sublicensing of trademark rights, the licensor should also ensure that it has adequate supervision of use of the mark by any sublicensees. This can be accomplished by requiring that the terms of any sublicense mirror the requirements of the primary license, as further discussed below.

5.2. Territory

The parties to a license agreement are free to limit the scope of that agreement to specific geographic territories covered by the licensed trademarks. Restricting the licensee to a limited territory will permit the licensor to continue using the mark, or license the same, in other territories.

5.3. Permitted and Prohibited Uses

A license agreement may include restrictions on the scope of permissible use of a licensed mark. These restrictions may include limitations on specific categories of goods or services included in any trademark registration, or a specification of permitted channels of trade. Such restrictions serve to allow a licensor to continue to use the mark with the remaining goods, or to license the mark in relation to such goods to a third party. Depending on the nature of the goods, a licensor may also include restrictions to ensure compliance with laws and norms, such as the prohibition against child labor or use of conflict minerals.

14. *FreecycleSunnyvale v. Freecycle Network*, 626 F.3d 509, 519 (9th Cir. 2010).

5.4. Sublicensing

Under United States law, sublicensing only is allowed with the express consent of the parties to a licensing agreement and the agreement should expressly state whether sublicensing is or is not permitted. Where a license does allow for sublicenses, it also should include additional safeguards to protect the integrity of the licensed brand. For example, additional safeguards may include: requiring that any sublicense be in writing; requiring licensor written approval of any sublicense; requiring sublicensees to comply with the license's quality control provisions; and providing the licensor with the authority to terminate a sublicense agreement based on any breach by the sublicensee—notwithstanding any wrongdoing by the licensee.

5.5. Assignability/Successors

A license agreement should address the rights of the parties to assign their rights and obligations to third parties, and the rights of their successors-in-interest to perform under the agreement. Given the personal nature of trademark licenses, licensors will typically seek to limit the assignability of a license agreement and require written consent prior to any assignment. This is especially necessary where the license is not terminable at will. As provided below, where the license agreement is for a set term or is automatically renewed, change in control or reorganization of the licensee may be included as express grounds for termination.

5.6. Non-challenge Clause/Ownership

A licensor should require its licensees to acknowledge its ownership of any licensed mark, acknowledge the mark's validity, and agree not to challenge the licensor's ownership of the mark or the mark's validity.

Use of a licensed mark by a licensee inures to the benefit of the licensor. Licensors should require licensees to expressly acknowledge the same and disclaim any rights accrued through use of the mark.

In addition to an agreement not to challenge the ownership or validity of the mark, a licensor may also seek express agreement that its licensees will not apply for a licensed mark, or any modification thereof, in any jurisdiction absent the written consent of the licensor.

5.7. Royalties and Fees

As provided above, any license agreement will require an exchange of consideration to be valid. While such consideration is not required to be monetary, a license agreement will typically require some form of payment from the licensee.

The terms of any payment will be heavily negotiated by the parties to the agreement and they are free under U.S. law to reach acceptable terms. Most often, the payment will be structured as a lump sum payment, a royalty payment, or a combination thereof.

A lump sum payment can be structured as a fully paid-up license whereby full payment is due at the beginning of the license. Such payments can be for the life of the license, or additional payments may be required upon renewal of the license. Payment of the full lump sum can also be delayed, such that periodic payments are made. Where the agreement calls for both lump sum payments and royalties, the lump sum payment may also be credited against future royalties.

Royalty payments require the parties to agree upon an appropriate royalty rate and measure. This can be structured as a set payment per unit, or a percent of a licensee's profits or sales. The parties to a license agreement may also negotiate a minimum or maximum royalty payment to provide greater predictability. Often, renewal of the license agreement may be conditioned upon benchmark royalty payments. Where royalty payments are due, licensors should secure the right to audit their licensees' records to ensure full payment of any obligation.

In addition to the foregoing, license agreements should also allocate responsibility for the payment of any fees associated with the prosecution of maintenance of the licensed marks. Typically for nonexclusive or sole licenses, licensors will pay these fees. But a different allocation may be agreed to in the case of an exclusive license.

5.8. Insurance

Licensors may require licensees to obtain and maintain appropriate insurance coverage for claims asserted against either or both parties. This typically will include claims for defectiveness of the products or services subject to a license agreement, or trademark infringement claims asserted by third parties. Depending on the nature of the license agreement, a licensor may also require business interruption coverage to ensure a steady income flow from a licensee in the event it ceases business operations.

Insurance clauses often allow licensors to approve the entity issuing the required coverage and set forth the amount of coverage to be obtained. Proof of insurance may also be required. Insurance clauses should also require licensees to notify their licensor in the event of loss, reduction or cancelation of coverage.

5.9. Representations and Warranties

The scope of any representations and warranties included in a trademark license agreement will be negotiated by the parties. At a minimum, both parties typically provide representations and warranties concerning their authority to enter and be bound by the agreement and that the agreement will not conflict with any existing contractual obligations.

Licensees likely will also seek representations and warranties regarding the licensor's valid ownership of the licensed trademarks and assurances that the licensed marks do not infringe any third party's trademark rights. The licensor's willingness to provide such warranty will depend on the strength of its marks and its historic uses of the same. Licensors will also often warrant that they will renew and maintain any licensed trademark registrations.

6. TERM AND TERMINATION

The parties to a licensing agreement will typically negotiate the term of their agreement and requirements for its renewal. Absent an express term to the contrary, U.S. courts have held that a license provided for an indefinite period of time is terminable at will by either party with reasonable notice.[15] Given the initial investment in the production of goods or rendering of services, the parties to a license agreement should arrive at an express term to ensure the appropriate protection of their interests.

Where the parties to an agreement provide for automatic renewal of a license, that renewal is often conditioned upon certain benchmarks. This is of special importance where the licensor has granted an exclusive license. Failure to provide such conditions may result in the licensor being unable to realize sufficient payments if the licensee is facing diminished sales or demand.

A license agreement should be drafted to plan for prompt termination under identified circumstances such as a licensee's failure to meet quality standards, unauthorized use of the licensed mark on unlicensed goods, failure to make an agreed-upon payment, or insolvency or change of control of licensee. It, therefore, is critical that any trademark license agreement: (1) identifies the circumstances that will result in immediate termination of the license; and (2) identifies the date for cessation of all use of the licensed mark by the licensee, including destruction of any existing inventory.

There are some important terms that also should be included to facilitate the licensor in exercising its legal remedies in the event of a breach. For example, the trademark license agreement should specify that breaching any terms will cause irreparable injury to the licensor. This will allow the licensor to obtain injunctive relief from a U.S. court. The license agreement should also identify liquidated damages for any breach so that the licensor can have a monetary recovery without having to prove actual damages. Finally, the license agreement should address recovery of attorney's fees for breach by a licensee.

In preparing termination clauses, consideration should be given to ongoing obligations of the parties. Typically, if confidential information was exchanged between the parties, continued maintenance of confidentiality or the destruction of documents is required. Similarly, any indemnification provisions will also likely survive termination. Where the license agreement provides for royalty payments, the license agreement should provide for the payment of accrued royalties upon termination.

Where the license concerns the productions of goods, the license agreement should address a sell-off period whereby the licensee may continue to fulfill orders and dispose of remaining inventory. This right is often conditioned upon the licensee not being in material breach of the agreement. Such a provision will provide the licensee a set period whereby it can continue to use the trademark to meet its obligations to third parties or to avoid a loss of inventory. Failure to provide this period may result in a licensee having to choose between destruction of remaining inventory or liability for trademark infringement.

---

15. *First Flight Associates, Inc. v. Professional Golf Co., Inc.*, 527 F.2d 931, 936 (6th Cir. 1975).

Absent a contrary agreement, termination of the license agreement will terminate any sublicenses. If a sublicense lacks terms consistent with the license agreement, the licensee may be liable to a sublicensee for breach of their agreement.

7. TRADEMARK INFRINGEMENT

The two primary issues that arise when a third party infringes a licensed trademark in the United States are standing and jurisdiction. Standing refers to the legal right of a party to bring a dispute before the Court, and jurisdiction refers to the power of the Court to hear the parties' dispute. It is incumbent upon the parties to a trademark licensing agreement to develop a strategy consistent with the metes and bounds of governing U.S. law to address infringement during the terms of any license agreement.

7.1. Standing

In assessing standing in the United States, it is important to note the difference in the law as it relates to registered versus unregistered trademarks. While there is some conflicting authority, generally speaking, a nonowner of a mark, such as a licensee, may not sue for trademark infringement under Lanham Act § 32(1), 15 U.S.C.A. § 1114(1) but is able to sue for trademark infringement under Lanham Act § 43(a), 15 U.S.C.A. § 1125(a).

The distinction has to do with the differences in the statutory language between the two provisions. Lanham Act § 32(1), 15 U.S.C.A. § 1114(1) provides that an infringer of a federally registered mark "shall be liable in a civil action by the registrant." However, Lanham Act § 43(a), 15 U.S.C.A. § 1125(a) says that a person who violates the prohibitions in that section shall be liable in a civil action "by any person who believes that he or she is or is likely to be damaged" by an act in violation of § 43(a). The language in Lanham Act § 43(a), as a general matter, confers standing to a nonowner of a trademark to sue in federal court so long as the nonowner is able to show a sufficient commercial interest in the trademark.

In fact, the Supreme Court in Lexmark circumscribed the language of the statute when it held that § 43(a) is not so expansive to allow "all factually injured plaintiffs" to recover.[16] The high court held that to have statutory standing, any plaintiff asserting a federal statutory violation must: (1) be within the "zone of interest" protected by the statute; and (2) show "proximate causation" between plaintiff's injury and the alleged statutory violation, at least for false advertising cases.[17]

7.2. Jurisdiction

Another issue that typically arises when a third party infringes a licensed trademark in the United States is jurisdiction. In terms of trademark infringement, federal and state

16. *Lexmark Int'l, Inc. v. Static Control Components, Inc.*, 572 U.S. 118, 129, 134 S. Ct. 1377, 1388, 188 L. Ed. 2d 392 (2014).
17. *Id.* at 129-134.

courts have concurrent jurisdiction over trademark matters. This means that both sets of courts have authority to hear a trademark dispute. Many times, an action for trademark infringement is brought with additional claims that may only be heard by a state court. As a general rule, if the action involves, primarily, a claim for trademark infringement, federal courts will have subject matter jurisdiction to entertain the claim for trademark infringement and also will have supplemental jurisdiction to hear any related state court claim as well.[18]

8. DISPUTES BETWEEN THE PARTIES

In drafting a license agreement, consideration should be given to how the parties will handle disputes regarding the agreement, including an agreement on governing law, venue and recovery of related costs and fees. The standard American rule is that each party will bear its own attorney fees, so any departure from this rule will need to be expressly provided for in the license agreement. Given the expense and resource drain associated with the civil litigation, the parties to a license agreement may elect to use alternative dispute resolution measures to curtail the time and costs associated with civil litigation.

The most common sources of disputes between the parties to a license agreement relate to their failure to anticipate changed circumstances such as new technologies, acquisition by competitors or new governmental regulations. To minimize risk of litigation, these issues should be accommodated, at the outset.

8.1. Standing

A trademark licensee does not have standing to sue a trademark licensor for trademark infringement. A licensee has no ownership rights in any licensed mark to assert against its licensor. In fact, the licensee's use of a licensed trademark inures to the benefit of the licensor. As such, a licensee's recourse against its licensor is largely limited to the remedies provided by contract law and the language of the parties' agreement.

8.2. Jurisdiction

As provided above, any dispute will involve a question of whether the dispute will be heard in a state or federal court. Should the litigation revolve primarily around a pure contract dispute between a trademark licensor and licensee, the matter will likely be addressed in state court. But, depending on the parties, federal courts may have jurisdiction where there is more than $75,000 in controversy and the parties are citizens of different states or of a foreign state.[19]

18. *See, e.g., Eureka Water Co. v. Nestle Waters North America. Inc.*, 690 F.3d 1139 (10th Cir. 2021).
19. 28 U.S.C. § 1332(a); *Johnson v. Columbia Properties Anchorage, LP*, 437 F.3d 894, 896 (9th Cir. 2006) (finding federal jurisdiction for breach of contract claim where parties were citizens of different states).

8.3. Estoppel

A trademark licensee is generally estopped from challenging the validity of its licensor's trademark during the term of their licensing agreement.[20] The licensee estoppel rule is founded on the view that a licensee of intellectual property should not be permitted to enjoy the use of the licensed property while at the same time challenging that intellectual property as being invalid.

9. CROSS-BORDER CONSIDERATIONS

Cross-border considerations come into play in two scenarios: (i) a United States company desires to license its mark for use on goods and services in jurisdictions outside of the U.S.; and (ii) a non-U.S.-based company desires to license its mark for use on goods and services in the U.S. In both instances, it is essential that the licensor ensures that its marks are registered in the relevant jurisdictions. Moreover, given the international nature of the arrangement, such agreements often provide for dispute resolution under the Arbitration Rules of the International Chamber of Commerce.

Given the possibility of misinterpretation due to language differences, it is also advisable that the parties resolve any ambiguities and clearly define the meaning of key terms in the agreement.

As discussed previously, in the United States, quality control by the licensor is a legal requirement to avoid abandonment of the mark. Therefore, a non-U.S.-based licensor should ensure that, in addition to quality control language in the license agreement, it puts in place concrete measures to control the quality of products sold under its mark.

In addition, in a cross-border arrangement, the licensor will likely have to rely on the licensee to police unauthorized third-party use of the mark. This requirement should be included in the agreement. If a licensing agreement includes manufacturing of products that will bear the mark, provisions should also be included in the agreement that address: safe and healthy working conditions; environmental conditions; nondiscrimination; no use of child or slave labor; and right of licensor to inspect manufacturing facilities.

20. *See, e.g.*, *Creative Gifts, Inc. v. UFO*, 235 F.3d 540 (10th Cir. 200); *Seven-Up Bottling Co. v. The Seven-Up Co.*, 561 F.3d 1275 (8th Cir. 1977).

www.ingramcontent.com/pod-product-compliance
Lightning Source LLC
Chambersburg PA
CBHW071331230926
51849CB00002B/365